THE CRAFT OF
THEOLOGY

THE CRAFT OF
THEOLOGY

FROM SYMBOL TO SYSTEM

—NEW EXPANDED EDITION—

Avery Dulles, S.J.

CROSSROAD • NEW YORK

1995

The Crossroad Publishing Company
370 Lexington Avenue, New York, NY 10017

Printed in the United States of America

Library of Congress Cataloging-in-Publication Data

Dulles, Avery Robert, 1918–
    The craft of theology : from symbol to system / Avery Dulles. —
New expanded ed.
        p. cm.
    Includes bibliographical references and index.
    ISBN 0-8245-1456-4
    1. Theology. 2. Catholic Church—Doctrines. I. Title.
BR118.D85 1995
230'.2'01—dc20   94-39432
                                                                      CIP

Nihil Obstat: Francis J. McAree, S.T.D., Censor Librorum
Imprimatur: + Patrick Sheridan, D.D., Vicar General,
    Archdiocese of New York
Date: February 11, 1992; July 26, 1994

Contents

Introduction to the Expanded Edition

More than two years after its original appearance, this book is being reissued in paperback. I have taken the occasion to add two new chapters, which I believe will fill in some gaps in the earlier edition. These chapters, composed as articles in 1992, were not published until after the original manuscript had gone to press, but now they can be reprinted as chapters 13 and 14.

Chapter 13, dealing with liturgy and the "rule of prayer" as a theological source, takes up a theme broached in the first chapter, but insufficiently developed there. Chapter 14, devoted to the quest of the historical Jesus, expands upon some material treated rather briefly in chapter 5. Each of these new chapters, in my opinion, deals with crucially important questions of method, sharply controverted in our day.

I have felt a certain temptation to add further chapters discussing subjects such as symbol and dogma, magisterium and reception, religious experience and praxis. It is difficult to set limits to a book on theological method, because that method is not a self-contained discipline. If the method is truly theological and ecclesial, as I have argued that it must be, it cannot be studied apart from disciplines dealing with revelation, faith, and the Church. My ideas of these last themes are expounded to some extent in other books, to which I refer in my text or in footnotes. I may add now my recent book, The *Assurance of Things Hoped For: A Theology of Christian Faith* (1994), which, like my works on revelation and ecclesiology, provides background for my reflections on method.

While recognizing the inevitable incompleteness of a book on method such as this, I hope that it can, in combination with these other works, supply the fundamental tools for the study of theology.

As any theologian knows, questions of method are never settled once for all. The method is subject to continual modification as theology grapples with new questions.

In this edition I have left chapters 1 through 12 unaltered. Even the pagination remains the same.

Michaelmas, 1994   Avery Dulles, S.J.

Introduction

During the 1940s, when I was a student of philosophy, one of my professors advised me against becoming a theologian on the ground that theology gave no scope for original thought. Many Catholics, I suspect, would have shared that assessment, but I found it rather puzzling even at the time. In any case I did go into theology, and I have found it an exciting and challenging career.

At Vatican II (1962–65) a certain number of theological opinions that had previously been suspect seemed to win official endorsement. This shift contributed to a new theological climate in which novelty was not only tolerated but glorified. Many took it for granted that the heterodoxy of today would become the orthodoxy of tomorrow. To be a leader, then, was to venture onto new and dangerous territory, and to say what no Catholic theologian had yet dared to say.

Abetted by journalists craving for headlines and publishers eager to market their latest wares, certain "progressive" theologians have been outdoing one another in originality. Practically every doctrine that had been constitutive of Catholic orthodoxy has been contested by some prominent author. Papal infallibility, the Immaculate Conception of Mary, the Assumption of Mary, the virginal conception of Jesus, his bodily resurrection, the divinity of Christ, and the Trinity itself were either denied or radically reinterpreted to mean what they had never before been thought to mean.

During the decade after Vatican II the Holy See and the bishops were almost powerless to prevent the dismemberment and reconstruction of Catholic theology by revisionist theologians. Any efforts by church authorities to set limits were denounced in certain quarters as repressive and inquisitorial. Under Pope John Paul II, since 1978, the papal and episcopal magisterium has in some measure reasserted itself, but its efforts are still met with great suspicion and, in some circles, bitterness. Liberal and radical theologians form coalitions, gather signatures, and issue manifestos deploring infringements of their autonomy. Meanwhile certain conservative factions, vainly striving for a restoration of the past, denounce the hierarchy for its alleged permissiveness.

It is quite possible, of course, for magisterial interventions to be inopportune, but in other cases they may be necessary to prevent the erosion of the faith. In any case, commands and prohibitions from the hierarchy cannot be a substitute for good theology. Theology should be able to discipline itself by consensus-forming procedures.

The present confusion is to some extent a reaction against the excessive uniformity that obtained in the decades before Vatican II. At that time a single theological school, neo-scholasticism, was dominant. Identifying their own theses too closely with Catholic faith, the neo-scholastic theologians resisted the emergence of other types of theology based more directly on Scripture, on the fathers, or on contemporary experience. They gave quasi-canonical status to concepts derived from Aristotelian philosophy.

Today, however, we are faced by the opposite problem. The different theological schools have drifted so far apart that what seems false and dangerous to one school seems almost self-evident to another. Theologians lack a common language, common goals, and common norms. Civil argument has ceased to function, and in its absence opposing parties seek to discredit one another by impugning the motives or competence of their adversaries.

In any field of learning such radical diversity would be debilitating. History would not be taken seriously if historians had no agreed method of resolving disputes about whether some past event had actually occurred. Medical experts are supposed to have commonly accepted norms about the signs of health and disease and about methods of curing diverse ailments. Even if the agreement is not universal, there is at least a prevalent and normative methodology. Members of the profession share a common vision of what they are about. The same can hardly be said of theology today, even within a single ecclesial body, such as the Catholic Church.

For the better health of theology I believe that its ecclesial character needs to be more clearly recognized. Theology must serve the Church and be accountable to it. While theology needs to have a measure of autonomy in order to perform its distinctive service, it loses its identity if it ceases to be a reflection on the faith of the Church. Needless to say, problems can arise about how to determine the faith of the Church, and these will be dealt with in the chapters that follow.

Within this ecclesial framework it is proper that there be a variety of theological schools. Different theologians can concentrate on different sets of problems, work with different presuppositions, consider different bodies of data, and address different publics. Many functional specializations can arise, but all must contribute to a common enterprise.

The twelve chapters of this book were originally composed for different occasions, as appears from the list of sources at the end. All twelve, however, have been reworked for inclusion in the present book, which is intended to have greater unity than a simple collection.

The first three chapters deal rather generally with contemporary problems of theological method. The first concentrates on the role of critical thinking, the second on symbolic communication, and the third on the use of models. All three chapters give reasons for holding that the neo-scholasticism of the recent past is no longer adequate for the present day. That system does not do justice to the personalist, symbolic, and mystical dimensions of faith. But theology cannot content itself with being merely descriptive or phenomenological. It must seriously grapple with questions of consistency and truth.

Chapter 4 deals with fundamental theology. It embodies a critique of certain types of apologetics that were until recently current in Catholic circles. At the same time it rules out an irrational leap of faith. It adverts to the illuminative and transformative power of the grace given through the gospel itself.

Chapters 5, 6, and 7 deal with three normative sources that are recognized by Vatican II as inseparable from one another: Scripture, tradition, and the ecclesiastical magisterium. Under the heading of the magisterium I take up the delicate problem of theological dissent.

In chapters 8 and 9 I explore the relation of theology to two cognate disciplines — philosophy and physical science. In the first of these two chapters I point out the intimate connection between systematic theology and the type of metaphysical realism that was embodied in scholasticism, both medieval and modern. Without calling for a specifically Christian or Catholic philosophy, I raise questions about whether certain modern systems can adequately replace this realist tradition, which has been presupposed in a great deal of papal and conciliar teaching. In the next chapter I propose a dialogic relationship between theology and the physical sciences. The principles developed in these two chapters would be applicable, with certain adaptations, to the relationship between theology and other disciplines not treated in this book, such as history, psychology, and the social sciences.

In chapters 10 and 11 I turn to the theme of university theology, which seems to require treatment in view of the growing importance of universities as theological centers. I give special attention to the currently debated problem of academic freedom, scarcely touched on in the classical treatments of theological method.

Finally, in chapter 12 I discuss the problem of method in ecumenical theology. After dealing in the first section with interreligious dialogue, I go on in the remainder of the chapter to treat at greater length the theology of intra-Christian ecumenism. Ecumenism, I contend, is best understood not as a separate branch of theology but rather as a dimension of all good theology.

I am aware, of course, that many of my ideas are personal, and will not be universally acceptable, even in Catholic circles. I hope, however, that this book will help to reestablish a broader community of discourse so that theology, building on its own past, can achieve greater consensus and more effectively serve the entire People of God as it builds itself up in unity and love.

Different people have inspired and assisted me with different chapters. I cannot here acknowledge them all, but I would like to express special thanks to two colleagues from the Theology Department of Fordham University. The Reverend William V. Dych, S.J., read most of the chapters in their formative stages, and the Reverend Richard J. Viladesau perused the final text. Both have given me valuable suggestions from which I have sought to profit. Among the efficient and helpful members of the staff of the Crossroad Publishing Company, I am especially indebted to Frank Oveis, senior editor. And finally, I must mention my assistant, Dr. Anne-Marie Kirmse, O.P., who in typing and editing took infinite pains to assure correctness of style, consistency, and accuracy in many places where these qualities were originally absent.

Feast of the Epiphany, 1992   Avery Dulles, S.J.

Abbreviations

AAS   *Acta Apostolicae Sedis* (Rome, 1909ff.).

ASS   *Acta Sanctae Sedis* (Rome, 1865–1908).

DS   *Enchiridion Symbolorum, Definitionum et Declarationum de Rebus Fidei et Morum,* ed. H. Denzinger, rev. A. Schönmetzer, 36th ed. (Freiburg: Herder, 1976).

EB   *Enchiridion Biblicum. Documenta Ecclesiastica Sacram Scripturam Spectantia.* 4th ed., rev. (Rome: Arnodo, 1961).

LTK²   *Lexikon für Theologie und Kirche,* ed. Josef Höfer and Karl Rahner.

PG   *Patrologiae cursus completus, series graeca,* ed. J. P. Migne (Paris, 1857ff.)

PL   *Patrologiae cursus completus, series latina,* ed. J. P. Migne (Paris, 1844ff.)

THE CRAFT OF
THEOLOGY

1.

Toward a Postcritical Theology

Many recent books on theology contain proposals for a restructuring of theology on the basis of principles proper to our own age. Various attempts have been made to show that we live in a new era in which the prevalent methods of the "modern" period are outdated. Many such works contain in their titles the term "postmodern" or some near equivalent.[1]

Labels such as "postmodern," "postliberal," and "postcritical" are likely to be rather manipulative. They seem to put unfair demands on people to conform to what the speaker proclaims as the spirit of the age, with the implication that previous approaches are obsolete. But at the same time the prevalence of such terminology indicates a widespread perception that we are moving, or have already moved, into a period radically unlike the past few centuries, necessitating an abrupt shift of theological style comparable in magnitude to the shift that occurred with the dissemination of printed literature in the sixteenth century. Without wishing to exaggerate the discontinuity, I share this perception to some degree. The history of theology over the centuries, I submit, can be clarified by the successive attitudes toward criticism; for example, the precritical, the critical, and the postcritical.

From Precritical to Postcritical

Was there ever a precritical era in theology? In a sense, no. Theology is by its very nature a disciplined reflection on faith, one that attempts to distinguish methodically between truth and illusion and to ground

3

its affirmations on principles rather than on blind impulses. In that sense it involves the use of criticism. In the patristic and medieval periods Greek philosophy, including Aristotelian logic, was used to refute heresy, reconcile the authorities, and establish particular doctrines as consonant with revelation. Everything was measured against divine revelation as enshrined in the canonical Scriptures and in the definitions of popes and councils. But criticism was not leveled at the canonical sources themselves. A privileged position was given to authoritative statements of the word of God. In this qualified sense the theology of the early centuries may be called precritical.

The critical era was ushered in when observation and mathematics were used to overthrow the authority of Aristotle in the realm of science. Francis Bacon and Galileo heralded the arrival of the new science. Shortly afterward philosophers, under the guidance of Descartes and Spinoza, attempted to erect comprehensive systems by adopting a quasi-mathematical method. Beginning with universal methodic doubt, they rejected whatever could not be verified by reduction to self-evident facts and principles. The critical program, after being launched in continental Europe, took an empiricist turn in England with Locke and Hume, both of whom applied their methodology to theological questions. Theologians, in their estimation, would be unwarranted in requiring the faithful to believe anything as true before it had been submitted to the acids of doubt and criticism. A few Protestant liberals and at least one Catholic theologian (Georg Hermes [1775–1831]) accepted the critical program, but the vast majority reacted defensively against it.

One reaction that became popular toward the end of the eighteenth century may be called the paracritical. Critical doubt and rational testing, it was held, were proper and necessary in the sphere of science and speculative knowledge. Faith and religion, however, were assigned to a separate sphere in which sentiment and volition were sovereign. Theology was seen as an attempt to describe and analyze the dictates of religious feeling. This dichotomy between scientific and religious discourse, having received its philosophical charter from Immanuel Kant, prevailed in Lutheran pietism, in nineteenth-century liberal Protestantism, and in Protestant and Catholic Modernism. Indeed, it still flourishes in certain circles influenced by neopositivism and linguistic analysis.

A second reaction to the critical movement was what may be called the countercritical. It strove to fight against criticism with its own weapons. Many theologians contended that the truth of Christianity could be vindicated by a rigorously critical approach to the sources and exact syllogistic logic. This approach, which insisted strongly on miracles as evidential signs, reached its culmination in early twentieth-century apologetics, both Protestant and Catholic. Hilarin Felder, O.M. Cap., in his two-volume work *Christ and the Critics*, which appeared in German in 1911, undertook to "summon the opponents of the Christian revelation before the bar of fair, unclouded history"[2] and to prove by strict historical method that the Gospels are "in their full extent and in the strictest sense of the word, historical authorities and scientific evidence."[3] The neo-scholastic theology of the nineteenth and early twentieth centuries, while rigorously orthodox, was heavily infected by Cartesian rationalism and mathematicism.

The Critique of Criticism

In the second half of the twentieth century the approach that I call postcritical has been emerging not only among theologians but among philosophers of stature, such as Michael Polanyi, Hans-Georg Gadamer, and Paul Ricoeur. Analogous themes may be found in the sociological writings of Peter Berger and Robert Bellah. Among theologians, authors such as Hans Urs von Balthasar and George Lindbeck are at least in some respects postcritical. Postcritical, indeed, may be used as an umbrella term to include a variety of positions, some more traditionalist and others more innovative. In the following presentation I shall give my own methodological proposals, without attempting to speak for any other theologian. Students of Michael Polanyi will find it easy to detect his influence upon this chapter.

Postcritical thinking does not reject criticism but carries it to new lengths, scrutinizing the presuppositions and methods of the critical program itself. It has drawn attention to the following five flaws.

First, the critical program was animated by a bias toward doubt, with the implied assumption that the royal road to truth consists in uprooting all voluntary commitments. In the estimation of critical thinkers, probity requires one to abandon any convictions that can be doubted rather than to maintain such convictions in the face of possible doubt. This bias was understandable enough in the time of the religious wars, when fanatical overcommitment was a major threat to civic peace, but is a distinct liability in a time when moral and religious convictions have been thoroughly eroded by skepticism. Our contemporaries, well aware that religious tenets are capable of being questioned, need to be shown how firm religious commitments may nevertheless be responsible.

In the second place, the critical program failed to recognize that doubt itself, and consequently criticism, rests on a fiduciary basis. If I doubt something I am implicitly affirming that it does not measure up to my standards of evidence. Such a doubt presupposes a network of beliefs concerning the possibilities of proof — beliefs that could in their turn be doubted. The postulates of Euclidean geometry and the testimony of the senses, taken as indubitable by some positivists, can be shown to be fiduciary in character.

Thirdly, it is impossible to apply the critical program consistently. We do not have stringent evidence for even the most obvious facts, such as the existence of the external world or the reliability of the physical and behavioral laws upon which all our ideas of worldly realities, past, present, and future, inevitably rest. Universal doubt is so repugnant to human nature that it is in fact unrealizable. If carried out, it would dissolve the very principles required for reconstructing the edifice of knowledge, as Descartes found when he tried to build a bridge between the mind and the external world.

Proponents of the critical program have rarely attempted to carry it through without restriction. Most have applied the program selectively with a view to destroying certain beliefs, such as those of revealed religion. In their hands the critical program has served to promote, in a covert way, liberal and naturalistic belief-systems such as positivism and scientific humanism.

In the fourth place, the critical program neglects the social dimension of knowledge. Implicitly it assumes that each individual is in a position to command all the evidence relevant for solving the question at hand. Although critical philosophers have in fact depended upon predecessors and colleagues, they tend to speak as though they were individually self-sufficient.

Fifthly and most fundamentally, the critical program overlooked the tacit dimension of knowledge. It gave no cognitive value to what Pascal meant by the "reasons of the heart" and what Newman meant by "presumptions," "antecedent dispositions," and the "instincts of an educated conscience." Yet these precritical orientations are essential. Even on the most primitive level of visual perception I have to depend on clues that I cannot specify, still less defend, by formal argument. Uninterpreted visual signals, if they may be said to exist at all, are situated at a level below that of explicit awareness. Still more palpably, tacit presuppositions are operative in all human knowledge concerning the facts of history, the findings of science, and the data of religious faith.[4]

The critical program has been under attack for at least a generation, not only in theology but also in philosophy, science, history, and literary criticism. The collapse of that program carries with it certain dangers, especially for theology. The critical program undergirded the not inconsiderable theological achievements both of liberal Protestantism and of various reactions against liberal theology such as neo-scholasticism. The widespread rejection of both the critical and the countercritical alternatives in our own day produces a vacuum and casts doubt upon the viability of the theological enterprise itself. Anticritical and paracritical theories that depict faith as a matter of arbitrary prejudice or blind emotion deprive theology of its cognitive import. We are faced today by an urgent need to overcome the present sense of drift and confusion and to establish an intellectually respectable method. My intention in the present chapter is to take a step in this direction.

The Sources as Clues

Postcritical theology, as I use the term, begins with a presupposition or prejudice in favor of faith. Its fundamental attitude is a hermeneutics of trust, not of suspicion. Its purpose is constructive, not destructive. This is not to deny that people are entitled to doubt what they have reason to regard as false or unfounded. The doubter can be a serious thinker, candidly examining the claims made for religion. But theology, as commonly understood, is the kind of inquiry that takes place from within a religious commitment. Drawing on the convictions instilled by faith, the theologian uses them as resources for the proper task of theology, which is the understanding of faith.

For the postcritical theologian the affirmations of faith cannot be rightly probed except from within the horizon of faith. A computer may be able to derive conclusions from creedal statements or dogmas considered as bare propositions. To the believer, however, the formulations of faith are binding and meaningful insofar as they express aspects of a total vision or idea that can never be fully objectified. The contents of faith are known not by merely detached observation but by indwelling or participation, somewhat as we know our own body with its powers and weaknesses.

Theology is, moreover, an ecclesial discipline. It is done in the Church because the Church is the primary bearer of faith. Christ delivered his revelation to a community of disciples; the Holy Spirit descended upon a gathered community. Any individual can lose or betray the faith, but the Church as a whole has the promise of indefectibility because Christ has promised to be with it through his Spirit to the end of the age. A theologian who departs from the Church and seeks to work without the support of fellow believers has forfeited a necessary resource for the theological enterprise.

Theology, then, is a methodical effort to articulate the truth implied in Christian faith, the faith of the Church. The method cannot be pursued by the techniques of mathematics or syllogistic logic, but it depends on a kind of connoisseurship derived from personal appropriation of the living faith of the Church.[5] The correct articulation of the meaning of the Christian symbols is not a science learned out of books alone but rather an art acquired through familiarity by being at home in the community in which the symbols function. To apprehend the meaning of the symbols, it is not enough to gaze at them in a detached manner as objects and dissect them under a logical microscope. The joint meaning of the symbols cannot be discerned unless one relies confidently on the symbols as clues, and attends to the realities to which they point. From within this stance of faith the theologian seeks to formulate in explicit terms what the Christian symbols have to say to the questions that call for solution.

Liturgy has regularly been recognized as a prime theological source and it is securely established in this role by postcritical theology. The rule of prayer, as the axiom has it, establishes the rule of belief. The Church was assured of the divinity of Christ and of the Holy Spirit because, or at least partly because, divine functions were attributed to them in prayer and sacramental worship. The Church was able to define that Mary was Mother of God because it had long invoked her as *theotokos*. It was certain that Christ was truly present in the consecrated elements because it worshiped him there. It knew that even infants needed to be redeemed by Christ because it had from the beginning practiced infant baptism.

If theology is not to regress, it must retain its close bonds with prayer and worship. In contemporary speculations about God theologians will do well to take account not only of abstract philosophical reasoning but also of the requirements of worship. If God were not personal and distinct from the world, how would our life of prayer be affected? Would we still be able to adore God, to call him Father, to thank him for all the blessings of life? If God were not sovereign over history, could we still have the kind of theological trust and hope that have been characteristic of believers? Theology should not allow truth to be subordinated to practical concerns, but it should turn to the praxis of the Church as a locus for the discernment of theological truth.

Postcritical theology gives new vitality to classical theological loci such as the "sense of the faithful." Johann Adam Möhler maintained that the Holy Spirit had imprinted on the Church "a peculiarly Christian tact, a deep sure-guiding feeling" that leads it into all truth.[6] Newman, in his famous essay *On Consulting the Faithful in Matters of Doctrine*, described it as "a sort of instinct, or *phronema*, deep in the bosom of the mystical body of Christ,"[7] enabling the faithful as a collectivity to distinguish between orthodoxy and heterodoxy. The theologian, quite evidently, must possess this subjective sense of the faith. Through indwelling in the community of faith one acquires a kind of connaturality or connoisseurship that enables one to judge what is or is not consonant with revelation. In applying this sense of the faith one apprehends the clues in a subsidiary or tacit manner and concentrates on their joint meaning.

The liturgy and the sense of the faithful are particular forms of tradition, which is likewise reckoned among the sources of theology.[8] As Maurice Blondel pointed out in his *History and Dogma*, tradition is not a mere surrogate for written records. It preserves the past not as a dead memory but as a living reality, and points toward the future, which it conquers and illumines. Tradition, says Blondel, "is the guardian of the initial gift insofar as it has not yet been formulated nor even expressly understood."[9] Consisting predominantly of tacit knowledge, tradition perpetuates itself not primarily by explicit statement but rather by gesture, deed, and example, including ritual actions. The theologian who wishes to draw on the full riches of tradition seeks to dwell within it so as to assimilate the unspecifiable lore that it transmits.

In addition to these nonwritten sources the theologian has the

Holy Scriptures.[10] In the words of Albert Outler, "the aim of post-liberal hermeneutics is to reposition Holy Scripture as a unique linguistic medium of God's self-communication to the human family" and "as the human medium of a divine revelation that has endured and will endure in and through the cultural metamorphoses that succeed each other as history unfolds."[11] The Bible for the theologian is not simply a mine of historical information or a collection of divine oracles, each having independent weight, regardless of literary genre and context. Postcritical theology treats the Bible in its totality as a set of clues that serve to focus the Christian vision of reality from manifold perspectives. Within the Bible the figure of Jesus Christ stands out as God's supreme self-disclosure. Any viable theological proposal must be seen as consistent with the biblical clues and as carrying forward the intentions imbedded in them.

Theology, to be sure, does not discount propositional speech. The Bible contains many clear doctrinal statements; others are embodied in the creeds and dogmas of the Church and in the accepted doctrines of the theological schools. Recognizing these statements as trustworthy articulations of the Christian idea, the theologian may use them as axioms around which to build a system. Such axioms prove their value by facilitating coherent discourse about the contents of lived faith. The axioms, however, cannot be reliably interpreted except by believers who have acquired the necessary skills through their participation in the community of faith. Systematization in theology can never be complete, for the true object of theology is the unfathomable mystery of God, attained by tacit rather than explicit awareness. Every theological system is deficient, but some systems are superior to others, especially for making the faith intelligible to a given cultural group at a given period of history.

The Validation of Discoveries

The questions confronting the present-day theologian arise from apparent gaps or contradictions in the normative sources, or from the deficiencies perceived in past theological syntheses, or from objections arising out of contemporary experience or knowledge. Theology, then, can never be static. It must deal with new questions put to the Church by the course of events and by the circumstances of life in the world. Continual creativity is needed to implant the faith in new cultures and to keep the teaching of the Church abreast of the growth of secular knowledge. New questions demand new answers, but the answers of theology must always grow out of the Church's heritage of faith.

Theology begins with wonder and with unanswered questions. These questions, arising in the minds of committed believers, stimulate a confident search for solutions that are foreseen to some extent by the shape of the problems themselves. On the trail of a solution the theologian combs the inventory of Scripture and tradition, including the statements of the magisterium and of previous theologians, hoping to find in these sources clues that can be integrated by a feat of imagination so as to provide an answer to the problem at hand. As one comes closer to a solution, one can experience the thrill of moving along what Polanyi calls "the gradient of deepening coherence" until one reaches the point at which one feels entitled to claim a discovery.[12] The solution, when it arrives, is already accredited in part by the anticipations that preceded it. It gives rise to a sense of heuristic satisfaction that is the surest test of an authentic discovery. Every major achievement in theology has aesthetic qualities that, as Hans Urs von Balthasar has taught our generation, reflect the glory of God shining on the face of Jesus Christ.[13]

The "eureka syndrome," as it may be called, makes a valid solution a happy dwelling place of the mind. By a kind of discernment of spirits the theologian becomes convinced that the proposed solution tallies with the tacit demands of faith. This single criterion, though it may serve to validate the discovery in the mind of the theologian, may require further validation, at least for the community of faith. Such confirmation may be provided by the cognitive fruitfulness of the theory and the approval of respected judges.

By the cognitive fruitfulness of the theory I mean its capacity not only to answer the precise question that was originally asked but also to illuminate problems not originally envisaged. By being applied to new questions the theory can, of course, be further enriched, even corrected, but if it does prove applicable, it is to that extent confirmed. In theology, as in the profane sciences, every genuine discovery opens up a path that leads to a host of further discoveries, each of which confirms, enriches, and in some measure corrects the initial discovery. Intimations of such cognitive fruitfulness are a powerful factor in winning acceptance for novel theories.

A further factor that can confirm or throw doubt upon a theological proposal is its acceptance by other believers, especially those whose openness and competence are recognized. Every new convert becomes a living witness to the value of the theory, and every prudent person who, after due deliberation, rejects the theory, becomes a source of doubt about the validity of the theory itself.

Among the "significant others" to whom theologians present their findings are pastoral leaders called to serve as judges of the faith.[14] They are not necessarily competent to assess the theory from the standpoint of its technical correctness, but they are commissioned, and presumably qualified, to decide whether the theological proposal is helpful or injurious to the corporate faith and witness of the Church. As trusted bearers of the tradition of faith, bishops must have a profound sense of orthodoxy. They normally draw on their tacit sense of the faith, and on that of their faithful, to decide what should and should not be preached in the community. The ecclesiastical magisterium need not always give reasons for its judgments, and the reasons, when given, need not be probative. In this respect the pronouncements of the magisterium may be compared to the decisions of a civil judge, who is trusted to make the right decision even when his or her explicit argumentation may be faulty.

Besides the official or ecclesiastical magisterium there is in the Church what some have called a "second magisterium" of scholars. Their concern is with theological competence rather than directly with the impact of scholarship on the community of faith. The theological confraternity exercises a kind of peer control over its members in much the same way as scientists do in the scientific community. The scholarly magisterium is by no means democratic. Like the ecclesiastical magisterium it perpetuates itself by co-option. Acknowledged scholars hold key positions in theological schools. They control the admission of new candidates into their ranks by teaching them, by awarding degrees, by voting on academic appointments, promotions, and tenure. These same professors usually control membership and appointment to office in scholarly societies; they are referees for scholarly journals and reviewers of books.

No one scholar is an authority on the whole field of theology. Rather, the scholars apportion the territory among themselves, so that some of their number are competent in each specialization. Individuals work primarily in their own specialties, but they are somewhat able to judge the work done in immediately adjacent fields, so that among them scholars can exercise a kind of joint control. By their mutual trust they are normally able to arrive at a mediated consensus regarding the value of new theories.

The control exercised by the dual magisterium of bishops and scholars is on the whole beneficial to theology. Since the Christian faith is knowable only from within the tradition, those who transmit the tradition must not be allowed to dilute it by ideas and values that have not been refined, as it were, in the fire of discipleship. Like other cognitive minorities, Christians have to take strong measures to prevent their special witness from being corrupted. It is essential, therefore, that the destinies of the community be in the hands of persons thoroughly steeped in the authentic tradition and loyal to it. Democratization, in the sense of an equal distribution of authority among the totality of the members, would bring about a rapid assimilation of the Church to secular society, as a result of which the salt might lose its savor.

From Faith to Understanding

It is much debated whether the methods and findings of theology must be public in the sense of being accessible to persons outside the community of faith. In critical and countercritical theology reliance was placed on hard evidence that would appear cogent to everyone capable of reasoning correctly. Paracritical theology, on the other hand, was content to operate in an intellectual ghetto and to address only the private experience of believers. Postcritical theology, as I use the term, takes an intermediate position. Avoiding the objectivism of critical theology and the subjectivism of the paracritical, it intends to speak about reality as actually constituted and to make statements of universal validity. It points to the deficiencies of any system that purports to dispense with faith. Recognizing that every affirmation rests upon some kind of faith, postcritical theology frankly relies on convictions born of Christian faith. It does not pretend that its arguments can be conclusive to thinkers who do not have the same faith-commitment. It nevertheless invites the uncommitted reader to enter into the universe of faith and seeks to foster conversion.

Postcritical theology, aware of the tacit dimension, avoids the rationalism of critical and countercritical apologetics.[15] It does not seek to argue people into faith by indisputable evidence. On the other hand, it avoids the fideism that substitutes emotion or blind choice for cognition in the sphere of religion. The postcritical theologian points to the necessity of conversion as a self-modifying act that enables one to look at the world with new eyes. To the extent that faith rests on a specific commitment, it is indemonstrable to outsiders. While the cognitive advantages of believing can be persuasively presented, the truth of the faith cannot be established from within the framework of the unconverted.

Not least among the merits of postcritical theology, in my view, is its ability to maintain a dynamic equilibrium between continuity and innovation. Looking on tradition primarily as the bearer of tacit knowledge, it recognizes that fidelity to the tradition may be consonant with certain innovations in the formulation of doctrine. While critical theology was unduly allergic to the authority of tradition, and while countercritical theology was unduly suspicious of originality, each is given its due in postcritical theology. Postcritical theology has its home within the Church as a community of faith, but it dares on occasion to break through the accepted frameworks in its passionate exploration of the mystery to which the Church bears witness.

Constructive innovations must be positively encouraged. The good health of the Church demands continual revitalization by new ideas. Nearly every creative theologian has at one time or another been suspected of corrupting the faith. When a new insight, apparently at odds with the tradition, is advanced by a theologian of stature, or by a group of such theologians, the magisterium and the theological community are put to the test. Mistakes are sometimes made, either in condemning theories that later prove to have been sound, or in failing to condemn theories that later prove detrimental to the faith.

Room must be made for responsible dissent in the Church, but dissent must not be glorified as though church authorities were generally ignorant, self-serving, and narrow-minded. Caricatures of this kind undermine the Church as a community of faith. Theology itself demands a basic confidence in the Church and its official leadership as the transmitters of the heritage of faith. In the last analysis the Church exists only to the extent that its members rely on its corporate decisions as predominantly correct.

Arising out of a passionate quest to articulate tacitly held truth that defies adequate formulation, postcritical theology is not a strictly deductive or empirical science. Yet it is deeply concerned with truth; it intends to put the mind in contact with a reality antecedent to itself.

The great masters of theology, such as John and Paul, Origen and Augustine, Aquinas, Luther, Barth, and Rahner, have brilliantly depicted how Christian faith can nourish the quest for understanding. Their output, comparable in some ways to masterpieces of music, painting, and literature, is a brilliant imaginative construction that exhibits the beauty and illuminative power of faith itself. Such theology continues to inspire multitudes of Christians who are influenced by it either directly or indirectly.

The critical program lost sight of the creative dimensions of theology, and the defensive theology of the countercritical movement shared the same blindness. Some romantic theology of the paracritical variety cultivated beauty and sentiment at the expense of truth. Postcritical theology seeks to reunite the creative with the cognitive, the beautiful with the true. In so doing it can greatly contribute to the vitality of the Church, which depends in no small measure on whether contemporary Christians can hold forth a vision of reality that is plausible, comprehensive, and appealing. Personally I am convinced that such a vision can be found in Christ and in full fidelity to the Christian sources.

2.

Theology and Symbolic Communication

Three Styles of Theology

In his intriguing book *The Nature of Doctrine*,[1] George Lindbeck discusses three styles of theology: the propositionalist-cognitive, the experiential-expressive, and the cultural-linguistic. Each of these theological styles has its own view of the nature of doctrine. For the first, doctrines are informative propositions about objective realities; for the second, they are expressive symbols of the inner sentiments of the faithful; for the third, they are communally authoritative rules of speech and behavior.

In Roman Catholic theology all three of these types are easily verified. In scholasticism, including the neo-scholasticism of the recent past, the first approach is dominant. Revelation is understood as divine doctrine — that is to say, a body of truth that is intended to inform people about the nature of ultimate reality so that they may rightly direct their lives to their last end. The primary content of this body of doctrine is God himself, three persons in one nature. Secondarily, revelation gives information about created realities in relation to God, and especially about Christ. Within Christology the central theme is the ontological constitution of the God-man, which is the ground of his redemptive action. Theology in this model is a deductive science that uses the propositions of revelation as premises.

In the second type of theology, revelation is held to consist of privileged inner experiences. The historical and dogmatic contents of faith are of interest only to the extent that they serve to intensify or illuminate present encounters with the divine. Doctrine

17

aims to express and communicate the experience of grace. In the words of Schleiermacher, "Christian doctrines are accounts of the Christian religious affections set forth in speech."[2] This type of theology flowered in Catholic Modernism. It also permeates much of the existential phenomenology and theological empiricism that became popular since Vatican II.

The most recent trend, and the most difficult to describe, is the third. It corresponds to what I have called in chapter 1 the postcritical turn. My own description of it will differ enough from Lindbeck's to merit a different name. Instead of cultural-linguistic I shall call it ecclesial-transformative. Revelation, I would say, is regarded as a real and efficacious self-communication of God, the transcendent mystery, to the believing community. The deeper insights of revelatory knowledge are imparted, not in the first instance through propositional discourse, but through participation in the life and worship of the Church. To become religious, says Lindbeck, "is to interiorize a set of skills by practice and training. One learns how to feel, act, and think in conformity with a religious tradition that is, in its inner structure, far richer and more subtle than can be explicitly articulated."[3]

The role of symbolic communication is differently conceived in each of the three approaches. In the first, symbol is subordinate to propositional speech; it is intended to illustrate for the senses and imagination what can be clearly understood only by discursive reason. The symbols of the Bible, like all other symbols, are obscure. In order to convey any definite truth or meaning, it is alleged, they must be fully translated into literal statements.

In the second approach doctrines are seen as "noninformative and nondiscursive symbols of inner feelings, attitudes, or existential orientations."[4] Symbols are products of the transformed consciousness, projections or constructions that express the immediate action of God on the human spirit. Besides manifesting religious experience, symbols serve to sensitize people to the presence of the divine in their own lives.

In the third approach symbols have greater cognitive importance. They are signs imbued with a plenitude or depth of meaning that surpasses the capacities of conceptual thinking and propositional speech. A symbol, in this perspective, is a perceptible sign that evokes a realization of that which surpasses ordinary objective cognition. Symbolic knowledge is self-involving, for the symbol "speaks to us only insofar as it lures us to situate ourselves mentally within the universe of meaning and value which it opens up to us."[5]

In this third view, with which I associate myself, religions are predominantly characterized by their symbols. The Christian religion is a set of relationships with God mediated by the Christian symbols. These symbols are imbedded in the Bible and in the living tradition of the Christian community. The symbols do not operate in isolation; they mutually condition and illuminate one another. Christianity, therefore, cannot be reduced to a single symbol, even that of Jesus Christ. The Christ-symbol does not function except in the context of the Old Testament background and the response of the Christian community to Jesus, as known fundamentally from the New Testament. "The basic biblical descriptions of Jesus as the Messiah, Son of God, Son of Man, Son of David, Lord, etc., not to mention more obviously metaphorical descriptions such as Light of the World, Good Shepherd, True Vine, and the like, are achievements of the religious imagination relying on symbolic materials made available by the religious traditions of ancient Israel."[6]

In the ecclesial-transformative approach, the primary subject matter of theology is taken to be the saving self-communication of God through the symbolic events and words of Scripture, especially in Jesus Christ as the "mediator and fullness of all revelation."[7] A privileged locus for the apprehension of this subject matter is the worship of the Church, in which the biblical and traditional symbols are proclaimed and "re-presented" in ways that call for active participation (at least in mind and heart) on the part of the congregation. The interplay of symbols in community worship arouses and directs the worshipers' tacit powers of apprehension so as to instill a personal familiarity with the Christian mysteries. The symbolic language of primary religious discourse can never be left behind if the dogmas and theological formulations of Christian faith are to be rightly appreciated. As Geoffrey Wainwright has said,

> This communion with God, symbolically focused in liturgy, is the primary locus of religious language for the Christian. *Theological* language belongs to the second order: it is the language of reflexion upon the primary experience. The language of worship mediates the substance on which theologians reflect; without that substance, theological talk would have no referent.[8]

This third approach leaves room for more than one concept of theology, more than one mode in which faith may be understood. Mystical writers such as Dionysius the Areopagite and John of the Cross have favored a "symbolic theology" in which the imagination is stimulated so as to evoke and invoke the presence of the spiritual world.[9] The purification and transformation of the human spirit through submission to the power of the symbols is regarded as essential for the attainment of contemplation, the primary concern of such theology. Less contemplative, more academic types of theology are also compatible with the ecclesial-transformative approach. The "scientific" theology that has developed in universities and other institutions of higher learning since the twelfth century does not commonly engage in symbolic discourse; rather, it reflects rationally upon the faith of the Church, including the nature and meaning of the Christian symbols.

Ecclesial-transformative theology, in a form that I can personally accept, rests on a kind of symbolic realism in which reality is held to have a symbolic structure. Karl Rahner, among others, has set forth an impressive ontology of the symbol, which will be the basis for some of the reflections that follow. He maintains that "all beings are by their nature symbolic, because they necessarily 'express' themselves in order to attain their own nature."[10] By a "symbol" or "symbolic reality" he means "the self-realization of a being in the other, which is constitutive of its essence."[11]

This ontology of symbol may be illustrated by reference to theological anthropology. The human person, it is held, consists of a spirit that realizes itself in the body to which it is dialectically united. The body is, so to speak, the self as other. It is not a mere appendage of a spirit that has its own existence, but is the self-expression of the spirit in a form other than its own. The two-in-oneness of body and spirit characterizes the whole of human life. The human spirit achieves selfhood and maturity not by withdrawal from the body but by developing its thoughts, attitudes, and commitments through the body.

To be human is to be socially and historically constituted. As social beings, human persons realize themselves through bodily communication, which is symbolic insofar as the bodily gestures and actions manifest the ideas and ideals of individuals in community. As historical beings, men and women achieve the benefits of culture by appropriating the insights of their forebears, as these insights are transmitted in the cultural heritage. The assimilation of social and historical symbols requires readiness to open oneself to the ideas and values that these symbols embody. The same principles apply to religion, which is an instance of social and historical existence. Christian symbols call for openness; they both demand and make possible a radical change in the hearers' attitudes and behavior. Thus revelation and redemption are two aspects of the same coin. Faith is not just an act of the intellect but a transformation of the whole person in response to God's initiatives, conveyed through the religious community and its tradition.

Theology and Communication

These preliminary remarks about symbol in relation to revelation and doctrine have considerable importance for one's understanding of the relationship between communications and theology, the topic of the present chapter. In the past the formal object, or subject matter, of theology has usually been identified in terms of what God is, or has done, but not in terms of communication, considered as a sharing of conscious life. To Karl Rahner, more than others, belongs the credit for having redefined the formal object of theology in a way that brings out the communications dimension.[12] Classical Thomism, he points out, held that the formal object of theology is "God in his godhead" (*Deus sub ratione deitatis*), but this definition was not very helpful in delineating the vital, mysterious, and salvific character of revelation. The classical view, according to Rahner, is acceptable if God is here understood not as a self-enclosed Necessary Being — the static object of some kind of natural theology — but precisely in his self-communication. The central concern of theology is with three great mysteries, all of which involve the divine self-communication. The first of these, the Trinity, is the inner self-communication of divine life within the godhead. The second, the Incarnation, refers to the self-communication of the divine Word to a particular human nature. The third great mystery is that of the divinization of human persons, either in this life through grace or in the life to come through what is called the light of glory. This divinization involves the self-communication of the Holy Spirit.

It may be objected, of course, that Rahner's redefinition of the formal object of theology is not particularly helpful for overcoming the gap between theology and communications, since he is evidently referring to the immediate self-bestowal of the divine, not to the external means whereby human beings communicate with one another. But when Rahner's concept of self-communication is linked up with his anthropology and his doctrine of symbol, as previously set forth, the implications for our subject become evident. God's revelation, if it is to come home to human beings as embodied spirits, must come to expression through tangible, social, and historically transmitted symbols. The divine self-communication, therefore, has a social and symbolic dimension.

It is not my intent in this chapter to deal with the complex question of the propagation of the faith in the modern world, or with the effects of the new media of social communication upon the prospects for Christianity.[13] In keeping with the plan of the present volume, I shall concentrate on the communications dimension inherent in theology as a methodical reflection on Christian faith. My contention will be that theology is at every point concerned with the realities of communication, and especially with what I have called symbolic communication.

Fundamental Theology

In certain theological disciplines, such as fundamental theology, the communications dimension has long been recognized. In classical scholasticism, revelation, the primary theme of this discipline, was understood as a type of communication from God to his intelligent creatures. This communication has been seen as mediated through words and confirmed by significant actions. Contemporary theologians of the ecclesial-transformative school would generally reaffirm this traditional view but, as I have already indicated, they would add that any event of revelation must have a symbolic character. Whether in their original bestowal or in their transmission by the faith-community, the revelatory signs must evoke what lies beyond the range of explicit statement; otherwise they could not be capable of radically reshaping the minds and lives of the recipients. As bearers of God's self-communication, these signs both call for, and have the power to effect, conversion. Revelation is salvific because it introduces one to a world of meaning and value that unaided human effort could neither disclose nor attain.[14]

Any revelatory sign or symbol may be called, in a generic sense, the word of God. As word it has three dimensions, corresponding to the three "persons" recognized in grammar.[15] In its first-person dimension the word is an expressive symbol, manifesting the previously hidden thoughts and attitudes of the speaker. In its second-person dimension the word is address: it summons others to hear and be attentive. In its third-person dimension the word has a content: something is communicated from the speaker or writer to the hearers or readers. Without all these three dimensions a theology of revelation would be incomplete. God by his symbolic action manifests himself as revealer; he summons human beings to be attentive and responsive; and he gives them ideas and insights that they would otherwise lack.

Fundamental theology has traditionally dealt with Scripture and tradition as sources, or preferably channels, of revelation. Holy Scripture, as the abiding symbolic self-expression of the People of God in the formative phase of its history, remains an essential resource for the Church in maintaining continuity with its divinely given origins.[16] But Scripture, as a stable sedimentation of the faith of the originators, needs to be supplemented by tradition, which presents the word of God in continually new forms, suited to the changing cultures and conditions in which the Church finds itself. Tradition is the process of diachronic communication whereby revelation, received in faith, perpetuates itself from generation to generation.

Scripture and tradition appear in a different light according to the model of theology that is chosen. In neo-scholastic propositional theology, each is used as an armory of authoritative statements to clarify and defend the teachings of the Church. The theologian is expected to bolster contemporary official doctrine by appropriate proof-texts from each source. In the experiential theology popular since the 1960s, Scripture and tradition are used to provide models or paradigms for the Christian community as it continues to reflect on its current experience. Where propositional theology accented stability and continuity, experiential theology emphasizes originality and innovation. The emerging ecclesial-transformative theology takes a mediating position. It looks upon Scripture and tradition both as expressing the faith of the original community and as shaping the faith of subsequent generations. The two "sources" in combination transmit the message less by explicit statement than by forming the imagination and affectivity of the Christian community. The biblical and traditional symbols impart a tacit, lived awareness of the God who has manifested himself of old. By appropriating the symbols and "dwelling in" their meaning, new believers are able to apprehend reality, as it were, through the eyes of their predecessors in the faith. Scripture and tradition are instruments through which God, who spoke of old, continues to address the believing community today.[17]

Practical Theology

In addition to fundamental theology there is another major branch in which the role of communication has long been recognized — namely, practical theology, which includes apologetic, missionary, and pastoral specializations. As is obvious, these disciplines deal with the ways in which the faith should be proposed in order to gain comprehension and acceptance from various audiences.

Apologetics, while distinct from the art of conversion, concerns itself with the human subjects to whom revelation is addressed and with the conditions that can favor or impede the acceptance of the Christian message. Neo-scholastic apologetics was greatly concerned with giving explicitly rational demonstrations of the truth of the Christian religion, based on philosophical and historical premises. Experiential-expressive theology substituted an apologetics in which Christianity was proposed as the most adequate symbolization of people's interior experience of grace. In the ecclesial-transformative style of theology apologetics concentrates on the discernibility of God's redemptive presence in the Christian community.

Missiology, which deals with the dissemination of the Christian message to peoples among whom the Church has not as yet been firmly planted, has usually taken some account of the various cultures and conditions of different peoples so that the preaching of the gospel could be adapted to their respective needs and capacities, enabling them to respond in an authentic manner. Modern missionary theology increasingly recognizes that this effort at adaptation requires the participation of the evangelized peoples themselves, for they alone have adequate sensitivity to the connotations of terms and symbols in their own cultural framework. It likewise recognizes the need for the indigenous cultural and symbolic structures to be transformed by the impact of the Christian symbols.

Pastoral theology has to do with the spiritual care of the Church's own members. In this field, likewise, communications is of crucial importance. Bernard Lonergan, following Rahner and others, emphasizes the importance of communications for enabling people to see the bearing of the Christian message on their lives and thus for building up the Church as a community of faith and witness. In this connection, Lonergan refers his readers to a five-volume work on pastoral theology by a team of German authors.[18] In these volumes, Lonergan states, the reader can contemplate theologians at work on communications, which in his own system he describes as the eighth functional specialization.

Pope John XXIII, in his opening allocution at the Second Vatican Council, cautioned that a magisterium that seeks to be predominantly pastoral must study and expound Christian doctrine according to the literary forms of modern thought. This is obviously essential for successful communication. But the Church, we may add, can never be content to take over the prevalent secular literary and artistic forms. In the great ages of faith Christianity has shown its capacity to forge new styles of art, architecture, music, and literature, corresponding to its God-given vision of reality.

In light of contemporary communications theory these practical theological disciplines are undergoing notable enrichment. More attention is being paid to the tacit dimension of communication. Here again, recognition of the symbolic or evocative character of revelation can be vitally important. Apologists, missionaries, and pastoral theologians cannot be content to establish doctrines by means of formal proof. They must be attentive to what is being communicated on the subsidiary and even the subliminal level by the Church's whole manner of speaking and acting.

Christian testimony invites its hearers to adhere with full freedom to the Church as a community of truth and love.[19] As Bernhard Häring points out, respect for truth in the abstract is not enough. Taking Jesus Christ as the pattern and norm of communication, Häring calls attention to "the inseparable unity of inner truthfulness and loving communication. A loveless use of facts and half-truths destroys our inner truthfulness and damages community. The authentically truthful person cannot deal with truth in a heartless and calculating way, for he is taken up heart and soul with truth."[20]

Systematic Theology

Although the bearing of communications on fundamental and practical theology has long been obvious, the same cannot be said regarding systematic theology. In Catholic and Protestant scholasticism systematicians have usually focused on the objective reality of God and on the "facts" of salvation history. They have discussed the physical and juridical aspects of sin and redemption, ecclesiology and the sacraments, but have not reflected deeply on the nature and efficacy of symbols. The experiential theology of the recent past regained some appreciation of symbol, but only in its subjective and expressive aspects. The recovery of the symbolic dimension in contemporary ecclesial-transformative theology may be able to shed new light on many traditional questions. In what follows I shall make some suggestions that appear consonant with the theological orientations of Karl Rahner. The further exploration and refinement of these suggestions must be left to specialists in the various disciplines.

Christology. We may suitably begin with the mystery of Christ, who has been described as "the perfect Communicator."[21] Since he is the central symbol of the Christian religion, every theological discipline must be developed in light of Christ and constantly return to him as its norm. In the words of Rahner,

> If a theology of symbolic realities is to be written, Christology, the doctrine of the incarnation of the Word, will obviously form the central chapter. And this chapter need almost be no more than an exegesis of the saying: "He that sees me, sees the Father" (Jn. 14:9). There is no need to dwell here on the fact that the Logos is image, likeness, reflection, representation, and presence — filled with all the fullness of the Godhead. But if this is true, we can understand the statement: the incarnate Word is the absolute symbol of God in the world, filled as nothing else can be with what is symbolized. He is not merely the presence and revelation of what God is in himself. He is also the expressive presence of what — or rather who — God wished to be, in free grace, to the world, in such a way that this divine attitude, once so expressed, can never be reversed, but is and remains final and unsurpassable.[22]

Christology, in many classical treatises, has been centered on the doctrine of the hypostatic union, conceived in rather essentialistic terms. This doctrine, true as it is, may be advantageously broadened out by a symbolic theology that contemplates the Incarnation as a mystery of communication. Every symbol, according to Paul Ricoeur, has two levels of meaning, the lower and more obvious being the key to the higher, latent meaning.[23] Symbolic realities consequently have a complex structure. The mystery of the incarnate Word, according to Vatican II, is "one interlocked reality, comprising a human and a divine element."[24] The humanity of Jesus is a symbolic manifestation of his divinity, which it in some sense also cloaks. This thesis does not contradict the classical doctrine of the hypostatic union, but rather clarifies and enriches it.

In Christ we have to do not merely with a literary symbol, a product of the fantasy of believers, but with a real symbol, presentative rather than simply representative. He is, in his very humanity, the "self-utterance of God outside himself."[25] By the act of coming into the world as a human being, Christ fully identified himself with those for whom he came. But the bare fact of the Incarnation, considered as the moment of origin of Christ's earthly existence, was only the inception of his communicative and redemptive career. He constituted himself as the unsurpassable symbol by all the mysteries of his life, including, climactically, his passion, death, and risen life. In the earthly ministry of Jesus each major event gives a further enrichment to his humanity and consequently to our ability to perceive him as God's definitive self-disclosure. The "mysteries of the life of Jesus," which were carefully pondered in some earlier theology, have often been passed over by late scholasticism in favor of an almost exclusive concentration on the passion and resurrection. In a symbolic Christology they can, however, be retrieved.

Among these mysteries the miracles of Jesus have their place, not simply as apologetic proofs that his teaching was true, but as having tongues of their own.[26] They symbolically express the redemptive mission of Christ and the quality of the kingdom that God was establishing through his ministry. In contrast to the miracles, which exhibit the power of Jesus, the passion and crucifixion show forth his weakness, which is really another form of power. By his total self-emptying Jesus manifested his identity with God, who alone acts out of pure, altruistic love. In his adoring surrender to the Father's will Jesus opened himself fully to the divine, which in him overcame every obstacle. The positive facet of this transaction, theologically inseparable from the death of Jesus, is of course the resurrection. By entering into the divine glory, the humanity of Jesus was fully constituted as the light that could never be overcome by the darkness of the world.

Some of the advantages of the symbolic approach become evident in soteriology, which in late scholasticism became unduly separated from Christology itself. The redemption cannot be adequately understood in the scholastic categories of physical efficient causality or in those of moral/juridical causality. As Rahner has persuasively argued, Christ is, through his whole being, and especially through his death and resurrection, the preeminent "real symbol" of God's grace and forgiveness. As symbol, Christ expresses what is at work whenever God communicates himself in grace. Being the high point of the permeation of the human by the divine, Christ is the source and goal of all other saving events, which in various ways anticipate or reflect his coming. He may therefore be called the "primordial sacrament of redemption."[27] Of him it may preeminently be said that the symbol effects what it signifies.[28]

Creation. In recent centuries the world of nature has provided the basis for a rather dessicated natural theology. Having supposedly grasped finite reality in itself, one then reasons from it to God the creator. These arguments, rather confidently proposed before the time of Kant, are now more cautiously advanced. Many retreat from finite objects and try to construct a natural theology on the basis of the aspiration of the human spirit for the unconditioned absolute.

In contrast to the moderns, the biblical authors had no difficulty in perceiving God at work in nature. For the Psalmist the heavenly bodies and the regular alternation of day and night formed a melodious chorus raising a great hymn of praise to God (Ps. 19:1–4). For Paul it seemed evident that God was constantly revealing himself — his invisible nature, his power, his divinity — through the attributes of the created world (Rom. 1:19–20).

This quasi-sacramental view of the world remained standard in Christian theology throughout the early centuries. Augustine, though he thought of God as ineffably exalted above all creatures, nevertheless found nature pointing the way to him. In the harmonies of music, the fragrance of flowers, and the sweetness of honey he found hints and traces of the God he was looking for — that brilliance which no space could contain, that sound which no time could carry away, that sweetness which no satiety could diminish. In Augustine's dialogue with nature the sea, the breezes, the sun, and the stars all gave testimony by their beauty to the God who had made them.[29]

This Augustinian approach survived in the Franciscan theology of the Middle Ages and reappears in modern religious thinkers such as John Henry Newman, who praised the Alexandrian fathers for their recognition of the sacramentality of nature. But can this approach maintain itself against the tide of Kantian criticism? Not perhaps if one insists on apodictic proofs. But there is no reason to deny that God the creator affords clues to himself in the visible cosmos. These clues, integrated by the religious imagination, may be interpreted as symbols of the divine. Jean Daniélou, building on the phenomenology of religion elaborated by Gerhardus van der Leeuw and Mircea Eliade, insists that the relationship between the symbol and the symbolized is by no means arbitrary and fantastic. "The symbol is a medium for a perfectly objective knowledge."[30] In various religions, Daniélou remarks, the same natural symbols, such as the sun, the sky, the rock, and the rain, symbolize similar realities. These analogies, he holds, are rooted in the analogy of being and in the permanent structures of the human spirit.[31]

What modern theology tends to add to the traditional approach to God through nature is that this method is viable only because the human spirit is, from the beginning, oriented toward the divine. God is at work in the depths of the human psyche, calling it to himself. The discovery of God in nature, like any discovery, depends upon a passionate eagerness to find and on an antecedent conviction that the quest is not in vain. This fiduciary component does not undermine the validity of the discovery, but on the contrary lends assurance that the truth was there, waiting to be found.[32]

A further distinguishing mark of the modern mind is its recognition that nature is not a static, immutable order. The heavenly bodies do not ceaselessly circle in their spheres. In fact, nothing in nature ever exactly repeats itself. Nature has a history in which each moment is unique and unrepeatable. Matter ceaselessly orients itself, under the direction of the creative energies by which it is permeated, toward the production of life and spirit. The striking breakthroughs whereby higher forms of life emerge suggest the presence and activity of transcendence in the heart of the cosmos. The continual thrust of nature toward spiritual being makes it clear that nature is not complete in itself, apart from humanity and its history.[33]

In the Christian view, nature comes to completion in Christ, who perfects it with his blessed humanity and initiates its glorious transformation. The symbolic significance of nature appears at its fullest when the eternal Logos assumes it to himself. In the light of this climactic event all the previous steps in the history of nature take on new meaning. This is perhaps what Paul had in mind when he described Christ as the firstborn of all creation. "All things were created through him and for him. He is before all things, and in him all things hold together" (Col. 1:16–17). Because this is true in the ontological order, it is also true in the order of symbol. The clues to the meaning of the cosmos cannot be fully integrated except in light of that clue which gives final meaning to all the others — Jesus Christ. He who completes the positive revelation given in the Law and the prophets completes also the primordial revelation given in nature.

Anthropology: sin and grace. The anthropology that corresponds to a symbolic theology has been briefly sketched above. It has been seen that to be human is, so to speak, to be a symbolic animal. As human, we live by meanings, and meaning, as Michael Polanyi has shown, is achieved through the creative imagination, which interprets clues that are subsidiarily perceived. Radically new meanings cannot be grasped by formal reasoning, for the mind in such reasoning remains fixed in the mental categories with which it began. When clues work on the imagination with symbolic power, however, fresh and unforeseen meanings arise.[34]

Vatican II asserted that humanity is revealed to itself in Christ. "Only in the mystery of the incarnate Word does the mystery of man take on light."[35] Theologically speaking, man may be described as what God becomes when God chooses to exist in a nondivine form.[36] In Christ, man is God as other. By contemplating the incarnate Word we can learn that humanity is, in its inmost reality, a capacity to share in the divinization preeminently realized in Christ. Human beings are potential or actual recipients of the Word that was spoken into the world by the Incarnation. They may be defined in terms of their obediential potency for, and their immanent finalization toward, divinizing transformation in Christ.

The movement toward the divine is, of course, continually crossed by sin. In a more rationalistic age theologians were inclined to look on sin too individualistically and legalistically as if it consisted only in deliberate, discrete acts. The mysterious and communicative aspects of sin were often overlooked. In contemporary ecclesial-transformative theology, hamartiology is enriched by a consideration of sin in its symbolic and communicative dimensions.

Paul Ricoeur, in the work already mentioned, emphasizes the value of symbolic language to describe sin as a stain or blemish, as missing the mark, as brokenness, as burden, and so forth.[37] Sin, in fact, transmits itself in society like an infection; it pollutes the social atmosphere we breathe. The "mystery of iniquity" is the counterpart of the mystery of redemption, as Antichrist is of Christ. Like redemption, sin begins its history with the first human generation and comes to a climax with Golgotha, in the crucifixion of the Lord of glory.[38]

What is communicated in sin, however, is anticommunicative. Sin is symbolized by Babel, the confusion of tongues. It produces blindness and deafness. Like static, it interferes with authentic communication. Those who immerse themselves in sin become isolated from their true selves, from other human beings, and from God. Critical sociologists such as Jürgen Habermas have attempted to expose some of the systematic blockages and distortions of communication in modern society.[39] His analysis confirms the judgment of Bernhard Häring: "The 'sin of the world' becomes visible in unhealthy and misleading communications."[40]

The theology of grace may be developed on the same principles as the theology of sin. Modern theology has generally been content to speak of grace as an invisible, interior gift whereby God elevates the subjectivity of the recipient into some kind of transcendental union with himself. This theology finds it difficult to take the traditional category of "external grace" seriously. The external and social elements inevitably appear as extrinsic to grace itself, whether as its occasion or as its manifestation.

In a symbolic theology this spiritualization of grace will be critically questioned. According to the New Testament the grace of God has appeared in Jesus (Titus 2:11; cf. 3:4). The word of life has been made manifest, so that it could be heard, seen, and touched by human ears, eyes, and hands (cf. 1 John 1:1). In Christ, therefore, grace expressed itself through a human and bodily form, which became the "realizing symbol" of God's redeeming action. To acknowledge the Christological character of all grace is to recognize that it never affects the mind or spirit without also influencing the body and its action. Grace, as Piet Fransen insists, affects our being also in its material aspect, already here on earth. "Both our body and the entire cosmos (which do not have to be thought of as divided from each other) receive a true germ of immortality, everlastingness and resurrection, in virtue first of Christ's redemption and second of our own personal grace of reconciliation."[41]

These observations are not without consequence for the communication of grace. Humanity, as Schoonenberg points out, is a community of education and companionship, both in the natural and in the supernatural order. Divine grace, therefore, is always connected with human mediation. However one may conceive the relationship between the inner grace and its outer manifestation, according to Schoonenberg, two affirmations must stand:

> First, each contact by which a person communicates his interior life to another person is, explicitly or not, a testimony about his relation to grace. Next, on account of our being human and especially on account of the humanity of God's Word there is no granting of God's grace in which the world and one's fellow man do not have a part.[42]

Grace therefore has an influence on the way individuals relate to one another. It makes its recipients, as Paul put it, "no longer strangers and sojourners but ... fellow-citizens with the saints and members of the household of God" (Eph. 2:19). Reversing the effects of Babel, grace restores the communicative structures of society. Every society is built on the twin pillars of fear and love. Where fear predominates, force prevails over freedom, but where love predominates, freedom flourishes. If freedom is the condition for authentic communication, the free society must be touched by the energies of love. Love opens people up to one another, causes them to care for one another and to accept the needs of others as their own. Henri Bergson rightly observed that a society cannot be truly and universally open unless it is animated by the dynamism of a love that comes from God.[43] Sinful social structures simply reflect the constricting effects of individual and social egotism. In an open society these must be replaced with structures of grace. Although this ideal will never be fully realized within history, it remains a potent norm and guide for all who have been touched by the gospel. To the extent that grace is effectively at work, society approaches what Habermas describes as the "ideal speech situation."

Latin American liberation theologians have shown how the biblical symbols of the Exodus, the Promised Land, and the Kingdom of God can be harnessed to give hope and motivation to Christians seeking to reconstruct the social order. Notwithstanding certain questionable elements in the social analysis of some members of the school, liberation theology deserves credit for its retrieval of neglected biblical symbols. It overcomes the excessive dualism that had developed in some circles between individual and community, between Church and society, between history and eschatology.

Ecclesiology, sacraments, ministry. The Church must be considered both as institution and, more fundamentally, as community. In its institutional aspect it was founded to be a structure of grace. Word and sacrament, which are constitutive of the Church, are the primary institutional forms through which Christ perpetuates his presence. There is always the danger that, in a superficial theology, the word of God will be seen as a mere word about God and that the sacraments will be regarded as actions pointing away from the Church to its absent Lord. In the symbolically oriented theology that I am here advocating Christ is viewed as making himself present, under symbolic forms, through word and sacrament. These forms, as symbolic, can be apprehended by the eye of faith, which discerns in them the presence and action of Christ.

Sacramental theology is the area of Catholic teaching in which the doctrine of symbolic communication has been most fully developed. The sacraments are regarded as signs in which the reality signified is truly and efficaciously present. Under one aspect the sacraments are effects of grace, since they express it, but under another aspect they cause grace, rendering it really present under symbolic forms. As Rahner says, the sacraments are efficacious inasmuch as they actualize the very nature of the Church as a "symbol of the eschatologically triumphant grace of God. . . . This visible form is itself an effect of the coming of grace; it is there because God is gracious to men; and in this self-embodiment of grace, grace itself occurs."[44] Symbolic communication, at least in this instance, is not merely an event in the order of cognition and psychology; it affects the entitative character of human existence and bestows a real relationship to God. Especially in the Eucharist, Christ really bestows himself in love and thereby establishes a very intimate communion among human beings and between them and himself.[45]

Edward Kilmartin explains how the recent advances in sacramental theology can be integrated with modern theories of human communication through symbolic actions and words used in the context of an established social situation. For the eyes of faith, he says, "Christ is the sender, receiver, and the medium of the dialogical event of the liturgy."[46] He quotes Alexandre Ganoczy's working description of a sacrament:

> The sacraments can be understood as systems of verbal and non-verbal communications through which those individuals who are called to Christian faith can enter into the communicative process of the ever concrete faith-community, participate in it, and in this way, borne up by the self-communication of God in Christ, progress on the path of personal development.[47]

The proclamation of the word, theologically considered, is not simply a communication of the gospel message, though it is obviously that too. The word of God is a revelatory, actualizing event, bringing with it that new life in God that it announces.[48] The sacraments themselves are instances of Christian proclamation, for in them the word achieves its fullest efficacy.[49] Seeking to account for the salvific efficacy of the word, Otto Semmelroth contends that the proclamation is symbolic. The mission of the Church to preach the word of God, he declares, is a symbolic continuation of the divine mission whereby the Word of God, through the Incarnation, entered human history. In this way "the Church's preaching of God's word becomes a portrayal and symbolic manifestation of the incarnation of God's Son in Jesus Christ."[50]

The theme of symbolic communication can enrich the theology of Christian ministry. In word and sacrament the primary minister is Christ himself. The ordained minister, as one through whom Christ speaks and acts, must be a symbolic figure, set aside from the rest of the community and standing in some respects over against it. The priestly role of the bishop or presbyter, though it calls for personal faith and holiness, is not simply a matter of personal qualities. As an individual, the minister remains simply a member of the community, as much in need of redemption as all others. In his public functioning, however, he takes on a symbolic role, representing Christ the head of the Church.[51]

Christ is dynamically present in the institutional Church and its ministries for the purpose of building up the Church in its second aspect, that is to say, as a community or communion of grace. We must therefore consider the Church, in its most fundamental reality, as the Body of Christ, the Temple of the Holy Spirit. As a great sacrament, it extends in space and time the physical body of the Lord. It is not a mere pointer to the absent Christ, but the symbolic manifestation of the present Christ. The members of the Christ, insofar as they are remade in Christ's image by the power of the Holy Spirit, represent Christ to one another and to the world. He identifies himself with them. Especially is this true of the saints, those who allow themselves to be totally transformed in Christ. The Church, in its most basic reality, is a holy fellowship built up through the self-communication of the triune God. As has been well said,

> The Church is a communion that exists to bring all persons into communion (fellowship) with God and thereby to open them to communication with one another. Its tradition or life exists in order to communicate its message; and its message is that salvation is participation in its community.[52]

Thanks to the divinely established structures of grace and the abiding presence of the Holy Spirit, the Church can and must aspire to a high degree of communicative openness. The Pontifical Commission for the Means of Social Communication, in an important pastoral instruction, called for "a responsible exchange of freely held and expressed opinion among the People of God" and for a "steady two-way flow of information ... at all levels."[53]

Pope Paul VI in his first encyclical called attention to the importance of sincere and respectful dialogue within the Church, but he also remarked on the distance between the empirical reality of the Church and the ideal set forth for it by the Lord.[54] At times, it may be admitted, authentic communication has been seriously corrupted in the Church, but even a deficient Church, if it humbly acknowledges its own unfaithfulness and its need for penance and reform, can continue to bear witness to the Lord. The sacramental model of ecclesiology allows us to distinguish between the symbol and that which it signifies.

The problem of communications within the Church is complicated by the fact that no one is simply a member of the Church. Every Christian is also a member of the larger secular society, and is subject to all the pressures and imbalances that affect the contemporary world. We live today in a "Church without walls," fully exposed to the power of secular movements and ideologies. This circumstance puts additional demands on the Church's internal systems of communication. Formally as Church, it strives to fashion its own members as disciples of the Lord, putting them on guard against excessive conformity to the world and worldly values. Living like "a pilgrim in a foreign land," and assailed by hardships that afflict it from within and without,[55] the Church seeks to protect its unique heritage and identity from adulteration. For this reason the Church as community cannot do without the authoritative structures that pertain to it in its capacity as institution.

Eschatology. The transition from the state of wayfarer to that of full possession brings with it a new mode of divine-human communication. In Scripture this transition is variously depicted as a shift from hearing to seeing and from seeing in a mirror to direct vision. What do these metaphors signify? Can the human mind under any conditions perceive God as an object spread out before its gaze? Theologians such as Rahner can help us escape from a simplistic understanding of the "beatific vision." God, they assert, can never be an object, for every object is perceived against a more comprehensive horizon or background. Since God is all-comprehensive, he is nonobjectifiable.[56]

A helpful analogy can be derived from self-knowledge. Whenever I know something else I am obscurely conscious of myself as knowing. In consciousness there is no gap between the knower and the known. I am immediately present to myself, without needing any representation to mediate the presence. When the graced subject passes into the state of glory, the veils that previously prevented it from being aware of God's interior presence fall away, so that it becomes focally conscious of the triune God who was already dwelling within it by grace.

What helps would be needed for the minds of the blessed to achieve this new awareness of their own divinization? Some have speculated that the glorified humanity of Christ would be the disposing cause.[57] If so, the eternal significance of the humanity of Christ for our redemption may be affirmed. The transfigured human reality of the Logos would, as Rahner puts it, remain "truly and perpetually the mediator of the immediacy of God."[58] For God to be seen in his own reality, it is essential for Christ in his risen condition to be "the permanent and ever-active access to God, which is always being used anew and can never be left as something passed over and past."[59]

For the communications dimension of the heavenly vision to be adequately treated, the social aspects must be taken into account. Too often eternal life has been depicted as a kind of lonely contemplation. It is as though each beatified soul were in a box of a theater, equipped with a pair of opera glasses, sharply focused on the divine essence, but totally oblivious to the persons sitting in the adjacent seats. The biblical imagery, however, suggests a communal experience. Heaven will be like a marriage feast or a liturgy in which all the saints will join in a single hymn of praise to God and to the Lamb who was slain (cf. Apoc. 5:12–14). Within the transfigured cosmos the saints will radiate the "light of glory" to one another.

In the treatise on eschatology, it would be necessary to spell out the communications dimensions not only of heaven but also of judgment, purgatory, and hell — a task far exceeding the scope of the present chapter. Judgment would be described as the manifestation of the hidden aspects of each person's true condition before God. Purgatory would be viewed as a passive purification removing whatever could impede the eternal vision. Hell, by contrast, would be the logical consummation of the path of sin, the total cessation of communication. Hell, far from being "other persons" (Sartre), would be isolation, darkness, deafness to God and to all other persons.

Trinity. The deepest mystery of communication we have reserved to the last. Negatively we may assert, from the general standpoint of this chapter, that the divine tri-unity is not simply a puzzling set of propositions. The mystery consists primarily in the reality and only secondarily in statements about it. The mystery, moreover, is not a lack of intelligibility but rather an excess of it. Our human eyes are blinded by its surpassing brilliance. The created analogies, while falling immeasurably short, point through their convergence to the communicative character of this exalted mystery. The Trinity is communication in absolute, unrivaled perfection, a totally free and complete sharing among equals.

In generating the Son as Word, the Father totally expresses himself, somewhat as the mind expresses itself in a concept. The Son is the eternal image of the Father, reflecting the brightness of the Father's glory. In his procession the Father communicates to the Son all that he himself is and has *excepto Patris nomine* ("except the name of the Father" — Athanasius). Thus the Son may, in an eminent sense, be called the symbol of the Father. "The Father is himself by the very fact that he opposes to himself the image which is of the same essence as himself, as the person who is other than himself; and so he possesses himself."[60] Just as the concept symbolizes the thought that it embodies, so the eternal Word symbolizes the divine self-possession through an act of knowledge that remains immanently in the knower.

In a way that is difficult to specify, the Holy Spirit completes the intradivine process of communication. It has been customary to elucidate this completion through the analogy of love as proceeding from the mind and its thought. Thus according to a well-known Augustinian formula, the three persons would be characterized as mind, knowledge, and love (*mens, notitia, amor*). The Holy Spirit is frequently called Subsistent Love, the sigh, breath, or kiss by which the mutual union of the Father and the Son is sealed.

Turning to a more consistently semantic model, George Tavard has observed that discourse comes to completion when it is interpreted. The third divine person, he concludes,

> is appropriately called Spirit, for it is characteristic of language that, as it is received, it is understood; the thought expressed, the reality conveyed, the discourse enunciated come to rest and fruition as spirit in the listener's mind. . . . The receiver of the Discourse is no foreign addressee: the divine Spirit is no other than the substance spoken by the Father in the Logos, as this substance comes to rest and fruition as divinely heard and received. The Third is the auditor and the audition.[61]

Because Christianity is first and foremost the religion of the triune God, it is preeminently a religion of communication, for God in his inmost essence is a mystery of self-communication. The entire work of creation, redemption, and sanctification is a prolongation of the inner processions within the Trinity. Creation is ascribed to the Father, who thereby fashions finite images and vestiges of his Son. Redemption is attributed to the Son, who communicates himself to human nature in the Incarnation. Sanctification is appropriated to the Holy Spirit, who communicates himself to the Church, the communion of saints. The mystery of divine communication, therefore, permeates every area of theology. The central thesis of this chapter could hardly be better summarized than in the words of Bernhard Häring:

> Communication is constitutive in the mystery of God. Each of the three Divine Persons possesses all that is good, all that is true, all that is beautiful, but in the modality of communion and communication. Creation, redemption, and communication arise from this mystery and have as their final purpose to draw us, by his very communication, into communion with God. Creating us in his image and likeness, God makes us sharers of his creative and liberating communication in communion, through communion, and in view of communion.[62]

3.

The Problem of Method:
From Scholasticism to Models

Several times in the last two chapters I have sketched typologies in the approach to theological problems. The use of types or models has become widespread in current theology. Numerous books can be found with titles such as *Models of God,*[1] *Models of Jesus,*[2] and *Models of Theological Reflection.*[3] I myself have used this device in many of my articles, and the word "models" appears in the titles of two of my books: *Models of the Church*[4] and *Models of Revelation.*[5] I gave some thought to making the present book an investigation of "models of theology." Even though I decided against doing so, it seems that some discussion of the use of models in theology is appropriate here. I can best explain my personal thought on the matter by means of some autobiographical reflections.

Scholastic Method

My own turn toward the method of models is partly in continuity with, and partly in reaction against, the neo-scholastic system in which I was trained in my own philosophical and theological studies. Characteristic of that system was the division of theology into tracts or treatises, each of which was broken down into a series of theses. The theses, generally formulated in language echoing the official teaching of popes and councils, were set forth in a standard pattern. After the enunciation of the thesis came the definitions of the key terms, followed by a listing of adversaries, and a theological

41

note indicating the degree of certitude and emphasis attaching to the thesis. Next came a series of proofs from authoritative church teaching, from the Bible, from tradition, and from theological reasoning. Finally the arguments of the adversaries were summarized and answered. The entire thesis was sometimes followed by corollaries and scholia dealing with connected questions.

I do not at all regret having been schooled in this scholastic method. It gave me a good exposure to the Catholic tradition and to the history of theological controversy. In addition it taught me something about how to mount a theological argument. Among the values of the scholastic system, in its twentieth-century neo-scholastic form, I would list the following ten:

1. Respect for the authority of distinguished predecessors and a desire to learn from them. The scholastics of modern times did not strive for originality. Their aim was to be faithful to the tradition handed down to them by the great masters of antiquity, especially Thomas Aquinas. St. Thomas and his contemporaries sought to be unoriginal or at least to conceal their originality. Above all they wanted to adhere to the teaching of the fathers.

2. Aspiration to reconcile the opinions of esteemed theologians. Ever since Abelard wrote his *Sic et non*, scholastic theologians were eager to "save the authorities." It was an unwritten rule that the fathers should never be contradicted. Their opinions were defended, if necessary, by subtle distinctions. This basic confidence in the ideas of orthodox Christians was beneficial to the Church as a community that perdures through the centuries.

3. High regard for official church teaching. The theses, as I have mentioned, were generally taken from the documents of popes and councils, and theological notes were an effort to assess the binding force of the theses on the basis of the authoritative sources.

4. The sense of working in and for the Church, and of having to contribute to its future. Scholastic theology was nothing if not ecclesial. The authors were all conscious of being collaborators in articulating the doctrines of the Church. Often enough the theses were proposed with a view to preparing the way for future official teaching, including dogmatic definitions.

5. The importance of proceeding systematically, ordering the questions logically, and avoiding unnecessary repetition. Thomas Aquinas, in his *Summa theologiae*, made a notable improvement on the order used by Peter Lombard in the previous century. In later cen-

turies some authors sought to improve on Thomas Aquinas. While recognizing that some anticipations and reiterations were inevitable, all agreed on the importance of not relying more than necessary on theses that were to be proved at a later point.

6. Clarity about the state of the question, the issues, and the meaning of the terms. The scholastics always took care to state what they were presupposing and what was the exact point at issue. With an accuracy that could at times be tedious, they explained what they meant by the terms in the theses, and when necessary distinguished between different meanings of the same term.

7. A sense of systematic responsibility. These theologians did not confine themselves to a single treatise, but looked upon each treatise as part of an all-embracing whole. They were at pains to see that their answer to any given question was compatible with the answers they would give to other questions. Often the connections between theses were illuminated by the objections and replies at the end of the thesis.

8. The necessity of taking a definite position and supporting it by explicit arguments. In contrast with some contemporary authors, who often leave their own positions to be gathered from the way in which they speak about other authors, the scholastics never contented themselves with simply expounding the views of others. The method constrained them to enunciate positions for which they took personal responsibility. They could not base their positions on emotional attraction, rhetorical appeal, or vague hunches. The method required them to give objective reasons.

9. The value of framing objections to one's own answers and of replying to adversaries. From the High Middle Ages to the middle of our own century, scholastic theologians strove to give the strongest arguments they could against their own positions, and then to answer those arguments. While the results were not always convincing, the method itself was sound.

10. The recognition that not all conclusions were equally certain. Each thesis had to have a theological note attached to it, indicating the degree of its certitude or probability, as the case might be. Reasons were given for the note in question: for example, the definitions of popes and councils, the clear teaching of Scripture, theological reasoning, the general consent of the fathers or of the theologians.

Limitations of Scholasticism

Educationally sound though the thesis method was, it could not be described as adequate. My own professors had no illusions about this. They read and recommended other pertinent literature to supplement the arid manuals. Studying theology in the early 1950s, when the *nouvelle théologie* was beginning to become popular, I treasured the opportunity to read books and articles by authors such as Henri de Lubac, Yves Congar, Jean Daniélou, and Karl Rahner. It was a period of renewal in Catholic biblical studies, and my professors introduced me to new developments in exegesis. The work of Roland de Vaux, Pierre Benoit, David Stanley, and John L. McKenzie, to name but a few, was closely followed. I had the opportunity also to read distinguished Protestant biblical theologians such as Oscar Cullmann and Rudolf Bultmann, though of course such reading was in those days considered strictly extracurricular and even dangerous.

Theological literature such as I have just mentioned formed a valuable supplement, and at some points a corrective, to the set theses of the manuals. The leaders of the *nouvelle théologie* showed how scholasticism itself had been narrowed down since the Counter-Reformation, and appealed for a recovery of the patristic roots. While retrieving the early Christian sources, they were able to exhibit the historically and culturally conditioned character of many of the scholastic categories that had been interpreted as if they were inseparable from reason itself. Some exposure to the new biblical theology reinforced the same lesson. It was misleading to quote isolated verses from the Bible as though the words meant in Scripture exactly what a modern writer might mean by them. It was necessary to study biblical texts in their own proper context. This exercise made it apparent that there were various biblical theologies, such as the Deuteronomic, the apocalyptic, the Pauline, the Matthean, and the Johannine.

Another major influence on my thought as a theology student was the ecumenical movement. Gustave Weigel, S.J., one of my professors, convinced me that the Catholic Church could not ignore the work of theologians such as Karl Barth and Paul Tillich, and that the World Council of Churches was making important advances in the quest for unity. Weigel himself had warm personal relations with many Protestant, Orthodox, and Jewish theologians, and was one of the pioneers of Catholic ecumenism in the United States in the

1950s. After Vatican II, which occurred when I was already teaching theology, it became evident to me that the kind of polemical theology pursued since the Reformation was no longer in order. It was necessary to adopt a dialogic method in which the views of Protestant and Orthodox theologians could be taken seriously, though not uncritically, as expressions of Christian faith.

During my early years as a professor of theology (beginning in 1960), I felt it important to familiarize myself with the history of my own disciplines, confident that I had much to learn from the past. As a result I was able to publish a history of revelation theology and a somewhat longer history of apologetics. From these and other studies I saw the advantage of moving beyond the thesis method in systematic theology and attempting to grasp the thought of individual authors and schools of thought as integrated wholes, which in turn had to be seen in light of the general movement of the history of ideas.

In my efforts at synthesis I found that thinkers tended to fall into certain types. For example, in the concluding pages of my *Revelation Theology* [6] I noted that three basic mentalities could be distinguished, giving rise to three distinct styles of revelational theology: the historical, the doctrinal, and the mystical. Some years later I was surprised to discover that Friedrich von Hügel had made almost the same division in his great work *The Mystical Element in Religion.*[7] Thinkers of any given type tended to agree with one another across the board, for their shared outlook and concerns predetermined their positions on a whole range of topics. The theologian, therefore, could not adequately deal with thinkers of another school by looking at their answers to isolated questions. Since each theologian's answers had to be considered within his or her own intellectual framework, it was necessary for system to confront system.

The scholastic method had to some extent recognized this need. The "adversaries" were grouped in types or schools, and the same adversaries continued to appear in thesis after thesis. But the thesis method, which took up individual questions in a piecemeal fashion, did not allow for any confrontation between systems as connected wholes. To the student it remained a mystery why anyone would choose to be an empiricist or an idealist in philosophy, a Lutheran or a Jansenist in theology. Scholasticism, at least in the forms familiar to me, did not seem to be able to deal with the different angles of vision from which theologians of different schools contemplated reality. It assumed too readily that everybody had an Aristotelian mentality.

A further weakness in scholasticism was that the authors were content to remain ensconced in their own battlements, treating all others simply as adversaries. Objections were raised, but only, it would seem, for the purpose of refuting them. No real dialogue was attempted. After Vatican II it became evident that a method was needed in which theologians of different schools could be treated with respect and understanding and in which all parties might hope to learn from one another. At this point I came to consider the advantages of the "models" methodology.

Models in Theology

While the term "model" is a relatively new one, perhaps imported from the physical and social sciences, the method is in its essentials rather traditional. Indeed, it goes back to pre-Christian times. Aristotle, in the first book of his *Metaphysics*, gives a typology of previous positions with regard to the first principles of reality. By surveying the views of the pre-Socratics and Plato and exhibiting their different "root metaphors" (to use a modern term), Aristotle attempts to gather materials for constructing his own "first philosophy." He finds it possible to synthesize and correct the insights of his predecessors by showing that they were concentrating on different but limited aspects of reality. While Aristotle made some real advances, his own philosophy belongs to a particular type, having its own characteristic metaphors. Thus the plurality of models remained.

Working as a theologian, I had certain assumptions based on faith. On the ground that Christians have never been unassisted by the Holy Spirit (cf. 1 Cor. 12:3), I presupposed that in speaking about matters of faith they are attempting to describe things of which they have some inner experience. If a major group of Christians has continued to regard some doctrine as a correct articulation of the faith, one ought to assume that there is some underlying truth in what they are saying, even though their formulations may be judged in some respects deficient. Augustine had asserted the importance of seeking out the truth in every heresy. Seeking to obey this injunction, I was inclined to find the truth-component more in what a given group asserted than in what it denied, since people tend to assert that of which they have experience and to deny that of which they lack experience. As a Catholic, of course, I was convinced that the tradition of my own Church, especially on the level of creed and dogma, was to be accepted, even though it might stand in need of further development or refinement, and that any contrary views were in need of correction. These methodological postulates seemed to me applicable not only to the relations between confessional groups but also to those between theological families. It followed that before refuting a theory one should make sure to have learned as much as one could from those who defended it.

In an ideal world it might be desirable to enter into dialogue with every theologian as an individual. To do this, however, one would have to compose lengthy historical disquisitions that would be distracting in a work of systematic theology. What was essential for theology was to identify the major points of view and to grasp the inner logic behind the characteristic positions. By giving a general overview of what significant groups of believers had held on different questions, it would be possible to exhibit where the principal agreements and disagreements lay.

Efforts to construct theological typologies had been common since Ernst Troeltsch's classic work *The Social Teaching of the Christian Churches* (1911). A remarkably successful example of the typological approach was *Christ and Culture* (1951) by H. Richard Niebuhr, who was in some ways a disciple of Troeltsch. In view of the manifest success of that work it was no longer necessary to apologize for using theological typologies.

In several of my works I refer to types as models. In a sense, every type is already a model. It is a schematic construction that enables one to make statements potentially applicable to an indefinite number of individuals. Just as the tailor's dummy is a help for producing clothes that can easily be adjusted to different individuals, so the theologian's models can be helpful for speaking about classes of theologians, even though every individual will have distinguishing characteristics.

If we consider theological systems in relation to the realities to which they refer, the concept of model takes on additional significance. The theologian, by vocation, deals with mystery. The primary subject matter of theology is God, the *Deus semper maior*, who infinitely excels all that can be thought or said about him. The theologian attempts to speak about God by using created similitudes that reflect, in limited ways, his infinite perfections. Quite under-standably, therefore, Holy Scripture uses a vast array of metaphors, calling God a husband, a rock, a fortress, a captain, a shepherd, and so forth.

The same problem confronts anyone who would speak about Christ or about the Church, or indeed about any properly theological topic. In the New Testament Christ is depicted under many images and metaphors, as shepherd, bridegroom, vine, door, light, king, and judge, to name but a few of the analogies. The Church is described under the likenesses of a sheepfold, an olive tree, a living body, a temple, and many other similitudes.

It might be thought that theology, by utilizing abstract concepts, would be able to leave these images and metaphors behind, but in fact it relies upon such devices, even while seeking to overcome their limitations. Stephen Pepper is generally credited with having first traced the divergences among metaphysical systems to their depen-dence on different "root metaphors." To understand the merits and limitations of a metaphysical system, Pepper contended, it is neces-sary to identify the root metaphor that is presumed in the system. He classified the characteristic metaphors under six headings: animism, mysticism, formism, mechanism, contextualism, and organicism.[8]

In the realm of physics, Niels Bohr maintained that certain phe-nomena such as light could not be accounted for except by invoking a plurality of metaphors, each of which was useful for dealing with certain problems. Thus light could usefully be considered for some purposes as a stream of particles and for others as a wave move-ment. Because of the inadequacy of our conceptual powers, Bohr contended, we had no way of accounting for all the phenomena by means of a single analogy.

The same may be said, mutatis mutandis, of theological systems. Mysteries such as the Holy Trinity are interpreted through models. Some use the analogy of a family, some that of the powers of the soul (memory, intellect, and will). But all the analogies limp. Often a failure to recognize the deficiency of the analogies leads to bitter disputes, even divisions in the Church. To heal these divisions it may be necessary to rediscover the limitations of theological models.

Since divine revelation always comes to people who have their own temperaments, their own memories, cultures, hopes, and fears, it is not surprising that they tend to speak of God's gifts in different ways. Some theologians take as their main reference point the ineffable peace and joy of contemplative union with the divine. Others find the most powerful manifestation of God in the explicit teaching of Scripture, popes, or councils. Still others think of God primarily as the Lord they have encountered in shattering experiences of death and rebirth. Relying on such diverse experiences or reference points, theologians use different root metaphors. They make statements that are difficult to harmonize in a single coherent system. The theory of models, I believe, helps to illuminate and to overcome the conflicts.

In my *Models of the Church* I attempted to show how different ecclesiologies are built upon different "metaphors" such as institution (army, state, school), living body (vine and branches, head and members), sacrament (baptism, Eucharist), herald (messenger, preacher), and servant (healer, helper). The differences between these ecclesiological visions, I maintained, could not be resolved by formal debate because the different schools were speaking out of different concerns; they employed different conceptual categories and different vocabularies. My intention in the book was not to support or deepen the existing divisions, but to facilitate dialogue and reconciliation. I hoped to make my readers more appreciative of the values of ecclesiologies other than their own, and at the same time conscious that their own preferred vision of the Church had its limitations and weaknesses. A truly adequate ecclesiology, I maintained, would have to take into account the insights contained in each of the five models.

In *Models of Revelation* I argued that comparable metaphorical divergences underlie the different theological types. Revelation is variously depicted as doctrine (propositional teaching), historical event (deed of God), mystical experience (loving union), dynamic word (event of proclamation), and new awareness (shift of horizon). In each of these styles of ecclesiology and revelation theology the basic metaphor seemed to be valid up to a point, but limited.

Although I was disposed to find some value in all major theological systems, I did not set all the models on the same level. Yet it was difficult to assign criteria by which they could be evaluated. Certain criteria were acceptable to members of a large variety of schools, but the criteria were differently interpreted and differently weighted, depending on the system. Only limited utility, therefore, could be found in criteria such as conformity with Scripture, rootedness in tradition, inner coherence, plausibility, illuminative power, practical and theoretical fruitfulness, and suitability for dialogue with outsiders.

In the presence of the many models the theologian is confronted with a limited number of options. First, it is possible to select a single model as the right one and dismiss all the others as misleading. Second, one may eclectically choose elements from different models, using some root metaphors for some problems and others for other problems. Third, one may seek to harmonize the models by showing that, rightly understood, they complement one another. Fourth, one may reject all the existing models and propose a new one.

For reasons explained in *Models of Revelation* none of these options, as stated, seemed fully satisfactory. I accordingly advanced still a fifth solution to which I gave the name "dialectical retrieval." Using the concept of symbolic mediation as a dialectical tool, I attempted to draw maximum value from each of the models and to harmonize them critically. To do justice to the values in each model, I maintained, revelatory symbols must themselves be understood not as projections of the believer's subjectivity but rather as means by which God chooses to bring people into living relationship with himself, especially through the incarnate Word. I argued the case for what I called "symbolic realism."

In *A Church to Believe In*,[9] seeking to go beyond the conclusions of *Models of the Church*, I proposed the concept of "community of disciples" as a tool by which to test and perfect the five ecclesiological models set forth in *Models of the Church*. Later I incorporated the model of "community of disciples" in the expanded edition of *Models of the Church*. As I did so, I was conscious that this "model" was not opposed to the other five. Rather, it was a "bridge model" that could not be adequately understood except in light of the previous five models, all of which were useful for illuminating different aspects of community and discipleship themselves.

Objections and Replies

In my discussions with colleagues and in the reviews of my work I have come across certain objections to the method of models. Some contend that the concept of models, taken from the physical and behavioral sciences, is inappropriate for theology. I am unable to see this as a serious difficulty. As I use the concept of models, it is grounded in faith and in the actual practice of theology. This should be evident from what has already been said.

Second, it is objected that the method involves an unfair pigeon-holing of theologians. To some extent this is inevitable, and therefore one would be well advised not to use this method to pass judgment on individuals. No one theologian conforms perfectly to type; many straddle two or more types. The typologist cannot replace the critical historian who presents and analyzes the work of individuals. The systematician's aim is rather to identify issues and options. Thus systematics can work at a level of generality that for history would be unacceptable.

A third objection is that by paying respect to a plurality of mutually incompatible models one falls into relativism and agnosticism. In the end, it is alleged, one endorses systems that clash with one another. This objection, in my opinion, might hold if the theologian did not pass on to the further stage of critical confrontation. The systematician cannot rest with an unresolved contradiction, but it may be that in theology, as in micro- or macrophysics, one must sometimes confess one's inability to overcome certain apparent contradictions. It belongs to the human condition that we are unable to grasp the Absolute except relatively and perspectivally. Even so, however, we can be aware of the limitations of our own words, concepts, images, and models. We are never completely imprisoned in these instruments of thought.

Fourth, it is objected that the method of models is bookish and uncreative. To this I would reply that, like the old scholasticism, the method is ecclesial rather than individualistic. The theologian practicing the method does not rely upon merely private religious experience but seeks to integrate his or her experience into that of the Christian tradition, as represented by other reflective believers. But the method makes ample room for the theologian to reflect on his or her own experience as a believer, participating in the prayer and worship of the Church. The theologian's own experience will inevitably show up in the way that the work of others is evaluated. But at the same time, the individual using this method submits to correction by allowing his or her personal insights to be refined or complemented by those of others in the community of faith.

Fifth and last, the method is impugned on the ground that it stops short of being truly systematic. This may or may not be the case. It is quite possible for the theologian, having pondered the models, to decide that some one model, with its characteristic root metaphor, is to be chosen as the primary basis for a coherent system. If so, he or she will select theological categories and terms suited specifically to that model and will apply them consistently to all the problems that have to be addressed. But I would also caution that in taking a variety of models seriously one will be sensitized to the limitations of any given system. According to my epistemology, any set of mental categories is necessarily limited and falls short of the unfathomable mystery with which theology has to deal. My preference, therefore, is for attempting to make use of a plurality of models, even if this procedure makes for less systematic unity.

Systematic theology aspires to deal in a consistent way with all significant questions pertaining to Christian faith and to develop answers to each of these questions in correlation with all the others. A theological system, as an original construal of the meaning of Christianity, is a major achievement of the creative imagination. Faithful to the data of Scripture and tradition, as well as to all that is known from other sources, the systematician integrates all these manifold elements by means of certain overarching principles into a complex and unified whole. Thomas Aquinas and the great medieval doctors were systematicians in this sense. So were Calvin and Suarez. In our own century the same may be said of a few authors such as Paul Tillich, Karl Rahner, and Wolfhart Pannenberg.

The greatest systematic theologians have always, in my estimation, been somewhat unsystematic. They have never been slaves to the logic of their system. Augustine never fully reconciled his Neoplatonic metaphysics with his commitment to the biblical vision of salvation through time and history. Thomas Aquinas, notwithstanding his preference for Aristotelian categories, never abandoned his attachment to Neoplatonism, even in the acute form represented by Pseudo-Dionysius. He interpreted Aristotle with extraordinary freedom and, when it suited him, shifted to biblical and juridical categories. Thus the method of models is helpful not only for mediating between different theological systems but for analyzing the inner tensions within a single theologian's work. No opposition exists between the approach through models and the practice of systematic theology.

4.

Fundamental Theology and the Dynamics of Conversion

In one of his better-known essays, Bernard Lonergan points out that theology is entering a new age and cannot continue to be what it has been since the sixteenth century.[1] Whereas it used to be a deductive science resting on premises taken from Scripture and church documents, it has become a predominantly empirical discipline, resting on data that have to be interpreted by complex processes and techniques. This new theology, if it is not to be the dupe of every fashion, needs a new foundation. In seeking such a foundation, Lonergan, building on the analogy with other empirical disciplines, concludes that it is possible for a science to have identity and unity even though all its laws and conclusions are subject to revision. By method Lonergan means a set of recurrent and related operations leading to cumulative and progressive results. Although methodology can to some extent be set forth in explicit rules, mastery of method requires long experience of the way the science operates. Each science is a particular dynamic way of generating knowledge.

Applying these principles to theology, Lonergan then points out that the empirical theology of today is a reflection on religion. The foundation is not a set of objective statements but rather the subjective reality of the persons who reflect upon their religious experience, and especially upon the basic process we call conversion.[2] Conversion, for Lonergan, means a radical shift in a person's apprehensions and values, accompanied by a similar radical change in oneself, in one's relations with other persons, and in one's relations to God. The subject of theology, then, is the person undergoing con-

53

version to God. Conversion, as an ongoing process, is for Lonergan correlative with living religion. Reflecting on conversion, he contends, can supply the new theology with the foundation it needs — a foundation that is concrete, dynamic, personal, communal, and historical. Religious conversion manifestly possesses each of these five properties.

My aim, in the present chapter, is not to analyze the nature of theology in general but rather to reflect upon the aims and methods of a single specialization, fundamental theology. The notion of fundamental theology is much controverted in recent literature. Some authors seem to look upon it as a kind of philosophy of religion; some as a strictly rational apologetics for Christianity; some as a generalized reflection on the categories of religious discourse, and some as an introduction to theological method. Karl Rahner has distinguished between "fundamental theology" and a "formal theology of foundations"; then again he has made a distinction between both of these disciplines, it would appear, and what he calls a "first-level reflection" on Christian faith.[3] I have no desire to dispute the terminology of Rahner or any other authority, but I intend in these pages to set forth, as simply as I can, one viable conception of fundamental theology as a reflection on the structures of religious conversion and, more specifically, those of conversion to Christianity. I do not claim that this is the only valid conception of fundamental theology.

Two Concepts of Fundamental Theology

The assignment of fundamental theology, in this context, is to show how the decision to become a Christian can be a responsible exercise of human freedom. In order to carry out this assignment, I shall contend, the theologian will have to adopt categories of thinking that would not be available apart from revelation and faith. He or she will have to look on reality from the believer's point of view and to experience faith, as it were, from within. Christian faith, in my estimation, cannot be justified by public criteria offered in common human experience.

It might be thought that by linking fundamental theology with conversion I am limiting the scope of the discipline so that it deals only with the initial approach to faith on the part of one who has hitherto been a nonbeliever. I would argue, however, that conversion is a continuous process demanded at every stage of the Christian life, and that fundamental theology is therefore of existential import to all believers. Being a Christian is not a static condition, for no believer has faith fully and securely in hand. Christianity, as Søren Kierkegaard well knew, is something to which we are constantly called, and the response to that call demands that we be ever and again extricated from the unbelief that threatens to engulf us.

The concept of fundamental theology just proposed will gain in clarity if contrasted with another, more familiar to most Roman Catholics. Fundamental theology is traditionally defined as that discipline which seeks to demonstrate the credibility of the Christian message and of the Church's claims by the unaided light of reason. This project, it seems to me, is flawed in three respects.

First, this discipline, by calling for *demonstration*, reflects a rationalistic understanding of reason and a faculty that possesses within itself, independently of experience, the principles needed to deduce unassailable conclusions. As I shall later contend, reason always operates within a fiduciary framework. I accept John Henry Newman's thesis that creative intellectual achievements are never attained or adequately justified by deduction or explicit proof.[4]

Second, standard fundamental theology is unrealistic insofar as it demands that the proofs be constructed by the light of *reason alone*, without the illumination of divine grace. This seems to me to be an artificial distinction, inapplicable in practice. The presence or absence of grace can never be verified by empirical tests. We never have the right to assume that our reason is operating by a purely natural light. To the Christian theologian it seems far more probable that reason, whenever it seriously engages itself with religious questions, is motivated by a God-given attraction to the salvation that theology understands as God's gift to us in Jesus Christ. That motivation affects the way in which questions are posed and in which evidence is assessed. Fundamental theology, if it is to consider what human reason actually does in reflecting on religious questions, must investigate the dynamics of a power that is open to the attraction and illumination of grace. The theologian cannot agree in advance to throw away what is, to his or her mind, the key to the phenomenon under investigation.

Third, the standard definition fails to elucidate what is meant by a demonstration of *credibility*. This involves either too much or too little, according to whether or not it implies that the truth of Christianity must be positively demonstrated. If reason alone can achieve this demonstration, then faith would seem to be superfluous; it could at most reduplicate what reason can do without it. If fundamental theology has to stop short of establishing the truth of the Christian faith, it fails to show the rationality of the decision by which one decides to embrace it, for it seems unreasonable to commit oneself decisively to that which is probably false.

In asserting that fundamental theology must study not only the preambles of faith but the dynamics of faith itself, I deliberately set out to pierce the supposedly impermeable wall between reason and faith. I hold that reason is at work not only in the approach to faith, but in the very act of conversion, and indeed in all the mental activity of the believer. Fundamental theology necessarily operates within the circle of faith, for the Christian believer cannot conceive of authentic religious conversion apart from the gracious self-communication of God and the gift of faith, which is known only from within the faith-commitment. To attempt an explanation of Christian faith that draws only upon data derivable from universal experience is to foreclose the very possibility of a satisfactory account of faith. To persons untouched by a grace-filled Christian experience, I submit, Christian faith can only appear as exorbitant and irrational. At best, it would be dismissed as an overcommitment.

Faith as Radical Conversion

In what follows I shall reflect on the process of conversion in two phases, which I distinguish for purposes of orderly presentation, although in actual practice the two are concurrent and mutually interdependent. I shall speak of conversion first from the standpoint of the individual who comes to a decision of faith and second from the standpoint of the believing community that mediates the action of God bringing about conversion. While pastoral theology commonly treats of the second phase, it has been generally neglected by fundamental theology. To study faith as though it were a purely individual decision, uninfluenced by the impact of the community of faith, would be foolish as to try to account for marriage by an investigation of a solitary individual, without regard for the interaction between the two prospective partners. Fundamental theology, I suggest, must ask not only how we get to God but how God comes to us. It must maintain a theological as well as an anthropological focus.

Looking at the process of becoming a Christian from the first of these two standpoints, I would insist that it must be seen as conversion. This term, as we have already seen, with Lonergan's help, signifies not just a change or development but a radical transformation, involving a transvaluation of all values. The convert apprehends differently, says Lonergan, because he has become different.[5] Michael Polanyi likewise describes conversion as a self-modifying act whereby one passes to a radically new way of seeing things. He speaks of the conversion needed to accept an irreducibly new scientific theory, such as those of Freud, Eddington, Rhine, and Lysenko.[6] The justification of religious faith presents problems similar to those encountered in justifying a scientific revolution.[7] The new outlook is not simply deducible from, or reducible to, anything knowable outside the framework it provides. It is separated by a logical gap from any other faith or ideology. No one who has not undergone a conversion is in a position to affirm that the conversion is an authentic one. And the believer, in making this affirmation, is expressing his or her own faith.

Any conversion, religious or other, is problematic. It may be asked on what grounds the process and the resulting act of faith are held to be responsible rather than blind or arbitrary. Before giving my own answer to this question, I should like to mention two solutions which seem to me to be inadequate. One group of theologians, perhaps including Lonergan himself, seems to hold that conversion occurs not in the very acceptance of the Christian message but in a more fundamental act of faith which is made possible by an interior gift of grace accessible even to the unevangelized. In order to have an experience of grace, or of the love of God poured forth into our hearts, these theologians would say, one does not need to have heard the gospel or the name of Jesus Christ. An accepting response to the workings of grace, as we experience these in our own lives, is or includes an act of divine and saving faith. Christian belief, in this perspective, is viewed as a particular thematization of the basic transcendental conversion, and hence not as requiring a new conversion for its acceptance.

This theory of basic of transcendental faith in my opinion contains much truth. I personally hold that the grace of God is at work everywhere, and that a fundamental act of saving faith is within reach of every human being. But I am also convinced that the gospel message, with its good news of what God has actually done for us in Christ, adds something that basically alters the structure of faith itself. Christianity tells us what we could never have spun out of our own private consciousness, namely, that God has appeared on earth in the person and career of Jesus of Nazareth. The gospel enables us to relate to God in a new way, thanking and trusting him because of what he has actually done for us in the incarnate life, death, and resurrection of his Son. Those theologians who treat faith simply as a transcendental experience of God, taking place in the inwardness of the human spirit, tend to minimize the historical element in the Christian religion and to overlook the crucial role of mediation through the living community of faith.

I conclude, therefore, that to come to Christian faith from any other stance, even from the theistic faith of Judaism, is a radically new discovery requiring that kind of heuristic process here described as conversion. The early Christians, in controversy with the Jews, appealed to the Hebrew Scriptures as proof-texts, but in fact they were reading these Scriptures in a new way, in light of the Christ-event, and hence were not giving deductive or syllogistic arguments. The Old Testament, indeed, teaches us to look in history for the work of a God who loves and saves, but the Christian interpretation of the Old Testament is a "new hermeneutic" which takes its starting point in the Christ-event as the key to the meaning of Scripture rather than interpreting Jesus in the framework of the previously accepted Jewish categories.

A second school of fundamental theologians, at the opposite extreme, speaks as though Christian conversion could be effected by demonstrative reasoning from historically accessible facts. This position corresponds to what I have already described as the traditional fundamental theology. In the early modern period, from the seventeenth century to the nineteenth, apologetics, in a deluded quest for objectivity, sought to establish the credibility of the Christian religion by means of historical proofs. Any reasonable person, it contended, looking at the data of history, would be obliged to admit that God had authenticated the prophets, Jesus Christ, and the Christian Church by prophecies and miracles. From this it followed that the Christian religion must be accounted a true revelation. This positivist approach was unsuccessful because it oversimplified the process of establishing the existence of fulfilled prophecies and miracles, including the resurrection of Jesus. As Hume conclusively showed, the academic historian, without the guiding light of religious presuppositions, will look upon error or deception in the accounts as far more likely than the actual occurrence of events such as the resurrection of a dead body.

Since the end of the nineteenth century, a host of Christian apologists have pointed out the inadequacies of the positivist approach. Henri Bouillard speaks for this newer tendency when he writes: "No historical proof could suffice to establish that these facts [i.e., miracles] manifest the presence of God and the advent of his Kingdom, unless these are spiritually discerned from the standpoint of a personal commitment."[8] Mere facts, viewed in the perspectives of positivist historiography, would be incapable of bringing about a conversion. For positivist historiography has its own principles which prevent it from acknowledging any such thing as divine activity in history. The decision of faith, therefore, must rest on a conversion process in which the data of history function in a different manner, still to be described.

Granted the insufficiency of the two approaches just outlined, we are left with the apparent irrationality of the decision of faith. If it cannot be grounded either in a commonly accessible transcendental faith or in rationally demonstrable historical events, how can conversion be distinguished from a blind and irrational leap into the dark? How can authentic faith be distinguished from fanaticism or delusion?

One may begin by retorting the objection against the objector. How does the non-Christian justify the nonacceptance of the Christian message? Careful scrutiny, I believe, can make it apparent that every intellectual stance, including all religions and all secular ideologies, rests upon a multitude of unspecifiable and unverifiable assumptions, and in that sense may be called a "faith." Agnosticism is itself a faith, insofar as it implies the assertion that we lack the capacity to attain sure knowledge about the transcendent. Although one may hold with Locke that it is unreasonable to be certain of anything about which we lack immediate evidence or demonstrative knowledge, this very principle is itself an act of faith, incapable of being made immediately evident or of being demonstrated from what is immediately evident. In point of fact, every world view, including positivism and skepticism, rests upon a matrix of presuppositions too complex and subtle for enumeration, let alone for proof.

As Polanyi shows at length, no intelligence can operate outside a fiduciary framework.[9] Whenever we judge or decide, we commit ourselves to something that could conceivably be false.

Everybody, then, operates on some faith or other, and each faith is, in the nature of the case, incapable of being cogently proved. In real life choice is between rival faiths, and there is no neutral ground from which to adjudicate their opposite claims, for every set of criteria itself presupposes some faith or other. Alternative systems, in religion as in the sciences, threaten each other, since the unbelief of people whom we respect imperils our own convictions. Each faith therefore propagates itself by seeking to win converts. It must overcome or die.

Practically speaking, however, there are norms that operate even in the case of conversion. Most people do have some criteria which serve as a rule of thumb for choosing among conflicting creeds. Some of these rules are so basic that they are almost inseparable from the inherent structures of the human mind. For example, few if any of us would defend a conviction that arose through simple inattention. Without fearing contradiction from others whose judgment we respect, we can reject certain systems as incoherent, superstitious, or fraudulent. But, having eliminated what is manifestly illusory and unhelpful, we are left with a number of systems of acknowledged competence — those which are regarded as credible and enlightening by people whose judgment we esteem.

At a second stage in selecting a faith for ourselves, I submit, we employ practical or pragmatic criteria. We eliminate as personally unacceptable those creeds which, in our estimation, would fail to enhance the quality of our lives. While the question of higher or lower quality cannot be settled by mechanical measurements, most of us would agree that qualities such as charity, joy, peace, patience, and the like are preferable to their opposites. To one who has experienced them, these qualities are self-validating. Paul made use of criteria such as these in instructing the Galatians regarding the kind of conduct that befitted Christians (Gal. 5:22). Similar criteria, I believe, can be applied to the choice between rival faiths. We are rightly inclined to accept a faith which promises to bring openness, generosity, mutual concern, and freedom to individuals and to the social body. We shy away from faiths that seem to foster hatred, misery, narrowness, violence, anger, impatience, and the like.

Still a third set of criteria focuses on those benefits which we expect specifically from a religion. People turn to religion, if at all, because they are looking for delivery from their situation of guilt and alienation and from the ever-present menace of death. Further, they expect religion to shed light on questions of ultimate meaning and to provide a coherent set of purposes and values for their lives. Religions differ notably from one another in their ability to furnish or credibly promise these benefits. A shift from one religion to another is frequently motivated by a judgment regarding the relative capacities of the two faiths to offer these specifically religious values.

In short, we may say that the chief criterion for a viable religious faith is its ability, or apparent ability, to satisfy those hungers of the human spirit which cannot be satisfied apart from faith. The concrete experience of these hungers will vary from person to person and from culture to culture; but there seems to be a generic human drive to be known, valued, and loved; to be drawn into communion with others; to be delivered from death and from the threat of final absurdity. A faith that offers even a provisional glimpse of ultimate meaning and abiding value will normally have great power to attract believers. Christians are convinced that the perception of God obtainable through Jesus Christ is able to provide these benefits more effectively than any other faith.

Influence of Word and Testimony

Thus far I have spoken as though conversion were the achievement of the solitary individual, dispassionately pondering the claims of different faiths and ideologies, which come into view as potential objects of choice. I have not shown how such deliberation brings about what Lonergan and others refer to as a conversion, a total transformation of the very person who accepts the faith in question.

This aspect of conversion can better be seen if we begin at the other end of the process and ask how it is that God brings a potential believer to the point of personal transformation. For it is certain that the kind of transformation required by religious conversion, if it is to be authentic, must be the work of God. We cannot convert ourselves by our own unaided powers.

Looking at this process from the point of view of faith, the Christian theologian will have good reason to suppose that God operates immediately in the depths of the human psyche, arousing selfless love, boundless hope, patience and gratitude of a kind that simply cannot be accounted for by any set of contingent circumstances. By responding to interior graces of this kind, a person may be raised to a very high degree of personal perfection. In this way an unevangelized person may be brought to a kind of nonobjective or transcendental faith, deserving of the utmost respect.

In the present chapter, however, I am concerned with the process by which people are brought to explicit Christian faith, that is to say, to an acceptance of Jesus Christ as Lord and Savior. Such a conversion, as is evident, commonly occurs through the ministry of the Church, which as a community of faith brings the message and the person of Christ within reach of potential believers. The Church makes its impact through committed testimony and through the symbolic embodiment of that testimony in the lives of Christians. Let me briefly touch on each of these two styles of impact.

It can scarcely be doubted that testimony, and indeed verbal testimony, plays an essential role in the transmission of Christian faith. For, as we have already noted, Christianity is an essentially historical religion. It looks upon a certain man, a certain series of events, at a certain time and place in the rather distant past, as the primary mediation of the saving message. No one can profess Jesus Christ as Savior, as incarnate Son, and as risen Lord, without dependence on Christian proclamation, either oral or written.

How does the proclaimed word bring about conversion? Words can be used to convey information, but mere information does not convert; it simply fits into previously existing thought categories, or if it fails to do so, it is ordinarily rejected as false. Words can also be used for discursive argumentation; but argument, even though it may convince, does not convert, for it necessarily appeals to the premises and presuppositions of the persons to whom the argument is directed. In inducing people to accept a new faith, we have to dispose them to accept new categories of thought and speech that previously seemed strange and incomprehensible to them.

Religious testimony is singularly well suited to achieve this precise effect. As an expression of personal conviction, testimony draws its power from its appeal to the trustworthiness of the speaker. Believers who proclaim a definite faith engage themselves as witnesses to what they affirm; they guarantee by their very persons the integrity and soundness of their message. To accept their testimony is to accept the witnesses as persons; to reject it, conversely, is in some measure to reject the witnesses themselves. When we bear witness to our religious faith, we make an offer of friendship; we expose what is most intimate and vulnerable in ourselves, most subject to ridicule and rejection. Trustingly we invite others to enter into a personal communion of shared faith, a communion constituted by a network of interpersonal relations. Whoever accepts such religious testimony becomes a member of a new community and is changed as a person by that very fact.

In light of these considerations we can easily see how religious testimony paves the way for conversion. In order to be genuinely open to the testimony of another, the hearer must put aside any natural tendency to judge and criticize the message according to a previously given set of expectations. The responsive listener, out of love and respect for the person of the witness, will seek to enter the latter's cognitive perspectives, to see the world from the witness's point of view. Through empathy it will be possible for the hearer to imagine what reality must look like to the speaker, and this vision, once grasped, may seem far more attractive than anything the hearer could have conceived apart from this testimony.

Fundamental theology, therefore, cannot neglect the crucially important factor of testimony. It must grapple with the difficult problem of drawing the line between credible and incredible testimony. Since religious testimony has the power to upset our expectations, we must beware of setting up rigid criteria, such as those conventionally used by academic history and by courts of law, both of which necessarily operate by rules which apply to common and repeatable situations. Still, criteria there are. The more extraordinary and unexpected the message, the more guarantees we normally demand from the witness.

Where a claim to divine revelation is made, the criteria are similar to those already outlined for the choice of religion. On the one hand, we must consider whether the message is evidently absurd or whether it can be explained away as a simple confusion, legend, fraud, or the like. On the other hand, we must consider whether the message has illuminative and transformative power, whether it brings promise of reconciliation with God, and does whatever else a divine revelation is supposed to do. As regards the witnesses, we shall seek evidence of their sincerity, their competence, their conviction, and the importance they attach to their message. We shall ask whether their testimony is corroborated by a plurality of independent witnesses. We shall also look to see what effects the message has had on the lives of those who already believe it. Are they more generous, joyful, open, and courageous than nonbelievers? If so, we shall have reason to suspect that by believing them we might ourselves achieve a richer and better life.

Because testimony is intimately connected with the person of the witness, credible testimony is never a mere matter of words. This is especially the case with testimony to religious faith, which touches the person at the deepest level. A witness to a revelation is not credible without being at least in some measure transformed by the message itself. If we are to bear effective witness to Jesus as risen Savior, we must be joyful, hopeful, and courageous; otherwise it will be apparent that our faith is not deeply and sincerely held. On the other hand, even a faith that is rather weakly held can be impressive in its own way. The most important thing will be the hearer's estimation of what effects the message would be capable of having on one who did fully accept it. Most Christian missionaries hold forth the examples of Christ and the saints, and are reluctant to propose themselves as examples of what Christian faith can do for people.

Christianity, then, propagates itself not only by explicit, or verbal, testimony but even more importantly by implicit, or factual, testimony — that is, by the testimony of transformed lives. In the measure in which faith is truly accepted, its adherents become living symbols of the creed they profess. The power of salvation takes over their existence and shines forth in their persons and in their actions. Such a transformation is particularly impressive when it is beyond expectation and when it defies the general patterns of human behavior. Paul was able to claim for himself that the life of Jesus was manifest in him, even when he was being given over to death for Jesus' sake (2 Cor. 4:7–11). A peace that is not troubled even amid danger and affliction can be a potent reminder of the transcendent power of divine grace.

The rationalistic apologetics of recent centuries was perhaps misguided in its attempts to prove that miracles were antecedently possible. If miracles could fit into the framework of what we already regarded as possible, they would be powerless to effect a conversion. The whole point of miracles, if one may put it in this way, is that they are beyond what we would have deemed possible. They shake us up and bewilder us, so that we acknowledge that our previous horizons were too narrow. The possibility of miracles, if it can be established at all, can only be established in the light of the conviction that miracles have occurred. Miracles, moreover, are most convincing when intrinsically connected with the message they accredit. The miracles of Jesus were not mere proofs that whatever he said should be believed; they were a way of telling his audience that the Kingdom he proclaimed was already being inaugurated. They were a kind of visible word. In the course of its history, Christianity has relied less on physical miracles, which are relatively remote from its message, than on the moral miracle of transformed lives. Such lives visibly embody the salvation which verbal proclamation promises and describes.

In order to complete this line of thought, it will be helpful to recall what has been said in earlier chapters about the nature of symbol. A symbol, we have seen, communicates by inviting people to participate in its own meaning, to inhabit the world which it opens up, and thereby to discover new horizons, with new values and new goals. Symbols do something to us. They shift our center of awareness and thereby change our perspectives and values. Symbols, therefore, have the kind of transformative power that is needed for conversion to come about. Without symbols, no revelation could be effectively communicated.

The message concerning Jesus Christ, then, must not only be spoken or written. It must also be symbolically enfleshed in actual life. This happens, to a greater or lesser extent, in the Church. Every community of faith stands under judgment to the extent that it fails to incarnate in its actual practice what it professes to believe. The successful proclamation of Christianity does not require, in the first instance, a better theory of apologetics. It does require that Christians be seriously committed to their faith, so as to make their communities living and corporate signs of the presence of Christ in the world. According to many contemporary ecclesiologists, with whom I align myself, the Church, in its basic reality, is a symbol or sacrament of Christ.

For the Christian believer the translation of the gospel into practice is not something extra, over and above the process of conversion. It is part and parcel of the conversion itself. As I have repeatedly insisted, conversion is not a mere change of ideas or objectives. More fundamentally it is a transformation of the person who is converted. The believer becomes a different being. The convert acquires a new identity, a new self, and for this reason it is customary for Christian converts, in baptism, to take a new name — a Christian name, signifying this new identity.

The new identity is one that each Christian shares with others. It is the corporate identity of the Christian community, into which the individual is integrated as an extension of his or her own self. Christians see and hear no longer with their own eyes and ears alone, but with those of the Church to which they now belong. They think its thoughts and it thinks in them. Their faith is a participation in the faith of the Church, to which they submit as the rule of their own believing. They know what the community knows, not with mere spectator knowledge, whereby one gazes at something, but by an inner familiarity, through indwelling, somewhat as we know our own bodies. The more completely the believer dwells in the community of faith and relies upon it, the more lively will be his or her sense of the Christian faith, and the better will he or she be able to discern what is and is not consonant with faith. The more believers make the faith of the community their own, the better will they be able to see the deficiencies in the ways that Christians have previously expressed their faith, and the more creative they will be in adapting Christian doctrine and symbolism to new and unprecedented situations. Paradoxically, commitment to the Church is a normal prerequisite for competently criticizing the Church.

In these last paragraphs I have passed quite deliberately from the individual to the ecclesial dimension of conversion. I would insist that no Christian conversion is complete unless it situates the convert solidly within the community of faith. But it is equally important not to stop with the ecclesial. The Church does not subsist in itself, nor is it intelligible in itself. It subsists in Christ. Christian initiation, therefore, is initiation into Christ, whose Body is the Church. Baptism sacramentally symbolizes both a death to one's former self (the self of the estranged individual) and a rebirth to new life in Christ, the life of the People of God. In the words of Paul, quoted by Lonergan in his essay on conversion, "If anyone is in Christ, he is a new creation; the old has passed away and, behold, the new has come" (2 Cor. 5:17).[10] The Christian already lives by faith in the transformed universe of the eschatological future.

To extend this line of consideration to its logical conclusion, we should not stop with Christ. We should have to discuss the doctrine of the Holy Spirit, who alone can account for the inner conviction with which Christians accept the person and teaching of Christ. The Spirit gives power and efficacy to Christian proclamation and arouses a positive response in the hearts of those who are called to believe. The full conviction of Christian faith is not achieved without both the outward and the inward testimony of the Holy Spirit. By reception of the Spirit the individual is incorporated into the Church, the Body of Christ.

William James treated religious faith as though it were a hypothesis to account for certain peculiar experiences. At a certain point, when one is moving in a tentative way toward faith, one's religion may in fact be nothing more than a hypothesis. But so long as one looks upon it in this light, one has not as yet been converted. A hypothesis is a tentative explanation that one is prepared to discard as soon as a better explanation is forthcoming. A religious faith, on the other hand, claims us totally, so that we are no longer in a position to discard it without loss of our new identity. As Polanyi remarks in answer to James, "a religion exists for us only if . . . it carries us away. It is not in any sense a 'hypothesis.' "[11] We do not so much grasp the faith as allow ourselves to be grasped by it, so that we are at its disposal rather than its being at ours. Our mind functions in a new way as God's thoughts break into it and possess it. It is possible, of course, for us to lose our faith, but such a loss, if we really had faith, would mean a shattering of our selfhood and of our world.

Antecedent Improbability

It may seem at this point that I have gone far beyond the proper limits of fundamental theology. If fundamental theology ought not to draw upon Christian doctrine, I have indeed transgressed the limits. But I hope that I have also succeeded in showing that the restriction is unwarranted, because it is impossible to account for Christian conversion, or to show the reasonableness of faith, in terms of merely human and created factors, and without reference to the Christian doctrine of God. The reasonableness can be sufficiently explained to the believer, but only from within the circle of faith. A non-Christian can see the coherence of the Christian explanation only if he or she is willing to accept the Christian doctrines in a hypothetical way, at least for purposes of the discussion.

If the basic thesis of this chapter is correct, it is a mistake to attempt, with certain theologians, to make Christian conversion plausible on terms other than those of Christianity itself. Every effort to account for Christian faith without the powerful interventions of God's Word and God's Spirit is in the last analysis foredoomed to failure. Such efforts, although well intended, necessarily end by giving the impression that faith, insofar as it is specifically Christian, must be either a tenuous conjecture or a fanatical overcommitment. It may be possible to show a non-Christian why one might use Christian symbols as a way of talking about one's boundary experiences, but such a use of Christian symbols is not yet an act of Christian faith. To justify Christian faith, one would have to show that it is proper to believe, with the firmness of faith, that Jesus really is what the New Testament and the creeds say he is.

Fundamental theology, as I understand it, can facilitate the approach to Christian faith by showing that there are real values that cannot be achieved except by undergoing conversion. It can show that the same kind of process that leads a person to accept the basic elements of morality and religion can lead on, with the help of grace, to Christian and Catholic faith. But it cannot establish the truth of the Christian dogmas by proofs convincing to persons who have no experience of the power of the gospel. The Christ of the New Testament is foolishness to the Greeks who seek after wisdom and weakness to the Jews who call for signs (cf. 1 Cor 1:18–25). One function of fundamental theology might be to show why the affirmations of Christian faith must seem implausible to all who do not experience the power of God's word in Christ.

5.

The Uses of Scripture in Theology

Holy Scripture, as I have said, is a medium of divine revelation, a self-expression of the original community of faith, and an abiding resource for keeping the Church faithful to its divinely given origins. For all its wonderful qualities, the Bible does not adequately certify or interpret itself to every individual. The theologian, at least in the Catholic view, must use it as a book of the Church. This principle, however, is not simply restrictive. On the contrary, it opens up immense vistas because of the variety of uses that are encouraged by the tradition.

Official Catholic Teaching

Over the centuries the Catholic Church has accumulated a vast body of official teaching on the interpretation of Scripture.[1] The Council of Trent, warning against the dangers of private interpretation in matters pertaining to the establishment of Christian doctrine regarding faith and morals,[2] declared that it is for the Church to decide on the true meaning and interpretation of Scripture and that Scripture is never to be interpreted contrary to the unanimous consensus of the fathers (EB 62).[3] Vatican I repeated the same warnings (*Dei Filius*, EB 78).

The popes in their biblical encyclicals reiterated the same restrictions but also added positive encouragement for biblical scholars and theologians. Leo XIII in *Providentissimus Deus* (1893) praised the medieval interpreters for their care to preserve both the biblical texts and the patristic tradition of interpretation, as well as for the greater precision with which they distinguished the various senses of the Bible, including those that were figurative or allegorical. While defending the primacy of the literal sense, Leo XIII pointed out the value of investigating the "other senses, adapted to illustrate dogma and confirm morality" (EB 108). Turning to theology, the pope laid down the principle, often repeated since his day, that "the use of Holy Scripture should influence the whole teaching of theology and should be practically its soul [*eiusque prope sit anima*]" (EB 114).

Benedict XV in his encyclical *Spiritus Paraclitus* (1920) was understandably defensive against the recent incursions of Modernism, but in the positive portions of his encyclical he exhorted Catholic scholars to imitate the scholarship of Jerome in seeking out the literal sense, and to see that any mystical interpretations are solidly based upon the literal. "For all the children of the Church," he concluded, "we desire that, being saturated and strengthened by the Scriptures, they may arrive at the all-surpassing knowledge of Jesus Christ" (EB 495).

Pius XII in *Divino Afflante Spiritu* (1943) exhorted Catholic exegetes to take as their principal task the discovery and exposition of the literal sense, "so that the mind of the author may be made abundantly clear" (EB 550). He reminded biblical interpreters of the need to take account of the various literary forms used by the ancient Semites so as to understand the texts correctly (EB 558–60). Emphasizing the freedom of Catholic biblical scholars, the pope mentioned that "there are but few texts whose sense has been defined by the authority of the Church, nor are those more numerous about which the teaching of the Holy Fathers is unanimous" (EB 565). At several points the pope exhorted exegetes not to confine themselves to historical and philological questions but to assist in determining the theological meaning of the sacred text, so as to be of assistance to professors of theology and to preachers (EB 551, 567).

The official teaching of the magisterium on the interpretation of Scripture was admirably summarized by Vatican II in its Dogmatic Constitution on Divine Revelation (*Dei Verbum*). In number 12, expressly devoted to biblical interpretation, the constitution distinguished between two levels of meaning, the literal sense intended by the biblical writers themselves and the further understanding that may be attained thanks to "the content and coherence of Scripture as a whole, taking into account the whole Church's living tradition and the analogy of faith," that is to say, the harmony that exists among revealed truths. In later numbers the constitution encouraged Catholic students of the Bible to pursue a deeper penetration of the Scriptures based on the teaching of the fathers and the testimony of sacred liturgies (no. 23). Repeating statements of Leo XIII and Benedict XV, the Constitution on Divine Revelation declared that the study of the sacred page is, as it were, the soul of sacred theology (no. 24). At many points *Dei Verbum* made it clear that the theological interpretation of Scripture requires faith (ibid.), since "Sacred Scripture must be read and interpreted in the light of the same Spirit through whom it was written" (no. 12). In the perspectives of Christian faith the council repeats the dictum of Augustine that "the New Testament is hidden in the Old, and that the Old Testament is manifest in the New" (no. 16).

One of the most instructive recent documents on the use of Scripture in theology is the statement of the Biblical Commission on *Scripture and Christology* issued in 1984.[4] This statement surveys eleven contemporary approaches to Christology and points out their respective assets and limitations.[5] While calling attention to what may be one-sided in these various approaches, the Biblical Commission adopts a basically positive attitude, accepting what is sound in each methodology. The commission concludes that an integral Christology must take account of the full content of the Bible and all aspects of the biblical witness.

In view of the profusion of approaches already current, the most pressing need is not for the elaboration of new methods but rather for a critical assessment of those already in use. The question is whether all the existing methods are legitimate, and whether they can comfortably coexist. Is the theologian compelled to choose certain methods and reject others? Although the methods could be multiplied almost endlessly, I shall try to summarize under ten headings the methods that seem most evident in contemporary theology.

Ten Approaches

The classical doctrinal approach. For many centuries theologians, both Protestant and Catholic, have been using the Bible as a treasury of doctrinal statements or as an armory from which doctrines of the Church can be textually vindicated. Taking the Bible as an inspired or inerrant book, or at least as a normative source of Christian doctrine, theologians quote biblical texts that seem to support their own positions or the positions of their Church.

The Bible, for instance, states repeatedly that there is one God, creator of heaven and earth, and that he is all-powerful, merciful, and faithful to his promises. It says further that the Word who exists eternally with the Father became incarnate in the womb of Mary, that Jesus Christ is the Son of God, that he died for our salvation, and rose glorious from the dead. The Bible also tells us that Christ founded a Church, that he will be present with it till the end of time, and that participants in the Eucharist receive his body and blood. To a great extent the creeds of the Church are a patchwork of citations from Scripture.

This use of Scripture was dominant in medieval and modern scholasticism. Today it is much in use in fundamentalist and conservative evangelical circles. No believing Christian will want to deny the value of scriptural affirmations for establishing or confirming points of doctrine. But in our time Catholic theologians, who have never accepted the idea that the Bible alone is the source of Christian truth, tend to be cautious about the conclusiveness of isolated "proof-texts." Three main reservations may be indicated. In the first place, the real meaning of a text cannot always be rendered by a quotation out of context. Often it makes a great difference who is speaking, to whom, and for what purposes. The classical dogmatic use of Scripture tended to overlook the importance of context. Second, critical approaches to the Bible have shown that the understanding of the biblical authors developed gradually, and that many statements in the Bible, especially those composed in the early stages of salvation history, fall short of definitive truth. Confessional statements that express the faith of the whole Church after Pentecost usually have greater value than statements embodying the personal theology of an individual author. It needs to be recognized, in the third place, that biblical language is often poetic, mythical, or metaphorical. The language of exhortation and of love differs from the language of doctrine. Although the Bible does contain propositional statements, excessive concentration on this aspect of Scripture can lead to an impoverishment or distortion of the true meaning.

These reservations do not invalidate the method itself. But the need to state these reservations indicates the importance of other methods that will be examined as this chapter proceeds.

Biblical theology. A healthy reaction against the use of isolated proof-texts came about with the rise of biblical theology, especially during the decade following World War II. Many biblical scholars at that time attempted to synthesize the teaching of the Bible in terms of biblical concepts such as creation and redemption, word and spirit. Some tried to capture the unity of the whole Bible under rubrics such as covenant (W. Eichrodt), the history of traditions (G. von Rad), or God's "elusive presence" (S. Terrien). Others produced studies on "biblical themes" (J. Guillet) or on key terms such as revelation (W. Bulst), work (A. Richardson), baptism (T. F. Torrance), and time (O. Cullmann). In the United States Protestants such as Paul S. Minear and James D. Smart and Catholics such as John L. McKenzie were prominent in the biblical theology movement. These scholars sought to do justice to the diversity as well as the unity of the biblical materials, and to exhibit how Old Testament themes became enriched and progressively transformed as they found their way into the New Testament.

In the biblical theology movement it was rather commonly held that the terminology of the Bible reflected specific styles of thought that should be contrasted with nonbiblical thinking, especially with Greek concepts, which were viewed as alien to Christian faith. This thesis was defended, for example, in Thorleif Boman's *Hebrew Thought Compared with Greek.*[6] Oscar Cullmann in his popular *Christ and Time*[7] gave the impression of holding that the biblical concepts of time were normative for faith, and that classical Greek philosophies of time were to be rejected as unbiblical. Thus divine authority was given not merely to the teaching of Scripture but to the very concepts and terms in which the biblical authors expressed themselves. Many Catholic theologians objected, correctly in my opinion, that the biblical message could be translated into other idioms, making use of different philosophical frameworks.

Spiritual exegesis. A number of Catholic theologians during the 1940s and 1950s, advocating a return to the biblical and patristic sources, revived the kind of "spiritual exegesis" that they found in the Greek fathers and medieval monastic theologians. For Louis Bouyer the Christian reader must seek in the Bible "not a dead word, imprisoned in the past, but a living word, immediately addressed to the man of today..., a word which affects him, since it is for him that it was uttered and remains uttered."[8] The spiritual meaning, for Henri de Lubac, interprets the Jewish past from the viewpoint of the Christian present. The contemporary Christian studies the Bible in order to live by it. "This is his own history, from which he cannot remove himself. This history interests him personally. It is a mystery which is also his own mystery, identically.... He 'searches the Scriptures' to discover God's thoughts and designs on him."[9] For de Lubac this point of view is not a matter of private devotion or spirituality, but of theology properly so called. In patristic times, he contends, the so-called mystical meaning was always considered the doctrinal meaning par excellence, as the meaning that disclosed the mysteries relating to Christ and the Church.[10] He quotes Dom Célestin Charlier to the effect that exegesis, for the fathers, "consists in drawing forth the profound and objective significance of a text, in the light of the entire economy of salvation."[11]

Hans Urs von Balthasar holds that God's word in Scripture has an essentially Christological form. Christ delivers himself to the Church under two forms, as Scripture and as Eucharist. The Holy Spirit as primary author leads those who read the Scripture in the Church to understand the inner spiritual meaning. "Scripture therefore is *God speaking to man*. It means a word that is not past but present, because eternal, a word spoken to me personally and not simply to others."[12]

Yves Congar, whose interpretation of Scripture likewise deserves to be called spiritual, holds that "the meaning of Scripture must be communicated by the Spirit of God in a revelatory action whose fruit in us is Christian knowledge, 'gnosis.' "[13] Such gnosis, accessible within the Church, manifests the unity of the two testaments and enables councils to achieve unanimity about matters of faith. Scripture, therefore, must be read within the Church, within the tradition.

This "spiritual exegesis," in my estimation, incorporates some of the finest insights of the biblical theology movement. It also comes close to the "pneumatic exegesis" of Karl Barth, who will be considered in the next section. It must be acknowledged, however, that an excessive enthusiasm for spiritual meanings led in some cases to fanciful allegorical interpretations, such as those developed by Paul Claudel, who exhibited an intemperate hostility to modern critical scholarship. A corrective may be found in historical-critical analysis, which, as we shall see, emphasizes the controlling importance of the literal sense.

Word theology. A Protestant counterpart to spiritual exegesis is provided by Karl Barth, who made use of "pneumatic exegesis" in his theology of the word of God. By the "word of God" Barth meant not the dead letter of Scripture but the living Christ who speaks to us here and now through the inspired words of Scripture. The word of God, for him, was not simply the text but the event in which the reader encounters God today. The canonical books are those in which the Church has heard God speaking in the past and in which it hopes to hear his voice again.

Barth insisted that the exegete must be a believer. To gain any understanding of the biblical message and of God, who is its essential content, one must have a personal affinity with God through faith. The Holy Spirit actively inspires not only the authors of the Bible but also believers who read it in the Church today. Divine life encounters us only when it is pleased to do so.

> Hence one cannot lay down conditions which, if observed, guarantee the hearing of the Word. There is no method by which revelation can be made revelation that is actually received, no method of scriptural exegesis which is truly pneumatic, i.e., which articulates the witness to revelation in the Bible and to that degree really introduces the Pneuma."[14]

Barth maintains, on the basis of Scripture itself, that God's self-revelation occurs principally in Jesus Christ, the incarnate Word of God. Through the Christ-event God personally encounters humanity. Theology, seeking to explicate the character of God as agent, listens to God as he speaks to the Church today through the Scriptures. Not only the express statements of Scripture, but the patterns of biblical narrative, including saga and legend, can mediate an encounter with God's living and personal word.[15]

Barth's theology of the word, as already noted, harmonizes well with some tendencies in Catholic biblical theology and spiritual exegesis. His emphasis on the personal action of the living Word seems to have influenced Bouyer, de Lubac, and von Balthasar. But Barth is more inclined than his Catholic colleagues to make a dichotomy between God's word and human understanding, and between the authority of the Bible and that of the Church. Questions can be raised about whether Barth himself succeeded in sealing the interpretation of Scripture off from his own philosophical presuppositions and from the influence of his own Church tradition as thoroughly as he claimed to do. But his summons to be attentive to the word of God, and to avoid imposing our own meanings upon it, retains its pertinence.

Existential hermeneutics; theology of proclamation. About the same time that Barth was working out his word theology, Rudolf Bultmann was attracting great attention with his existential hermeneutics. Influenced by the philosophy of the early Heidegger, Bultmann contended that the real intention of the Bible was to impart an authentic self-understanding to the human person struggling to attain authentic existence. The New Testament kerygma, according to Bultmann, speaks to man as a historical (*geschichtlich*), responsible, future-oriented being. The biblical message of the cross and resurrection of Jesus comes to the reader or hearer as a summons to radical obedience, detachment, freedom, openness, and trust. It rids us of fear and anxiety in the face of suffering and death.

The biblical message, according to Bultmann, is encased in ancient mythological structures of thought and language that make it difficult for contemporary readers, whose world view is shaped by science and technology, to grasp the real meaning. Bultmann therefore instituted a program of demythologizing the New Testament. He tried to strip away the mythological structures in order to retrieve the existential meaning that lies hidden beneath them. As a scientific exegete he felt entitled to take a very skeptical position regarding the historical value of the Bible, including the words and deeds of Jesus as reported in the Gospels.

During the 1950s and 1960s some disciples of Bultmann, notably Ernst Fuchs and Gerhard Ebeling, somewhat modified Bultmann's positions under the influence of Heidegger's later philosophy. The Bible, they held, must be understood as a stage in the history of the word of God. The biblical word is efficacious; it produces a history of transmission and interpretation, and this "effective history," in turn, illuminates the original word. The word of God, as a living subject, challenges the reader and demands a response. Hermeneutics, as a study of the word-event, aims to clear the way for effective proclamation of the word and to remove obstacles to contemporary interpretation. Theology, as a hermeneutical discipline, must attend to the word of God and contribute to the effective proclamation of the word in the Church today, so that hearers are challenged to respond with trust and submission.

The hermeneutical theology of the Bultmann school proved helpful to many readers who wanted to remain Christians but found it hard to accept the miraculous and apparently legendary features of the Bible. Conservative Protestants, who based their faith on the authority of the Bible, regarded Bultmann as a dangerous heretic. Catholics, who believed that the Bible always had to be interpreted in light of philosophical and scientific knowledge, saw some merits in the Bultmannian program. But they objected that its purely existential exegesis was too narrow. The Bible, they insisted, had a lot to tell us about God and not only about human self-understanding. The Bultmann school, I would agree, concentrated too narrowly on existential categories of address and response. Many members of the school, including Bultmann himself, had an exaggerated antipathy to the supernatural. Thus this school, like many others, was more valuable in what it affirmed than in what it dismissed or denied.[16]

The experiential-expressive approach. A widespread trend in the use of Scripture may be characterized, in the terminology of George Lindbeck, as "experiential-expressive."[17] This approach, which may be traced back to Friedrich Schleiermacher, is a theological counterpart of the philosophical "turn to the subject" commonly attributed to Immanuel Kant. Karl Rahner, though he uses more than one approach, speaks of Scripture primarily as a historically and situationally conditioned deposit in which the utterly simple "experience of the divine grace of faith" comes to expression.[18] Scripture, he says, is "one of the ways, although a preeminent way, in which God's revelatory self-communication to man becomes explicit and thematic in history."[19] The theologian turns to the Bible to recover the foundational experiences of the early community, to make those experiences intelligible to men and women of our day, and to express them in ways that evoke and confirm the contemporary experience of grace, which, prior to all theological reflection "has already been experienced and lived through more originally in the depths of existence."[20]

This experiential approach is widespread in current theology. Gregory Baum, for example, writes: "The Bible is the test, norm, and judge in the church by purifying and reassuring Christians in their own experience of life."[21] David Tracy uses the concept of the religious classic as his point of departure for understanding Scripture. By classics he means "certain expressions of the human spirit [that] so disclose a compelling truth about our lives that we cannot deny them some kind of normative status."[22] The Scriptures are "the normative, more relatively adequate expressions of the community's past and present experience of the Risen Lord, the crucified one, Jesus Christ."[23]

Unlike the schools previously examined, theologians of this experiential school are reluctant to speak of the Bible as the word of God. They tend to place the locus of authority not in the text itself but in some prior experience that is regarded as compelling and therefore normative. Edward Schillebeeckx, at least in his *Jesus* volume,[24] is more concerned with reconstructing Jesus' "original *Abba*-experience,"[25] and the "Easter-experience" of the disciples[26] than with the biblical testimonies to the message of Jesus and the resurrection. These original experiences, for Schillebeeckx, are important insofar as they can serve as paradigms and catalysts for Christian experience today. The word of Scripture is brought into "critical correlation" with our own experience so that the relative adequacy of each can be assessed.[27]

A major difficulty in this approach is the ambiguity in the term "experience." It is widely recognized today that we do not have some pure experience prior to thought and word, but that our experience is largely molded by the presuppositions and interpretative categories with which it is bound up. Religious experience is not a mere matter of God being perceived in the depths of the soul. To classify any experience as "religious" is a matter of interpretation, and the interpretation is inevitably dependent on social and historical factors. The Bible may indeed intensify and direct our spiritual experience, but it can hardly do so unless we are prepared to accept the interpretation that the biblical authors put on their own experiences and on the tradition that had come down to them. Thus the experiential approach to Scripture cannot stand on its own.

Authorial intention. A broad current of biblical scholarship still looks upon the Bible as a trustworthy rendition of the truth that God intended to disclose through the inspired authors. Using all modern techniques of investigation, these scholars seek to establish the literal meaning, that is to say, the meaning that the inspired authors intended and expressed by their words. This method of interpretation is identified with notable Catholic exegetes such as Raymond E. Brown and Joseph A. Fitzmyer, who have recently written defenses of their approach against critics from within the exegetical community.[28] They do not contend that the meaning established by their discipline is determinative for tradition and dogma, but that it needs to be taken into account, and that the divinely intended meaning, at the very least, cannot contradict the literal meaning. Shared by many Anglican, Lutheran, and other Protestant scholars trained in the universities of Europe and North America, this approach has proved very useful in ecumenical dialogues for arriving at a measure of consensus about the meaning of the Bible as the basic document of Christian faith. Historical-critical biblical studies of this kind have been fruitfully used in ecumenical dialogues, for example, in the volumes on Peter, Mary, and justification commissioned or executed by the Lutheran-Catholic Dialogue in the United States.[29]

The method of interpreting texts by seeking out the intention of the authors has come under attack from new trends in literary criticism, which assert that the meaning of any text is separable from what the author intended by it. Texts, it is argued, take on meaning from the context in which they are handed down and from the perspectives of the readers. In the case of Scripture we have the additional problem that for many texts there may have been no author in the modern sense of that word. The so-called author is simply the redactor of an oral tradition or fragmentary documents that originated and grew anonymously. For other texts, which presumably have an author, we cannot identify the place and time of composition.

Admitting that these difficulties are not without force, defenders of the "authorial intention" position reply that for many texts one can say approximately what the author must have intended and what would presumably have been understood by readers in the Old Testament and New Testament communities. Besides, as Brown and others assert, the meaning intended and expressed by the first author is not terminal. Historical-critical study can identify trajectories of development within the Bible and thus point the way to later doctrinal developments in church tradition.[30] The Church may well insist on traditional and dogmatic meanings that go beyond the intention of the first author, but the original literal meaning, which was divinely inspired, can be used to correct misinterpretations that may have arisen at a later time. Brown himself has written extensively on the "more-than-literal" meanings that flow from the text as taken up into the canon, the tradition, and the teaching of the Church. This series of hierarchically ordered meanings (which begins with the literal meaning but goes well beyond it) can be very helpful to the theologian; it harmonizes well with the teaching on the interpretation of Scripture in Vatican II's Dogmatic constitution *Dei Verbum*, number 12.

With these reservations and modifications, the method that seeks out the authorial intention merits approval. The more we know about the original text and the author's intention, the better shall we be positioned to propose and evaluate further interpretations that purport to go beyond the literal.

Historical reconstruction. Another form of historical-critical study tends to probe beneath the texts in order to find a meaning anterior to them. Liberal Protestants such as Adolf Harnack believed that by identifying the earliest sources, those closest to the actual events, it would be possible to achieve a reliable historical reconstruction. In particular, Harnack tried to get to the words and deeds of Jesus by using a combination of the Gospel of Mark and a hypothetical source named Q. The nineteenth-century effort to set faith on a secure basis by means of scientific historiography, based on positivistic postulates, ended in the impasse brilliantly described in Albert Schweitzer's *Quest of the Historical Jesus*.

The project of finding the true Jesus somewhere behind the New Testament witness is still carried on, though more soberly than a century ago. In the late 1950s some of the post-Bultmannians, including Fuchs and Ebeling, reconstructed the aims and intentions of Jesus, and his impact upon his contemporaries, with the help of a kind of existential history. Wolfhart Pannenberg, distrusting this existential approach, attempts to ground faith on rational knowledge. Since the Enlightenment, he maintains, it is no longer possible to argue from the Scriptures as inspired and inerrant sources. "For the unified 'essential content' of Scripture, which, for Luther, was the basis of its authority, is for our historical consciousness no longer to be found in the texts but only behind them, in the figure of Jesus who is attested in the very different writings of the New Testament in very different and incongruous ways."[31] The exegete, according to Pannenberg, must engage in a kind of detective work, inferring what must have happened from a critical examination of the various testimonies.[32]

He believes that this method, rightly pursued, will confirm the truth of Christian teaching, at least in its main lines.

Hans Küng insists that historico-critical exegesis may constitute a challenge to dogmatic theology.[33] Since Vatican II, he asserts, "Catholic theology has committed itself in a positive manner to *the facts of the Bible, as elucidated by criticism.*"[34] Accordingly he holds that the source, norm, and criterion for Christian faith is the Jesus of history, to whom we have access through historico-critical method.[35] "We have no choice but to apply the historico-critical method (in the comprehensive sense) strictly in order to find out what were the established facts, what is known with scientific certainty or great probability about the Jesus of history."[36]

This approach to Scripture is not without value insofar as, by showing that the Christian story has a solid foundation in fact, it can serve to strengthen faith. In addition, believers cannot fail to have a keen interest in all that throws light on the ways of God with his people, and especially on the words and deeds of Jesus, whom all Christians seek to follow. As contrasted with the experiential school, this school respects the objective givenness of the contents of faith and refrains from equating redemption or revelation with a direct experience of the transcendent. But still there are difficulties. The scholars who reconstruct the events of sacred history have not succeeded in achieving an agreed reconstruction of the past. It is all but impossible to prevent the bias of the historian from predetermining what will be found. All too often the historians adopt methodological presuppositions that are alien to Christian faith and achieve only fragile hypotheses, incapable of sustaining the weight of faith or serving as the basis of a solid theology. The deeds of God in salvation history are not Christian revelation except as taken up into the preaching and memory of the Church, which treasures Scripture as a privileged text.

Narrative theology; the cultural-linguistic approach. A number of contemporary theologians, dissatisfied with the dogmatic, experientialist, and historicist approaches, are returning to something like the biblical theology of the mid-twentieth century. Professing what they call a narrative theology, they hold that the Bible consists primarily of stories and that it should be accepted on its own terms rather than forced into alien categories by people who read it with an agenda formed by the contemporary secular world.

From the Catholic side, Johann Baptist Metz is prominent for his insistence that Christianity is a community that cherishes the "narrative and evocative memory of the passion, death, and resurrection of Jesus. The logos of the cross and resurrection has a narrative structure."[37] In fact, he maintains, Scripture has from beginning to end a fundamentally narrative character. As a consequence, Metz believes, theology must have a narrative and practical structure. While admitting that argumentation may have a legitimate place in theology, he insists that its primary function is "to protect the narrative memory of salvation in a scientific world, to allow it to be at stake and to prepare the way for a renewal of this narrative, without which the experience of salvation is silenced."[38]

In the United States the late Hans Frei of Yale University maintained that the meaning of the Bible can only be the fruit of the stories themselves, which communicate the subject matter to the reader by the interaction of persons and events. Interpretation must appropriate the narrative in its own right and not pose questions that arise out of a different horizon.[39]

George Lindbeck, influenced by his Yale colleague Frei, proposes a "cultural-linguistic" theology. From the patristic age until after the Reformation, he notes, Scripture served as "the lens through which theologians viewed the world" rather than as "an object of study whose religiously significant or literal meaning was located outside itself."[40] For the reinvigoration of Christianity, he maintains, the Scriptures must regain their position as canonical texts, in the sense that they create their own domain of meaning. "A scriptural world," he writes, is "able to absorb the universe. It supplies the interpretive framework within which believers seek to live their lives and understand reality."[41] For this cultural-linguistic approach it is not crucial to distinguish between certain biblical passages that are, and others that are not, historically or scientifically exact. The Bible can be taken seriously even when its history or science is challenged. "As parables such as that of the prodigal son remind us, the rendering of God's character is not in every instance logically dependent on the factuality of the story."[42]

These theologians are correct, I believe, in holding that the revelatory power of the Bible is diminished if one does not allow the stories to work in a symbolic way on the reader's affections and imagination. Modern rationalistic criticism has often neglected this dimension. But it must be asked what task remains for theology.

Ronald Thiemann, who like Lindbeck is a follower of Hans Frei, holds that "theology is primarily concerned with the interpretation of text and tradition and only secondarily, if at all, with speculations about the true nature of the self and the deep structures of human understanding."[43] He goes on to say that the conception he espouses

> sees the primary theological task to be the critical redescription of the Christian faith in categories consistent with the church's first-order language. It eschews the systematic correlation of Christian concepts with those of a philosophical anthropology and thus resists theology's "turn to the subject." Its primary interest in biblical narrative is in discerning God's identity as agent in the text and in the on-going life of the Christian community.[44]

Although I recognize real value in the narrative theology fashioned along the lines proposed by Thiemann and Metz, I am not convinced that the predominantly narrative structure of the Bible requires that theology retain the narrative mode. Theology, as a reflective discipline, cannot content itself with describing or redescribing the biblical story. It may be expected to explore the deeper implications of that story, as it has done in elaborating the attributes of God and the doctrine of the Trinity. Pheme Perkins wisely observes:

> Narrative analysis does not yield the kind of conceptual syntheses which might provide the introductory paragraphs to systematic expositions of Christology, ecclesiology, Christian discipleship, or ethics.... In the Christian tradition our stories have provoked theological and ethical reflection, but they do not hand us theology or ethics on a platter ready for consumption.[45]

While using a biblical framework, theology can ask questions not asked in the Bible itself, and in answering these questions it need not confine itself to biblical concepts and categories. Augustine and Thomas Aquinas can provide models of how to insert questions arising out of Platonic and Aristotelian philosophy into a domain of meaning established by the Bible.[46]

Liberation theology. Metz's narrative theology already leans somewhat in a liberationist direction, since the "dangerous memories" of the passion of Jesus, in his view, provoke protests against the injustice and violence reigning in our world. A more specific and constructive social program is involved in Latin American liberation theology as typified, for example, in the work of Gustavo Gutiérrez, Juan Luis Segundo, J. Severino Croatto, and José Míguez Bonino.

In general, these authors may be said to adopt a kind of hermeneutical circle, which begins and ends with the existing social reality. Analyzing the situation in which they find themselves, these theologians consciously adopt a partiality based on a commitment to the poor and the oppressed. In light of that commitment they adopt a "hermeneutics of suspicion," contesting all readings of Scripture that do not favor their own social orientation. Conversely, they select in the Bible passages that confirm their own preferences. Then they announce the gospel as they have interpreted it within the context of their commitment to liberation. Only in that context, they hold, is it possible to understand the implications of the gospel and give it a real impact.

According to Segundo, Latin American liberation theology "is known to have a preference and a partiality for the Old Testament in general, and for the Exodus event in particular,"[47] for in no other portion of Scripture does God the liberator reveal himself in such close connection with the political plane of human existence. On the other hand, Jesus and Paul seem to be almost unconcerned with, if not opposed to, liberation from political oppression.

An approach similar to Segundo's may be found in the black liberation theology of James Cone and in the feminist exegesis of Elisabeth Schüssler Fiorenza. Fiorenza, for example, starts with an analysis of the oppression of women today, then proceeds to unmask the oppressive patriarchal structures in the Bible, and finally calls attention to nonandrocentric elements in Scripture that can be used for grounding a theology of feminist liberation.[48]

In favor of liberation hermeneutics one may say that a deliberately partial reading permits one to see certain implications that might otherwise escape notice, but at the same time this selective approach can blind the interpreter to lessons that ought to be gained from the text. Gregory Baum, in a sympathetic critique of Segundo, calls attention to the need for the originating experience to stand up under the verdict of Scripture. As Segundo analyzes it, the initial experience seems not to be subject to any critical examination at all. For this reason, says Baum, Segundo neglects the personal dimension of life in favor of the social. He has little to say about central features of human life such as birth and death, friendship and love.[49] In an official critique, the Congregation for the Doctrine of the Faith in 1984 called attention to the danger of radically politicizing the affirmations of faith and thus reading the Bible in too narrow a framework. More specifically, liberation hermeneutics tends to overlook the transcendence and gratuity of grace and to secularize the Kingdom of God.[50]

The Values of Diversity

I am aware that the ten categories described above do not exhaust all the possibilities of hermeneutics. Other approaches are in use among historians and literary critics. I have attempted to keep my eye fixed on the theological literature, and to ask how systematic theologians have in fact been using the Bible.

All ten of the approaches are in my opinion verifiable on the contemporary theological scene. It would be a mistake to dismiss any of them as worthless. All have their distinctive values and would defy incorporation into a single unified methodology. The coexistence of different styles or models is healthy and desirable. Different methodologies may be useful, depending on the precise questions being asked.

A given theologian, pursuing a particular project, may legitimately adopt one approach or another as a primary tool of investigation. My own present leaning would be toward a method that makes use of historical critical studies to assure a solid foundation in the biblical sources themselves, but does so under the continuous guidance of tradition and magisterial teaching. An adequate theological use of Scripture, I believe, would build also on the achievements of biblical theology and the kind of spiritual exegesis described above. An interpretation that limited itself to the historical-critical phase would overlook the tacit meanings conveyed by the biblical stories, symbols, and metaphors. A comprehensive approach, combining scientific and spiritual exegesis, does better justice to Catholic tradition and the directives of Vatican II, and better serves the needs of systematic theology.

6.

Tradition as a Theological Source

One characteristic of Catholic theology, as distinct from most Protestant theology, is its adherence to tradition as a divinely authoritative norm, on a par with Scripture itself. A proper understanding of Catholic theological method requires careful study of the meaning of tradition. For a proper understanding of the Catholic approach to Scripture, the doctrine of tradition is essential.

Trent: The Insufficiency of Scripture

In the sixteenth century, immediately before the Council of Trent, there were three main schools of thought.[1] According to one school all the truth needed for salvation was contained explicitly or implicitly in the canonical Scriptures. Tradition was required for the correct interpretation of Scripture, especially for spelling out what was merely implicit in the text. This view, which some scholars regard as the "classical" one, is represented by many church fathers, including Vincent of Lerins, and was dominant in the High Middle Ages, in theologians such as Thomas Aquinas. In the sixteenth century this was essentially the view of John Driedo, Cajetan, and Kaspar Schatzgeyer.

A second view held that Christian revelation is partly contained in the canonical Scriptures and partly in apostolic traditions passed down orally from the apostles through their disciples. This view was represented in the fifteenth century by Thomas Netter and, at least in certain writings, by Gabriel Biel. In the sixteenth century, Albert Pigge has been judged to belong to this school of thought.

According to the third view, dominant among curial canonists and curial theologians in the late Middle Ages, the Holy Spirit abides constantly with the Catholic Church, giving new inspiration or illumination. The teaching of popes and councils, even though not supported by the canonical Scriptures or by apostolic traditions, is binding on all the faithful. Pierre d'Ailly is cited as a fifteenth century champion of this view. In the sixteenth century this opinion was defended by Sylvester Prierias, Johann Cochläus, and Nicholas Ellenbog. Other authors such as Johann Eck and Thomas More, without implying that new public revelation has been given since the age of the apostles, speak of the vital consciousness of faith, "written on the heart of the Church."

In the fifteenth and sixteenth centuries the humanists advocated a return to the sources. Some of them, such as Giovanni Pico della Mirandola, had a great enthusiasm for ancient traditions, including cabalistic traditions allegedly stemming from Moses, but others, such as Johann Rucherat von Wesel, gave a clear priority to Scripture. The latter group paved the way for some Protestants to appeal to "Scripture alone" as finally normative.

At the Council of Trent it was almost unanimously agreed that the canonical Scriptures are not sufficient as a source of doctrine. Even if it contained all truth, Scripture could not be sufficiently understood without reliance on tradition, enshrined in the works of the fathers and in ecclesiastical decisions. Beyond this, there was little agreement. All three of the main schools had their champions.

An important breakthrough in framing Trent's Decree on the Sacred Books and Apostolic Traditions (Session 4, April 8, 1546) was the exclusion of disciplinary decisions.[2] The council fathers agreed to pronounce only on traditions "pertaining to faith and morals [*mores*]." In confining its attention to traditions of a dogmatic character, the council intended to exclude merely ceremonial traditions, having a merely temporary or local binding force. The council traced all dogmatic traditions to the apostolic age, attributing their origin either to the teaching of Christ or to the inspiration of the Holy Spirit and ascribing their permanence in the Church to the continuous influence of the same Spirit. Apostolicity was seen by Trent as the hallmark of revelation. By implication the council rejected the idea that new articles of faith, not based on the apostolic heritage, had been revealed in the course of history. Vatican I and the anti-Modernist documents were to make the same point even more emphatically.

The draft text adopted by majority vote at Trent seemed to favor the theory that not all revelation was contained in Scripture. It stated that Christian revelation is contained "partly" in written books and "partly" in unwritten traditions. In the final text, for reasons that are not entirely clear from the acts of the council, the terms *partim...partim* were dropped. Thus the decree left open the possibility of holding that all revelation was contained either in Scripture alone or in tradition alone. It did, however, affirm the value and importance of both as means of transmission. Trent said nothing about "two sources of revelation." On the contrary, it declared that the gospel, promised beforehand by the prophets and then proclaimed by Jesus Christ, was "the source of all saving truth and moral discipline [*fontem omnis et salutaris veritatis et morum disciplinae*]."

The council refrained from specifying the contents of apostolic traditions. Relying on authors such as Tertullian and Clement of Alexandria, some of the fathers at Trent held that practices such as infant baptism, prayer for the dead, and the invocation of saints, and beliefs such as the perpetual virginity of Mary might be examples. But the council did not involve itself in these historical questions. It contented itself with asserting the principle.

Trent held that the authority of tradition was not less than that of Scripture. Both, coming from God, had divine authority. Asserting that Scripture and tradition are to be received with equal reverence (*pari pietatis affectu ac reverentia*, DS 1501), the council took over an expression of Basil the Great.[3]

In the Counter-Reformation Trent was usually interpreted as though it had said *partim...partim*. Tradition was often described as a deposit of apostolic doctrines not attested by the canonical Scriptures. This tradition was, moreover, seen as constant and static. Little place if any was allowed for development in tradition. The Catholic theology of the post-Tridentine period was polemically directed against the Protestant principle of *sola scriptura*, particularly as represented by Lutherans such as Johann Gerhard and Abraham Calovius.

Post-Tridentine Catholicism

During the late seventeenth century and on through the eighteenth, a contest developed within the Catholic Church about the locus of authority. The Roman theologians increasingly emphasized the prerogatives of the Holy See in defining the contents of tradition. Gallicans and Jansenists resisted this tendency toward centralization and received considerable support from monarchs and parliaments in Catholic nations. With the secularization that followed the French Revolution, these dissident movements lost much of their force.

In the Enlightenment the concept of tradition fell on evil days. Rationalistic thinkers exhorted people to think for themselves and to shake off the yoke of dependence on the authority of others. Positivist thinkers in the nineteenth century continued to look on tradition as an impediment to progress, which could only be achieved through critical reasoning and experimentation. As scientific historical study of the early Christian sources advanced, it became increasingly evident that the teachings of the Catholic Church in modern times were far more detailed and complex than the beliefs of the first-century Christians. The Tridentine expedient of defending current beliefs and practices on the ground that they had been continuously handed down from apostolic times became ever more difficult to maintain.

Certain trends in the nineteenth century were more favorable to tradition. The romanticism of the early nineteenth century was, in part, a rebellion against the dessicated rationalism and individualism of the eighteenth. By emphasizing the organic structure of society and the emotional and imaginative aspects of religion, the romantics brought new appreciation for the value of roots and tradition. Some of the romantics (such as Walter Scott and François René de Chateaubriand) were enamored of the Middle Ages. French romanticism gave rise to the traditionalism of Louis de Bonald and Félicité de Lamennais, who contended that all human knowledge came from revelation by way of tradition.

In Germany Johann Adam Möhler, influenced by romanticism, by the incipient nationalism of the day, and by Protestant idealists such as Schelling and Schleiermacher, drew analogies between the collective spirit of the nation (*Volksgeist*) and the sense of the faith abiding in the Church as a whole. Especially in his early work, he emphasized the subjective aspects of tradition. "Living tradition," for him, was a collective sense of the faith instilled in the Church by the Holy Spirit. In his later work Möhler balanced this one-sided concept with greater attention to the apostolic deposit of faith transmitted by the Church.

John Henry Newman as an Anglican distinguished between apostolic (or ecclesiastical) tradition and prophetic tradition.[4] The former, he held, was continuous, invariant, and infallible. Prophetic tradition, on the other hand, was an ongoing but unofficial commentary on apostolic tradition, and was primarily the responsibility of preachers, catechists, and theologians. Prophetic tradition mediated the apostolic tradition to particular publics; it suggested new ways of understanding and presenting the apostolic faith, but added nothing substantial to the latter.

As a Catholic Newman abandoned the distinction between the two kinds of tradition. He held that Scripture never exists by itself alone, and that it cannot be adequately interpreted without ongoing ecclesial commentary. The interpretation can express itself in irreversible doctrinal decisions, such as creeds and conciliar definitions. Tradition is not constant and immutable, as Vincent of Lerins had maintained; it develops through a harmonious interaction between the ecclesiastical magisterium and the sense of the faith inherent in the Church as a whole. In his letter to Pusey on the occasion of the latter's *Eirenicon*, Newman held that, while Catholics may accept the Anglican view that the whole Christian faith is contained in Scripture, they add the proviso that "not every article of faith is so contained there, that it may thence be logically proved, independently of the teaching and authority of the Tradition."[5]

The Jesuits of the Roman school, who were close collaborators with the Holy See, emphasized the role of the magisterium not only in safeguarding the ancient faith against corruptions but in developing the explicit content of faith.[6] They promoted the definition of the Immaculate Conception (1854) and the dogmas of Vatican I concerning papal primacy and infallibility (1870). These theologians (notably J. B. Franzelin and L. Billot) distinguished between "active tradition" and "passive tradition." For them, the role of the magisterium, as the bearer of "active tradition," was not simply to authenticate what was believed by the faithful as a body, but to clarify and explicate the contents of faith. The "passive tradition" borne by the faithful as a body was simply a reflection of what had been taught by the magisterium.

During and after Vatican I a few theologians such as Ignaz von Döllinger resisted the centralizing of doctrinal authority in the Holy See. Döllinger himself came close to reasserting the positions of the seventeenth-century Gallicans, as did his English disciple Lord Acton. In the name of critical scholarship Döllinger challenged the Vatican I dogmas as unwarranted by tradition.

Toward the end of the nineteenth century new movements of thought such as pragmatism and neo-Kantianism exerted an influence on the theology of tradition. Maurice Blondel, a Catholic layman on the fringes of the Modernist movement, developed an original philosophical system in which action was seen as a source of understanding.[7] Applying this theory to the theology of tradition, he denied that tradition is necessary, or particularly helpful, as a source of information regarding facts not attested by written records. For him, tradition was required for the transmission of the "tacit" component in faith, that is, the aspects that could not be spelled out in verbal statements. Tradition, he held, sustains in the community a vital sense of the realities to which Christians are committed in faith. The primary vehicle of tradition is not word but faithful action, including the liturgy of the Church.

In his own day Blondel was suspected of being too close to Modernism, with its doctrine of "vital immanence." Well into the twentieth century the neo-scholastic theologians, dominant in Catholic universities and seminaries, adhered to the Tridentine idea of tradition as a deposit of apostolic teachings not contained in Scripture. In 1942 the French Dominican Louis Charlier was censured by Rome for identifying tradition too closely with the teaching of the magisterium. In 1950 Pius XII in *Humani Generis* favored the concept of the "two sources of revelation" that had come down from the Counter-Reformation. He depicted the living magisterium as a third theological locus, which is dependent for all its teaching on the testimony of Scripture and apostolic tradition.

During the 1950s many avant-garde Catholics struck off in new directions. Biblical scholars, liberated from previous restrictions by Pius XII's encyclical *Divino Afflante Spiritu* (1943), sought to renew Catholic theology by a fresh study of the word of God in Scripture. Patristic theologians such as Henri de Lubac and Jean Daniélou launched a movement of theological *ressourcement* inspired by the Greek and Latin fathers. Historical theologians such as Josef Rupert Geiselmann, reviewing the teaching of Trent in the light of the nineteenth-century Tübingen theology, challenged the Counter-Reformation thesis that there were revealed truths in no way attested by Scripture.[8] Yves Congar, a Dominican Thomist familiar with the work of Möhler, Newman, and Blondel, attempted to build bridges with other Christian bodies and worked closely with theologians involved in the Faith and Order movement. His masterly studies on the theology of tradition began to appear shortly before Vatican II.

Vatican II: Subjectivity and Dynamism

The official schema drawn up in 1962 by the Preparatory Commission for Vatican Council II followed along the lines of *Humani Generis*. It spoke of Scripture and tradition as "two sources of revelation" and affirmed that there were some revealed truths not taught by Scripture but by apostolic tradition alone. The living magisterium was declared to be the divinely authorized custodian and interpreter of both Scripture and tradition.

In the debates of November 14-20, 1962, this schema met with severe criticism, partly because of its inadequate treatment of tradition. It was considered unecumenical because it denied the "material sufficiency" of Scripture — a point seen by that time to have been left open by Trent. Many members of Bea's Secretariat for the Promotion of Christian Unity spoke against the schema as damaging the hopes of reconciliation with Protestants. Also, some theologians influenced by Möhler, Newman, and Blondel considered that the concept of tradition in the schema was too static. Alternative drafts for a schema on revelation by Rahner and Congar were privately circulated among the bishops.[9] After a stormy debate and a preponderantly negative vote, Pope John XXIII intervened to appoint a mixed commission jointly chaired by cardinals Alfredo Ottaviani and Augustin Bea, with the mandate to prepare a new text for discussion.

Especially after March 7, 1964, when he was appointed to a subcommittee to revise the new schema on tradition, Yves Congar exerted major influence on what was to become chapter 2 of *Dei Verbum*. His proposed schema on Scripture and tradition, mentioned above, strongly emphasized that tradition is not merely verbal but also "real," and that it is handed down not mechanically as a dead reality, but as a living reality that progresses in the Church. Congar's close contacts with non-Catholic theologians, including those in Faith and Order, no doubt contributed to the ecumenical tone of the document, which we shall discuss below.

The final text of the chapter on tradition in *Dei Verbum* reaffirms the basic positions of Trent but draws likewise on the dynamic, developmental concept of tradition defended by Congar.[10] Whereas Trent had emphasized the objective elements in tradition, its continuity from the apostles, and the verbal element in transmission, the themes of subjectivity, progress, and action are more prominent in the utterances of Vatican II.

Six main points of chapter 2 of *Dei Verbum* may be summarized as follows:

1. *Tradition and traditions.* Whereas Trent, interested in objective content, spoke of traditions in the plural, Vatican II, in *Dei Verbum*, speaks of tradition in the singular.[11] Its concern is with tradition as an organ of apprehension and transmission rather than as a set of doctrines or precepts. Tradition is the mode in which the Church perpetuates its faith and its very existence (DV 8).

Although *Dei Verbum* focuses on apostolic tradition as a unitary reality, other documents of Vatican II discuss traditions in the plural. The Decree on Missionary Activity (*Ad Gentes*) directs the young churches to borrow "from the customs and traditions of their people ...all those things which can contribute to the glory of their Creator, the revelation of the Savior's grace, or the proper ordering of Christian life" (AG 22). The "particular traditions" developed in this way "can be illumined by the light of the gospel and then taken up into Catholic unity." The individual young churches "adorned with their own traditions," will have their own place in the ecclesiastical communion (ibid.).

The Decree on Ecumenism (*Unitatis Redintegratio*) speaks at some length of the different "traditions" in the Eastern (Orthodox) and Western churches. It states:

> The heritage handed down from the apostles was received in different forms and manners, and from the earliest times of the Church it was explained variously in different places, owing to diversities of character and of conditions of life. (UR 14)

The churches of the East have their own liturgical forms, spiritual traditions (UR 15), disciplines, customs, and observances (UR 16). Still more significantly, the council adds that in the expression of doctrine "sometimes one tradition has come nearer than the other to a full appreciation of some aspects of the revealed mystery, or has expressed it to better advantage" (UR 17). The "authentic theological traditions" of the Orientals are declared to be "admirably rooted in holy Scripture" and to be sustained by the living apostolic tradition as well as by the writings of the Eastern fathers and spiritual authors (ibid.). Thus the different theological formulations accepted in the East and the West "are often to be considered complementary rather than conflicting" (ibid.).

2. *The means of "traditioning."* The Constitution on Divine Revelation, to which we now return, insists on the nonverbal elements in tradition: Christ communicates the gospel not by his words alone but also by his dealings with others and his behavior (DV 7). The apostles transmit the gospel not only by preaching but also by example and ordinances (*institutiones*, ibid.). "In its preaching, life and worship...[the Church] hands on to every generation all that it is and all that it believes" (DV 8). Thus tradition is identified with the total life and praxis of the Church.

Until almost the last draft the sentence just quoted affirmed that by tradition the Church hands on "all that it is, all that it has, and all that it believes." Cardinal Albert Meyer of Chicago, in a speech of September 30, 1964, objected that this wording seemed to canonize all particular traditions, including some that were deficient in the light of the gospel. In response to the criticism the Theological Commission dropped the words "all that it has." According to the *Relatio* this change was made to make it clear that only what is substantive to the Church should be ascribed to apostolic tradition.[12] Ratzinger remarks that the change was insufficient to meet Meyer's difficulty, which called for a discussion of the criteria of genuine tradition.[13]

3. *Development.* The forward thrust of tradition is stated: "This tradition which comes from the apostles progresses in the Church under the assistance of the Holy Spirit.... Thus, as the centuries advance, the Church constantly tends toward the fullness of divine truth, until the words of God reach their consummation in the Church" (DV 8). This progress does not occur by mere logical inference or by continuous, organic evolution, but through "the practice and life of the believing and praying Church" (ibid.). It comes about through contemplation and study, through spiritual experience, and through the preaching of the bishops who possess "the sure charism

of truth" (ibid.). Tradition develops under the influence of the Holy Spirit, thanks to whom the Church is in constant conversation with its divine Lord (ibid.).

The idea of "growth" in tradition was criticized by some of the fathers at Vatican II. Cardinal Ernesto Ruffini, from a neo-scholastic point of view, wanted the council to cite Vincent of Lerins on the immutability of Catholic teaching, but the Theological Commission refused on the ground that Vincent was favoring the neo-Pelagians and opposing the Augustinian developments in the doctrine of grace.[14]

The concept of "growth" was deemed unsatisfactory from an ecumenical standpoint by Cardinal Paul Emile Léger, who felt that the Church was committed to the sufficiency of the apostolic deposit, which needs no increment. Much the same criticism was taken up after the council by Protestant theologians such as Oscar Cullmann and J. K. S. Reid. According to some commentators, favorably disposed toward the text, this line of criticism overlooks the inevitable historicity, and the consequent perfectibility, in the subjective appropriation and understanding of the gospel.[15]

4. *The relation between Scripture and tradition.* The two are said to constitute a single mirror in which the Church, during its earthly pilgrimage, contemplates God (DV 7). They derive from one wellspring (*scaturigo*) — a term that recalls the statement of Trent that the gospel is the one source (*fons*) of all saving truth (DV 9; cf. DS 1501).

Within the Scripture-tradition tandem, Scripture is described as being the word of God consigned to writing (DV 9). Vatican II accepts the idea, affirmed in Vatican I, that the word of God exists in a twofold form: as canonical Scripture and as tradition. Scripture is the *verbum Dei scriptum*; tradition is the *verbum Dei traditum* (DV 10; cf. DS 3011). Echoing Trent, Vatican II affirms that "both Scripture and tradition are to be accepted and honored with like devotion and reverence" (DV 9).

In accordance with its characteristic stress on the dynamic, Vatican II describes tradition primarily in terms of what it does: it preserves and hands on the word of God (DV 9). This does not mean that tradition is not itself the word of God, or that it is merely derivative or secondary. The process of traditioning begins before the composition of the inspired books and continues without a break throughout the ages. Thus tradition has a certain priority, in view of which *Dei Verbum* found it advisable to treat tradition before turning to Scripture.

Scripture is formally insufficient. In other words, tradition is needed for a sufficient grasp of the word of God, even though it be assumed that all revelation is somehow contained in Scripture. It is not from Scripture alone that the Church draws its certainty about everything that has been revealed (DV 9). Tradition is the means by which the full canon of the sacred books becomes known, and by which the meaning of the biblical text is more profoundly understood and more deeply penetrated (DV 8). While asserting the formal insufficiency of Scripture, the council leaves open the question of its material sufficiency. According to the Theological Commission, by stating that the word of God is faithfully transmitted by Scripture and tradition, *Dei Verbum* intended to teach that "the same revelation is transmitted by both" (no. 9). Here and throughout the chapter, the council sedulously endeavored to avoid deciding the question whether tradition contained any revealed truth not present somehow in Scripture.[16]

5. *The problem of distorting tradition.* Although the issue of corrupt tradition had been raised by Cardinal Meyer, as mentioned above, the council did not expressly address this question. It nowhere describes Scripture as a norm for validating tradition, but its teaching on the authority of Scripture implies that nothing contrary to God's word in Scripture could have any claim to be authentic tradition.

The council also attributes a discriminatory function to the ecclesiastical magisterium. For instance, it states, with a reference to Irenaeus, that the apostles set up the succession of bishops to keep the gospel intact and alive (DV 7). Those who succeed to the apostolic office "receive the sure charism of truth" (DV 8). The successors of the apostles, "enlightened by the Spirit of truth," are commissioned to preserve, interpret, and disseminate the word of God (DV 9). The task of authentically interpreting the word of God, either written or handed on, is entrusted exclusively to the living magisterium, which exercises its authority in the name of Christ (DV 10).

6. *Tradition and magisterium.* Tradition, according to *Dei Verbum*, has been committed not to the magisterium alone but to the People of God as a whole (DV 10). All believers are responsible to hold fast to the faith and bear witness to it (ibid.). The magisterium is not above the word of God but under it: it must serve that word (ibid.). Yet the magisterium is the sole authentic interpreter of the word of God, whether in written or nonwritten form.[17]

In summary, Scripture, tradition, and the magisterium are inseparable and mutually interdependent (DV 10). Since the three are
reciprocally coinherent, no one of them can be used as a totally
independent source to judge or validate the other two. Theologically, Scripture has no normative value except as read in the light
of tradition and under the vigilance of the magisterium. Tradition
and the magisterium, conversely, have no value except as referred
to Scripture. Thus Vatican II seems to cast its weight in favor of
the "classical" position of pre-Tridentine theology and against late
medieval attempts to play off Scripture and tradition against each
other, by making the one or the other an independent and adequate
source.

Assessment of Vatican II

Some commentators on Vatican II have judged that its presentation
of tradition as a dynamic process was its most important theological
achievement.[18] Three major benefits may here be mentioned.

1. The council's teaching on tradition is highly ecumenical. It
emphasizes the transmission of the basic Christian message, contained in the Scriptures and the ancient creeds. It does not reaffirm
the post-Tridentine thesis that some revealed truths are contained in
tradition alone. In handling controversial questions such as the development of doctrine and the role of the hierarchical magisterium,
Dei Verbum shows sensitivity to Orthodox, Anglican, and Protestant
concerns.

The convergences with the Faith and Order report from Montreal on Scripture and tradition have often been noted.[19] Montreal,
like Vatican II, describes tradition as a "living reality transmitted
through the operation of the Holy Spirit" (no. 46).[20] The Faith
and Order report further resembles *Dei Verbum* in viewing tradition
as logically and chronologically prior to Scripture (no. 42) and in
maintaining that, "when the canon of the New Testament had been
finally defined and recognized by the Church," tradition needed to
be understood in relation to Scripture (no. 49). Like Vatican II,
again, Montreal looks upon the life of the Church as a "continuous
recalling, appropriation, and transmission" of the once-for-all event
of Jesus Christ (no. 56) and dwells on the "dynamic element in the
Tradition, which comes from the action of God within the history

of his people and . . . looks to the consummation of the victory of the Lord at the end of time" (no. 64).

Yet there are significant differences between the two documents. *Dei Verbum* goes beyond Montreal by seeming to acknowledge cumulative progress in tradition, whereas Montreal is more concerned with finding criteria to distinguish genuine tradition from "impoverished tradition or even distortion of tradition" (no. 48). While recognizing that the letter of "Scripture alone" is not an adequate criterion (no. 49), Montreal does not speak of the magisterium as a criterion except when describing the Roman Catholic position (no. 53). Montreal goes beyond Vatican II in raising the question about the legitimacy of different denominational traditions (a question it leaves unresolved in nos. 57-59) and in recognizing that different cultures require different expressions of tradition (nos. 65-66, 69). But Vatican II, as we have seen, treats these questions in *Unitatis Redintegratio* and in *Ad Gentes*.

Even the agreements between the two documents, impressive as they are, do not reflect a consensus among all Christians. A significant minority, consisting primarily of conservative evangelicals, have found fault with both Montreal and Vatican II in the name of "Scripture alone."

2. Besides having ecumenical value, Vatican II's statement on tradition may be welcomed for helping Catholics to account for the dogmatic teaching of their own Church. It liberated them from the burden of feeling obliged to justify all their present beliefs as having come down unchanged from the apostles, or even as being logical deductions from what the apostles had taught. It thus made room for rather striking developments of dogma and practice. As a result of the council, Catholics can now cheerfully admit that some of their dogmas would have been unknown and even unintelligible to Christians of the early centuries. A new dogma such as the Immaculate Conception may emerge in the course of centuries with only the slenderest apostolic warrants and yet be "traditional" insofar as it is inspired by the Holy Spirit, who remains continuously active in the Church.

3. Finally, by linking tradition directly to the Holy Spirit as transcendent subject, and by uncoupling it from traditions (in the plural), the council legitimized the program of renewal and reform that was at the heart of Vatican II. It allowed Catholics to be critical of certain aspects of their own heritage and to shuffle off

whatever might be regarded as culturally conditioned. Many Catholics felt authorized by the council to become full-fledged citizens of the modern world, to open themselves to the spiritual riches of non-European cultures, and to engage in dialogue with other religions.

The council responded to a widespread desire on the part of Catholics in the 1960s. Many of them were becoming restive under the medievalism that still prevailed in their Church. Thanks to Vatican II, the Church in the West was able to break away from the Latin language in liturgy and theology, from scholasticism in philosophy, and from a predominantly monastic style of spirituality. During the decade after the council the Catholic Church experienced greater changes than in the century — or probably several centuries — prior to Vatican II. Many of these changes were desirable, inevitable, and overdue.

It must be admitted, however, that Vatican II's teaching on tradition was not received with enthusiasm by all Catholics. The vital, realistic, forward-looking concept of tradition promoted by the council struck many conservative Catholics as a capitulation to the modern spirit. Many loyal Catholics, who had been trained to look upon modernity and innovation as sources of confusion and heresy, were bitterly disappointed. "Traditionalist" movements broke out in many countries, calling for greater loyalty to the full Catholic heritage. Archbishop Marcel Lefebvre, one of the most outspoken traditionalists, composed in 1974 a profession of faith in which he stated:

> [W]e formally hold everything that has been believed and practised, whether in the faith, the customs, the worship, the catechetical teaching, the formation of priests, or the institution of the Church, by the Church of all ages as codified in the books that appeared prior to the modernist influence of the Council, while we wait for the true light of Tradition to dispel the shadows that darken the sky over Eternal Rome.[21]

Seeking to justify Vatican II's reforms in the face of traditionalist criticism, apologists for the council took over from the Montreal report on "Scripture, Tradition, and the Traditions" (no. 39) the distinction between the *Tradition* (with a capital T) as the revealed message, *tradition* as a process of transmission, and *traditions* as diverse forms of expression of the gospel. This threefold distinction is reflected in an address of Paul VI of August 7, 1974:

> Here we should explain what we mean by tradition, in this religious sphere, both as a constituent, together with Sacred Scripture, of revelation, and as authentic and compelling transmission, with the assistance of the Holy Spirit through the teaching of the Church, of revelation itself. We consider that these are ideas acquired from our common culture and are held distinct from those commonly so-called traditions which can rather be said to be usages, customs, styles — transient and changeable forms of human life without the charism of a truth which renders them unchangeable and obligatory. We add, rather, that these purely historical and human traditions not only contain many contingent and perishable elements, towards which criticism is liberal in judgement and reform. They often indeed must be criticised and reformed because of the ease with which human things age, or are distorted, and they need to be purified and even supplanted. Not for nothing do we speak of "modernization" and renewal: and you know with how much energy and breadth of application.[22]

The Tradition/tradition/traditions distinction was certainly useful in ridding the Catholic Church of the encumbrance of culturally conditioned accretions from the Middle Ages and the baroque period. But in the 1990s the problems have changed again. Catholics today have less reason to feel weighed down by the accumulated baggage of past centuries. They are no longer forced into the rigid patterns established by their ancestors. In countries such as the United States, young people cannot even imagine what it must have been like to live in the Catholic Church of fifty years ago. They frequently worship in churches or auditoriums barren of shrines and statues. They are ignorant of the answers that their parents or grandparents memorized out of the catechism. They know practically no prayers by heart, and are perhaps unable to say the Angelus or the Rosary. They are so open to the world that they are almost drowning in secularity. Everything familiar to them came into existence yesterday and will probably vanish tomorrow. Nothing in their lives seems to be settled and secure. Not surprisingly, many of them hunger again for the richness and stability of a Catholic tradition to which they have almost lost access.

While the recovery of stable tradition will not be easy, the signs of the times in the 1990s are in some respects more favorable to "traditions" than those of the early 1960s. Four considerations may here be proposed:

1. The historicism of the recent past exaggerated the transitoriness of all things human. The deep structures of nature, including human nature, are surprisingly resistant to change. When we read Homer or Sophocles, Exodus or Proverbs, we are struck by how little things really change. Religious traditions provide symbols that express, in vivid and concrete ways, the permanent and universal situation of human beings before the transcendent otherness of God. Gestures such as bowing and kneeling, the use of candles and incense, water and oil, and the maintenance of sacred spaces in houses of worship — these and a thousand other usages put the faithful in contact with the deep structures of reality and foster authentic religious experience. Nothing in the contemporary situation calls for an abandonment of these aids to worship.

2. Religious traditions, precisely when they are out of phase with secular fashions, perform an important service, disposing worshipers for communion with the sacred and the divine. We should not overlook the importance of chant, icons, and ancient sacral languages — such as, for Christians, Hebrew, Greek, and Latin. Even the vernacular used in worship, if it is to evoke reverence for the divine, should be distinct from the ordinary jargon of the marketplace.

3. In historical faiths such as Christianity tradition has still another function. It binds the contemporary believer to the founding events on which the community rests. Traditional feast days, readings, and rituals reactualize in a powerful way the experiences of the Exodus, Sinai, the conquest of the Holy Land, the return from the Babylonian Exile, and, for Christians, the redemptive deeds of Jesus Christ. Communal actions such as the blessing and pouring of water, or the consecration of bread and wine, do more than build on the symbolic potentialities of nature. They enable us to participate in the saving events that lie at the very sources of our religious existence.

4. Traditions are needed to initiate and socialize individuals into any community that requires loyalty and commitment on the part of its members. For a nation the flag, national holidays, anthems, and pledges of allegiance do much to establish solidarity among citizens.

The Church needs similar traditions. Without its network of cruci-
fixes, feast days, hymns, and professions of faith, Catholicism could
scarcely maintain itself as an enduring worldwide society. Many of
these traditions were severely shaken in the years following Vatican II. Today they need to be reconstituted and reinforced. Without
a more effective socialization into the Church, the faithful may no
longer be in a position to accept or to interpret correctly the Scriptures, the normative symbols, and the statements of faith that have
come down from the past.

Toward a Catholic Consensus

In view of the persistent debates and fluctuations in Catholic theology discussed in this chapter, it should be evident that Catholics
have considerable scope for variety in their theology of tradition.
Yet certain agreed positions can be discerned. Thanks to the clarifi-
cations of Vatican II, the following ten theses would probably receive
broad, if not almost universal, support from Catholic theologians
today.

1. Tradition involves a communal "sense of the faith" aroused
and continuously sustained in the Church by the Holy Spirit.

2. Access to tradition is gained primarily through a grace-filled
life within the community of faith. Rather than being known in a conceptual or objective manner, tradition is grasped through familiarity
or participation as a result of dwelling within the Church, taking part
in its worship, and behaving according to its standards.

3. Although tradition necessarily includes a tacit component, it
has to some degree found normative expression in the writings of the
fathers, in liturgical texts, and in other ecclesially certified "monuments of tradition." These "monuments," in turn, serve to sharpen
the community's sense of the faith.

4. Tradition, as a sense of the faith nourished in the Church by
normative texts or "monuments," provides an element of continuity
in the development of Christian doctrine.

5. Tradition is "divine" insofar as it is aroused and sustained by
God; it is "apostolic" insofar as it originates with the apostles; it is
"living" insofar as it remains contemporary with every generation.

6. Thanks to its divine source, tradition is of equal dignity with
Scripture. It is temporally antecedent to, concomitant with, and sub-

sequent to Scripture. But it falls short of Scripture insofar as it is not available in inspired and canonical texts.

7. The Church drew on tradition as a resource for recognizing the canonical Scriptures and continues to rely on it for interpreting Scripture theologically.

8. Divine tradition gives rise to a variety of human traditions that mediate it to particular groups at particular times and places.

9. Human traditions, while needed to make divine tradition concrete and tangible, must constantly be scrutinized for their soundness and relevance. They are subject to correction and to updating.

10. The ecclesiastical magisterium, making use of Scripture and tradition, is the authoritative judge of the conformity of particular doctrines and practices, including human traditions, with the word of God.

7.

The Magisterium and Theological Dissent

In its Dogmatic Constitution on Divine Revelation, Vatican II declared that "sacred tradition and sacred Scripture together form a
single deposit of the word of God, entrusted to the Church" (DV 10).
The council then added: "The task of authentically interpreting the
word of God, whether in its written form or in that of tradition, has
been entrusted only to the living magisterium of the Church, whose
authority is exercised in the name of Jesus Christ" (ibid.).

Having considered in the last two chapters the relation of Scripture and tradition to theology, we may now turn to the magisterium,
not indeed to examine it in all its aspects, but to comment on its relationship to theology. In this connection it will be necessary to discuss
whether theologians ever have a right or obligation to dissent from
the magisterium, and if so, under what conditions.

Interplay between Magisterium and Theology

Theology, as Christians have come to understand the term, is a distinctively Christian discipline. It is a methodical inquiry into the
meaning and grounding of what, in faith, is taken to be the word
of God (*logos theou*). Because revelation proceeds from the divine
intelligence and is addressed to human intelligence, it calls for reflective assimilation. It encounters in the believer a dynamism toward
rational appropriation and loving contemplation.[1]

As a discursive and contemplative reflection on revelation, theology depends on reliable access to God's prior word. According to
Catholic faith, revelation is mediated through Scripture and tradi-

tion, both of which are constitutive of the Church. The Church, as the bearer and interpreter of revelation, has the capacity to approve what is consonant with, or reject what is dissonant with, the word entrusted to it. The organ that authoritatively expresses the mind of the Church is known as the ecclesiastical magisterium. The ordinary bearers of this magisterium are the pope and the bishops.

Some might question whether there is any need for a continuing magisterium. After all, the revelation by which Christians live was completed nearly two thousand years ago, and it has, in substance, been committed to writing in the canonical Scriptures. Scripture alone, however, was never intended to be, and has not proved to be, a self-sufficient rule of faith. From the early centuries it has been supplemented by creeds and doctrinal formulations. Popes and councils were called upon to decide doctrinal questions that arose as the faith became rooted in Hellenistic soil and as it interacted with the culture and philosophy of the ancient world. For the same reason, a living magisterium continues to be needed in every century. The message of Christ has to be proclaimed in new situations and interpreted for new audiences who have their own perspectives and their own questions. The ecclesiastical leadership must decide whether new hypotheses and formulations are acceptable in light of Christian faith.

Tensions can arise between the hierarchical authorities and theologians. From some literature one gets the impression that the two groups are engaged in a perpetual contest, and that every advance of one group is achieved at the expense of the other. The magisterium, according to this scenario, would be asking theologians to "knuckle under," to abandon their own judgment and sacrifice the integrity of their own discipline. Theologians, on the other hand, would be seen as seeking to achieve full freedom and autonomy by declaring their independence from the magisterium. This journalistic portrayal of the relationship is a caricature.

The respective tasks of theologians and the magisterium have been clarified in several recent documents of the International Theological Commission and likewise in the statement "Doctrinal Responsibilities: Approaches to Promoting Cooperation and Resolving Misunderstandings between Bishops and Theologians" adopted by the United States bishops in their meeting of June 16-19, 1989. Still more recently, on May 14, 1990, the Congregation for the Doctrine of the Faith (CDF) issued an important "Instruction on the Ecclesial Vocation of the Theologian."

These various statements agree in recognizing the relative autonomy of the hierarchical magisterium and the theologians in the performance of their specific tasks. The official teachers and the theologians use different methods and have different goals. The magisterium, which is charged with authoritatively formulating and safeguarding the faith of the Church, does not have to establish its positions by strict theological reasoning. Theologians, whose essential task is to understand and explain, cannot be content to appeal to the authority of popes and bishops. While respecting the judgment of the official teachers, they have to use distinctively theological methods to achieve the insight proper to their discipline. Both theology and the ecclesiastical magisterium must operate in the context of the whole Church as the primary recipient and bearer of divine revelation. The diversity of functions, since it exists only within the prior unity of the People of God, cannot be understood as separation or antagonism. Within the Church, theologians and hierarchical teachers depend in many ways upon each other.

Catholic theology in every century has been profoundly molded by the previous teaching of the magisterium. Councils such as Nicaea and Chalcedon, Trent and Vatican I have given rise to distinct eras in the history of theology. Twentieth-century Catholic theology has depended heavily on the encyclicals of the popes and, since the 1960s, on the teaching of Vatican II. Without the directives of the magisterium Catholic theology would lack adequate guidance.

The dependence of the ecclesiastical magisterium on theology is no less evident. Every great council has made ample use of theologians, some of whom were bishops, but many of whom were not. What would the documents of Trent look like had it not been for the work of papal theologians such as Lainez and Salmeron? What would Vatican I have been able to say without the preparatory texts supplied by Franzelin, Kleutgen, and others? How would Vatican II have been able to accomplish its task in the absence of Congar, Philips, Rahner, Murray, and their colleagues? Nearly every papal encyclical has been drafted with the help of theologians, and the day-to-day functioning of the Roman congregations and episcopal doctrinal commissions involves the collaboration of innumerable theologians. By their preliminary research theologians help to mature the judgment of the Church. By their technical skill they assist the bishops in the precise expression of Catholic doctrine. And even after the magisterium has spoken, theologians play an important role in the reception and interpretation of doctrinal declarations.

The role of theology in reception and interpretation is emphasized in the recent statement of the International Theological Commission on the hermeneutics of dogma. Dogmatic proclamation, according to this document, takes concrete form "as a real, symbolic expression of the content of faith" and "contains and makes present what it designates."[2] All doctrinal formulations, moreover, point beyond themselves to the mystery of God's own truth, which abides in the Church as a living subject. In a certain sense, therefore, even dogmatic declarations cannot be final. "The definition of a dogma, therefore, is never just the end of a development, but always a new beginning.... After definition follows reception, i.e., the living assimilation of a dogma into the entire life of the Church and deeper penetration into the truth to which the dogma gives testimony."[3] To be correctly interpreted in light of the gospel and Christian tradition, the pronouncements of the magisterium require the service of theology. The theological interpretation, in turn, presupposes a purification of the heart and the God-given light of faith.[4]

A further reason for continuing dialogue is that the abiding truth of the gospel never comes to human beings except in provisional, historically conditioned forms. In the words of Walter Kasper, "The definitive content of statements of faith is given only in and through history."[5] Pronouncements made in a particular historical and cultural situation may require reinterpretation or modification with the passage of time. The core teaching is constant, but the forms in which it is conceptualized and verbalized are fluid.

Four Categories of Magisterial Statement

The balance between permanence and timeliness in doctrinal declarations varies in different types of pronouncements, which partly for this reason differ from one another in their obligatory force. Four categories seem to be distinguished by the CDF instruction (23-24):

1. Statements that definitively set forth something that all Catholics are to accept as divinely revealed. Such statements are dogmas in the strict sense.

2. Definitive declarations of nonrevealed truths closely connected with revelation and the Christian life.

3. Nondefinitive but obligatory teaching of doctrine that contributes to the right understanding of revelation.

4. Prudential admonitions or applications of Christian doctrine in a particular time or place.

The first of these four categories is accepted by all Catholics. It is explicitly taught by Vatican I and Vatican II that the pope or the universal episcopate may solemnly define that some truth has been divinely revealed and is contained at least implicitly in Scripture and apostolic tradition. The universal body of bishops may also teach revealed truth infallibly, without solemn definitions, by exercising their ordinary (or day-to-day) magisterium, provided that they agree in proposing some truth as contained in Christian revelation. The response due to strictly dogmatic teaching is called "divine and Catholic faith."

The second category is not explicitly mentioned in either Vatican I or Vatican II, but it appears to be implied by the teaching of both councils. At Vatican I, the pope was declared to have the power to teach infallibly "doctrine concerning faith and morals to be held by the whole Church."[6] The word "held" (*tenendam*) was selected so as to include not only revealed truths to be "believed" (*credenda*), the primary object of infallibility, but also nonrevealed truths closely connected with the revealed deposit and required for its proper explanation and defense. Again at Vatican II, in the Dogmatic Constitution on the Church, the bishops chose their words carefully so as not to seem to be restricting the infallibility of the episcopate to revealed matters. The Theological Commission explained that the object of infallibility included not only the contents of the revealed deposit but also "all those things which are required...in order that the same deposit may be religiously safeguarded and faithfully expounded."[7] Theologians rather commonly assert that the infallible teaching authority of the pope and the united episcopate extends to the principles of the natural moral law, even if these principles are not themselves revealed.

According to the CDF it is a doctrine of faith that moral norms that are revealed but that could per se be known by natural reason can be infallibly taught by the magisterium.[8] Even if this be granted, it may be debated whether the magisterium can definitively teach *all* matters that pertain to the natural law. One commentator on the recent Profession of Faith asserted: "One can include in the object of irreformable definitions, even though not of faith, everything that pertains to the natural law, this also being an expression of the will of God."[9] Francis Sullivan in his commentary on the Profession of Faith rejected this broad interpretation.[10] In his commentary on the CDF instruction he points out that the instruction nowhere asserts that the magisterium can infallibly teach matters of the moral law that go beyond the content of revelation, still less that it can infallibly teach all matters pertaining to the moral law.[11]

The response due to definitive but nonrevealed teaching is firm assent. Some authors, pointing out that the motive is one's trust in the reliability of the magisterium, designate such assent as *ecclesiastical* faith, a term chosen as a counterpart to *divine* faith. Other authors, who prefer to restrict the term "faith" to submission to the word of God, dislike the term "ecclesiastical faith." But this debate about terminology is not substantive and does not require further discussion here.

The third category has long been familiar to Catholics, especially since the popes began to teach regularly through encyclical letters some two centuries ago. The teaching of Vatican II, which abstained from new doctrinal definitions, falls predominantly into this category.[12] In view of the mission given by Christ to the hierarchical magisterium, it is evident that when the magisterium formally teaches something as Catholic doctrine, it is not uttering a mere opinion that Catholics are free to disregard. The teaching has a real, though not unconditional, claim on the assent of the faithful.

The response due to teaching of this third category has been called, since Vatican II, "religious submission of will and intellect" (*religiosum voluntatis et intellectus obsequium*, Vatican II, *Lumen Gentium*, no. 25; cf. CIC, can. 752). Some theologians hold that such *obsequium* necessarily involves actual assent, whereas others interpret *obsequium* as meaning a reverent inclination of the will that normally, but not inevitably, leads to intellectual assent.[13] Theologians of both groups agree that a person who reveres the authority of the magisterium may, in a given case, be unable to proffer a sincere interior assent. The CDF instruction, apparently describing what it understands by *obsequium religiosum*, states that "the willingness to submit loyally to the teaching of the magisterium on matters per se not irreformable must be the rule" (24; cf. 29). The implication seems to be that *obsequium*, while inclining a person to assent, need not in every case result in actual assent.

The fourth category, that of contingent prudential applications, appears to be new in the CDF instruction. The instruction itself gives no examples, but Cardinal Ratzinger, in his press conference on the instruction, was quite specific. He said:

> In this regard one can refer to the statements of the Popes during the last century on religious freedom as well as the anti-modernistic decisions of the Biblical Commission of that time. As a warning cry against hasty and superficial adaptations they remain fully justified; a person of the stature of Johann Baptist Metz has said, for example, that the antimodernist decisions of the Church rendered a great service in keeping her from sinking into the liberal-bourgeois world. But the details of the determinations of their contents were later superseded once they had carried out their pastoral duty at a particular moment.[14]

Utterances of this fourth category generally refer to what may be done, taught, or written in the public forum. In such cases the proper response would seem to be external conformity or obedience. The official directives do not in every case call for interior assent though, as the instruction notes, Catholics would not be justified in holding that the magisterium was habitually mistaken in its prudential judgments (24).[15]

Dissent and Its Limits

The problem of dissent does not normally arise in connection with pronouncements of the first two categories, for these are, in the nature of the case, very rare and are not issued, in practice, except where there is already an overwhelming consensus in the Church regarding their truth. Anyone who flatly rejected such pronouncements, sealed as they are by an anathema, would thereby cease to be a Catholic. But it is possible for a theologian to have personal doubts about whether the conditions of infallibility have in fact been verified in the case of some supposedly irreformable[16] statement. For example, John Henry Newman hesitated for a time after Vatican I before recognizing that there was sufficient consensus among the bishops so that that council's definition of papal infallibility could be recognized as binding. Then again, questions may arise about whether a given statement of these first two categories was prudent and opportune, whether the concepts employed in the definition were suitable, whether the arguments were persuasive, and whether the language was felicitous. Doubts of this kind are not the same as dissent, but they can prevent a person from giving the wholehearted assent that is normally expected.

The problem of dissent arises more commonly with respect to pronouncements of the third and fourth categories. Since no claim of infallibility is here made, such statements could, in principle, be erroneous. It stands to reason that the theologian, like any other Catholic, must be antecedently disposed to accept the reformable[17] teaching of the magisterium, which has the divinely given office of determining the doctrine of the Church. But it may happen that an individual theologian, as already mentioned, could be unsuccessful in attempting to achieve personal conviction.

Contrary opinions are possible because a nondefinitive magisterial statement is not the sole or overriding source of knowledge about the matter under scrutiny. Other sources to be used by theologians in forming their judgment include the teaching of Scripture, the testimony of ancient Christian tradition, the prayer and worship of the Church, the opinions of other theologians, the sense of the faithful, and the evidence of history, experience, or reason. If a reformable teaching appears to be at odds with one or more of these other sources, a theologian who has personally looked into the matter may be inclined to doubt or disagree. Because of the esteem in which theologians are held (at least in some circles), their doubts and denials can lead to widespread disagreement in the Church.

The problem of dissent within the Church was acutely raised when Vatican II seemed to modify, and even perhaps to reverse, previous papal teaching on several subjects such as biblical inerrancy, the ecumenical movement, religious freedom, and criteria for membership in the Church.[18] As a result the council brought about the rehabilitation of a number of biblical scholars, together with well-known systematic theologians such as Henri de Lubac, Yves Congar, Karl Rahner, and John Courtney Murray, all of whom had been under suspicion during the 1950s for their apparent disagreement with certain official teachings.

After the council, the problem of dissent became still more acute. Many right-wing Catholics dissented from the social teaching of the Church, and a few, including Archbishop Marcel Lefebvre, frankly dismissed Vatican II as a heretical council. On the left, many progressive theologians differed from papal teachings such as, most particularly, the doctrine of Paul VI on birth control (*Humanae Vitae*, 1968).

The United States bishops in 1968, in their pastoral letter *Human Life in Our Day*, stated that it was sometimes licit to hold and express views contrary to nondefinitive church teaching. "The expression of theological dissent from the magisterium," they declared, "is in order only if the reasons are serious and well-founded, if the manner of the dissent does not question or impugn the teaching authority of the Church and is such as not to give scandal."[19] The three criteria here given for licit dissent proved difficult to apply. Who was to say whether the reasons were well-founded? How could one establish that the authority of the magisterium was not being impugned when its teaching was being denied? How could scandal be avoided when theologians were openly saying that the pope's teaching was wrong?

The recent instruction of the CDF treats the question of dissent more fully than any previous official document. Some commentators have interpreted it as prohibiting all dissent and thus as contradicting the American bishops' pastoral cited above. A group of theologians (including Hans Küng and Edward Schillebeeckx), in the so-called Tübingen Declaration of July 12, 1990, accused the instruction of attacking the legitimate freedom and autonomy of Catholic theology in a repressive and totalitarian fashion. This accusation, in my judgment, rests on an excessively restrictive interpretation of the instruction.

The instruction does not specify in detail what is to be done in every case of disagreement with the teaching of the magisterium. It does, however, lay down some limiting principles. On the positive side, the instruction explains the grounds that might lead competent theologians to withhold assent. Because of the mingling of permanent truth and historically conditioned perceptions in the formulation of doctrine, certain magisterial documents, according to the CDF, "have not been free from all deficiencies."[20] Especially in their prudential instructions, the bishops and their advisers have sometimes failed to take account of certain aspects of the complex questions under consideration (24). A span of time is often needed to filter out what is contingent and imperfect. In such cases the critical response of theologians may provide the magisterium with "a stimulus to propose the teaching of the Church in greater depth and with a clearer presentation of the arguments" (30). For this reason theologians who feel unable to give intellectual assent may have a positive duty to inform the hierarchical teachers of the problems they find, whether in the doctrinal content, the arguments, or the manner of presentation (30). Through dialogue of this kind, tensions between theologians and the magisterium can contribute to doctrinal progress.

While admitting that candid exposition of honest difficulties can be an impulse to constructive dialogue, the CDF instruction goes on to state that certain kinds of opposition are harmful to the Church as a community of trust and faith. Theologians, according to the instruction, should refrain from giving "untimely public expression" to their divergent opinions and from presenting such opinions as though they were "non-arguable conclusions" (27). They should not give normative status to their own views, thus setting up a "parallel magisterium" of theologians (34). In particular, they should avoid turning to the mass media and seeking to mobilize public opinion to bring pressure on ecclesiastical authorities (30, 39). These reservations are in my judgment valid and important.

The instruction devotes considerable space to certain factors in the contemporary cultural situation that encourage strident public opposition. It mentions fallacious concepts of the rights of conscience, sociological pressures to conform to secular public opinion, the power of the mass media to manipulate ideas, and the influence of political activism with its tactics of conflict and protest.

Cardinal Ratzinger in his press conference pointed out that when dissenting theologians organize themselves as a pressure group, passing from the sphere of thought to that of power play, theology falsifies its own scientific nature. Max Seckler, in commenting on the instruction, observed that the very nature of the Church as a communion is here at stake. What the instruction condemns, he notes, is "a very precise model of conflict with a corresponding strategy of opposition and protest." Agitation, pressure, and threats are, in the long run, a poor method of arriving at truth and consensus in matters of faith.[21]

Rejecting these unseemly methods, the instruction discountenances dissent, equating the latter with "public opposition to the magisterium of the Church" (33). But the instruction does not deal with everything that might be called dissent in the etymological sense of the term. It adopts a rather narrow concept of dissent, not uncommon in political and ecclesiastical usage. The Latin *dissentire,* from which our English word is derived, has a broader meaning, "to be of a different sentiment or opinion, not to agree" (Cassell's *New Latin Dictionary,* 1959 edition). The English verb "dissent" is defined in Webster's *Ninth New Collegiate Dictionary* (1987) as having two meanings: "to withhold assent" and to differ in opinion."[22]

Does the instruction permit theologians who disagree with a reformable teaching to make their views publicly known? Some interpreters have taken the recommendation to make one's difficulties known to the magisterium (30) as though the only option were to approach the ecclesiastical authorities in a private manner, avoiding all publicity.[23] Archbishop Quinn, in my opinion, is correct in pointing out that the "public dissent" repudiated by the instruction has to do with organized opposition and pressure tactics, and that the instruction does not discountenance expression of one's views in a scholarly manner that might be publicly reported.[24] I do not find in the instruction any prohibition of a measured discussion of theological difficulties in scholarly journals, professional societies, seminars, and the like.[25] Such means of dissemination do not imply political pressure or propaganda, but on the contrary invite scholarly response in a spirit of openness to the truth.

The question of classroom teaching is more complex. The Church is quite properly concerned to assure that its official teaching is credibly passed on to those who will have the responsibility of instructing others in faith and morals, for otherwise the faithful would be deprived of their right "to receive the message of the Church in its purity and integrity and not to be disturbed by a particular dangerous opinion" (37). Religious instruction can at times be closely related to preaching and catechesis. It may be intended to train future priests and ministers of the word. Such students should certainly be familiarized with the various grades of authority attaching to different magisterial statements, and with the arguments given by Catholics who dissent. It is important, however, that the teaching of the Church be presented fairly, respectfully, and in a favorable light. A professor who seriously disagrees with church teaching on a broad spectrum of issues might be disqualified from teaching or preaching with an ecclesiastical mandate.

To assure the faithful transmission of its official teaching, the Church has introduced a number of controls, such as public professions of faith (the *professio fidei*), ecclesiastical permission to publish (the *imprimatur*), the licensing of seminary professors and members of ecclesiastical faculties (the *missio canonica* or its equivalent), and warnings (*monita*) against books that are deemed to contain dangerous or fallacious doctrine. Measures such as these are capable of being too restrictively used, at the expense of freedom and honesty in the Church, but these risks can usually be avoided. At all events, care should be taken to prevent the official positions of the Church from being treated as mere opinions, or as having no practical force, as has happened in some branches of Protestantism. Some restrictions on the freedom of theologians may be acceptable in order to prevent the authentic teaching of the Church from being ignored or obscured.

Prudential Norms for Magisterium

The recent instruction of the CDF concentrates primarily on the norms by which theologians should conduct themselves in order to avoid destructive collisions with the magisterium. It speaks more briefly of the obligation of pastoral leaders to safeguard unity and "to see that the tensions arising from life do not degenerate into divisions" (40). In this connection it exhorts bishops to build up "relations of trust with theologians in the fellowship of charity" and in joint service to the word of God (42). The United States bishops, in their statement on "Doctrinal Responsibilities," give a number of suggestions as to how the local bishop can establish cordial and constructive relationships with theologians. Some of these principles seem to be applicable also to the papacy and the college of bishops in their teaching ministry. Even so, as several theologians have noted, there is need for further clarification of the measures that can help to avoid any abuse of authority on the part of the ecclesiastical magisterium.[26] It may be possible to learn from the sufferings unjustly inflicted on creative theologians who have eventually been vindicated. As an initial suggestion I should like to offer the following five ground rules:

1. The magisterium can avoid issuing too many statements, especially statements that appear to carry with them an obligation

to assent. Until the twentieth century, ecumenical councils and dogmatic decrees were rare. Popes issued relatively few doctrinal decisions, and then only at the end of a long process of theological discussion. But encyclicals, conciliar documents, decisions of Roman congregations, and pastoral letters from bishops have increased in number and length. Ecclesiastical authorities are continually being pressured to make statements about every controversial issue that could be seen as having a moral or religious aspect. Unless the authorities exercise great restraint, Catholics can easily feel overwhelmed by the multitude of views they are expected to profess, even on issues where Scripture and apostolic tradition appear to be silent. Wherever diversity seems to be tolerable, theologians and others should be given freedom to use their own good judgment. Newman and, later, Pope John XXIII were fond of the ancient dictum: *In necessariis unitas, in dubiis libertas, in omnibus caritas.*

2. The hierarchical teachers can use their influence to protect legitimate freedom and to moderate charges and countercharges among theologians of different schools. Authority can be used permissively as well as restrictively. The American bishops, in "Doctrinal Responsibilities," proposed some procedures for screening out groundless complaints.[27] The Holy See has at times forbidden theologians to brand one another's views as heretical, for example, in the famous dispute between Jesuits and Dominicans about actual grace in the seventeenth century.

3. The magisterium should be on guard against efforts of any given school or party to gain official endorsement for its own theological positions. Before issuing binding statements of doctrine, the pope and bishops would do well to consult widely with theologians of different schools.[28] The sense of the faithful should likewise be ascertained, with care to discriminate between views actually inspired by faith and mere opinions that could well be due to the influence of the secular climate.

4. The hierarchy, before it speaks, should anticipate objections and seek to obviate them. This goal can more easily be achieved if preliminary drafts are published and subjected to open criticism. When possible, the faithful should be forewarned and prepared for decisions so that they do not feel suddenly commanded to adopt new views.

5. Those who speak on behalf of the universal Church must be sensitive to the variety of situations and cultures in different parts

of the world. At times statements are read in a context other than that of the authors and are taken as referring to problems that were not envisaged. Sometimes, also, concise and objective doctrinal statements, especially as excerpted by the news media, give an impression of abruptness and pastoral insensitivity. Advance consultation with episcopal conferences can be, and has often proved to be, of assistance in finding palatable formulations or permitting the preparation of timely explanations.[29]

In the last analysis, however, popes and bishops cannot be infinitely permissive. They have the painful duty of setting limits to what may be held and taught in the Church. There is no guarantee that true doctrine will always be pleasing to the general public. Jesus uttered hard sayings, with full awareness that in so doing he was alienating some of his own followers. Peter spoke for the believing minority when he exclaimed: "Lord, to whom shall we go? You have the words of eternal life" (John 6:68). The whole Church, including the theological community, depends on the courage and fidelity of the hierarchical magisterium in continuing to hand on these words of life.

8.

Theology and Philosophy

It is impossible to carry through the project of systematic theology without explicit commitment to particular philosophical options. Hitherto Catholic theology has relied principally on the axioms and categories of Greek philosophy, filtered, in some cases, through Roman or Arabic thinkers. After early experiments with Stoicism, the fathers came to prefer some variety of Platonism. Although Aristotle had long been an influence, his philosophy did not become dominant until the High Middle Ages. Thomas Aquinas, the greatest of Catholic theologians, constructed his system on the basis of a Platonized form of Aristotelianism.

Revivals of Thomism

Thomistic philosophy became the principal partner for Catholic theology since the Reformation. Not only Dominicans but also Carmelites and Jesuits, in their great systematic summas, relied heavily on Thomas Aquinas both for philosophy and for theology, even while not following his opinions slavishly. In the eighteenth and nineteenth centuries a number of Catholic theologians tended to make use of Descartes, Leibniz, Malebranche, Wolff, and Kant to provide them with philosophical principles. In the mid-nineteenth century, however, Thomism was revived, especially through the influence of Dominicans and Jesuits in Naples and Rome.[1]

Pope Leo XIII in his encyclical *Aeterni Patris* (1879) called for a restoration of philosophy that would build on the "golden wisdom" of St. Thomas, while leaving behind any of his opinions that might be incompatible with modern discoveries. In 1880 Leo XIII established the Institut Supérieur de Philosophie at Louvain, which became a major center for promoting a renewed Thomism. At Louvain Désiré Mercier, Désiré Nys, and Maurice De Wulf published an influential *Cours de Philosophie*.[2]

Pius X gave a further impulse to Thomistic orthodoxy by making the *Summa theologiae* the textbook for all pontifical institutions. Under his pontificate the Congregation of Studies issued, in 1914, a list of twenty-four theses, drawn up by Guido Matiussi, S.J., which were considered to summarize the central philosophical positions of the Angelic Doctor. Many of these theses were directly contrary to the Suarezian system, still taught at that time in most Jesuit houses of study. It took another generation to staff Jesuit philosophates with professors who could accept the twenty-four theses.

Between the two world wars Thomism rose to new heights through the brilliant writings of Etienne Gilson, Jacques Maritain, and the able research of the Pontifical Institute of Mediaeval Studies at Toronto. Indicative of future rifts among Thomists was the debate that occurred at this time about the possibility and nature of "Christian philosophy." Some held that revelation and faith exerted an intrinsic influence on philosophy (Gilson, Maritain, Chenu); others, that the influence was merely extrinsic. All agreed, however, that revelation could serve at least as a negative norm, since philosophy could not contradict revealed truth.

Thomism, however, was not the sole philosophical option for Catholic theologians. In Germany many of the leading theologians, such as Karl Adam and Romano Guardini, were strongly influenced by the phenomenology of Edmund Husserl. Several of Husserl's followers, including Max Scheler, Dietrich von Hildebrand, and Edith Stein, became Catholics.[3] At Juvisy in 1932 the Société Thomiste held a study session, attended by Thomists such as Jacques Maritain and Etienne Gilson and by phenomenologists such as Alexandre Koyré and Edith Stein, to discuss whether Catholics could adopt the phenomenological approach without, of course, committing themselves to the conclusions of Husserl and Heidegger. The spirit of the discussion, according to Herbert Spiegelberg, seemed to favor the affirmative answer.[4]

A number of other currents were in the air. Blondel's philosophy of action, Maréchal's transcendental Thomism, and Teilhard de Chardin's evolutionary humanism were popular in Catholic circles. In France phenomenology was given an existential twist by Gabriel Marcel, who became a convert to Catholicism. Emmanuel Mounier popularized a personalist philosophy that sought to reconstruct society in a way that would avoid the evils of capitalism and socialism. The advocates of the so-called *nouvelle théologie*, notably Jean Daniélou, lamented the sterility into which Catholic theology had fallen because of its excessive commitment to scholasticism. He advocated making use of the dynamic and historical categories of Hegel and Bergson, and of linking theology to modern philosophies such as existentialism and Marxism.[5]

Scholastic philosophers and theologians were quick to sense the new threats to the dominance of Thomism. They vigorously attacked the *nouvelle théologie* as leading to relativism and modernism. Pius XII in his encyclical *Humani Generis* (1950) seemed to take the side of the Thomists. The method of the Angelic Doctor, he declared, "is singularly preeminent both for teaching students and for bringing truth to light; his doctrine is in harmony with divine revelation and is most effective both for safeguarding the foundation of the faith and for reaping, safely and usefully, the fruits of sound progress" (no. 52). The Catholic Church, he explained, has accepted as part of its patrimony a philosophy "that safeguards the genuine validity of human knowledge, the unshakable metaphysical principles of sufficient reason, causality, and finality, and finally the mind's ability to attain certain and unchangeable truth" (no. 48). This philosophy had permanent value. "Truth and its philosophical expression cannot change from day to day, least of all where there is a question of the self-evident principles of the human mind or of those propositions which are supported by the wisdom of the ages and by divine revelation" (no. 49). Philosophical systems such as immanentism, idealism, dialectical materialism, and existentialism are incompatible with Catholic dogma (no. 56).

Vatican II and Scholasticism

One of the central questions at Vatican II was whether the council would reaffirm the scholastic tradition or accept a measure of philosophical pluralism. Most of the preparatory schemas of 1962, drawn up principally by Roman professors, were strictly scholastic in thought and expression. But when the bishops assembled they rejected many of the schemas and established new commissions to write their documents. The majority of the members and experts now came from the liberal "European Alliance" and its supporters.[6]

In the end, the council documents were not written in scholastic style. Care was taken, in fact, not to adopt any philosophical option. The council chose to focus on pastoral aims and to avoid hard theoretical questions. As its dominant method, the council used phenomenology. In a decisive intervention on December 4, 1962, Cardinal Léon Josef Suenens proposed as the chief theme of the council: "We therefore ask of the Church: What do you say of yourself?"[7] In submitting the text to the Central Commission, he added the suggestion that the relationship of various classes of people to the Church should be set forth in concrete terms. According to John F. Kobler, the idea of concrete reflection on human relationships was a signal that the phenomenological method should be adopted. As supporting evidence Kobler refers to the views of Gabriel Marcel on the way in which "concrete interpersonal relations" impart a haunting sense of "the 'mystery' of our inescapable involvement with others."[8]

However that may be, it is indubitable that many of the council's theological experts, such as Bernhard Häring, Karol Wojtyla, and Edward Schillebeeckx were thoroughly at home with phenomenological method. Many of the documents consciously seek to pursue a method that is "objective, phenomenological, and as little interpretative as possible."[9] The council thus became a corporate pastoral reflection on the self-consciousness of the Church as it finds itself in its present life-world. In his book on the implementation of the council, Wojtyla has a pivotal chapter entitled "The Consciousness of the Church as the Main Foundation of Conciliar Initiation"[10] He points out that in answering the question, "Church, what do you say of yourself?" the council reflects on itself as a conscious subject, responsible for its own faith and practice. Similarly, Pope Paul VI, in his homily at the close of Vatican II, recalled how the Church had "gathered herself together in deep spiritual awareness...to find in herself, active and alive, the Holy Spirit, the word of Christ."[11]

The extensive use of scholastic philosophy at Vatican II was practically ruled out by the purposes of the council, as articulated by Pope John XXIII and as accepted by the bishops themselves. The council was to be pastoral in nature, in the sense of being concerned with the effective proclamation of the gospel and with enabling the Church to show forth, in its actual practice, the features of Christ the Good Shepherd. Scholasticism was not oriented toward proclamation or toward spiritual renewal, but rather toward subtle and abstract discussions that were rather remote from conduct.

Second, Pope John desired that the council should relate the Church more positively to the modern world. His program of *aggiornamento* militated against the tendencies of scholasticism, which had become the special preserve of Roman Catholics and which had adopted a negative attitude toward almost all modern philosophic systems. A positive orientation to modernity would imply receptiveness to alternative systems and a disposition to reconcile them, insofar as possible, with Catholic faith.

Third, the pope wanted the council to contribute to Christian unity. In his opening address he insisted that the council was intended not to repress and condemn errors but to exhibit the Church as "the loving mother of all, benign, patient, full of mercy toward the brethren who are separated from her."[12] This ecumenical concern was unfavorable to the dominance of scholasticism — a system with very little appeal in Orthodox and Protestant circles, even though it had some admirers among the high Anglicans. Eastern Orthodoxy retained traces of Platonism and Neoplatonism; some Russian Orthodox theologians were influenced by German idealism. Most Protestant theologians of the nineteenth and twentieth centuries took philosophical positions that depended on Kant, Hegel, and their successors. A common basis for dialogue with non-Catholic Christians could surely be found in the Scriptures and often also in the fathers, but scarcely in scholasticism.

Finally, as became apparent in the conciliar discussions, the continued progress of Catholicism required that the faith be stated in language accessible to non-European cultures. Scholasticism in its present and past forms is a Western European phenomenon arising out of the demise of classical culture and the various revivals of learning that had occurred since the time of Charlemagne.

About half of the bishops at Vatican II came from missionary lands. "They wanted theological reflection to have some practical relevance and benefit to the real world in which their people lived."[13] Scholasticism could not cope with the flood of new experiences registered from non-European parts of the world. Phenomenology, on the other hand, was designed to invite dialogue on the basis of intersubjectivity and thus to establish communication between people with differing perspectives on reality.

For all that, Vatican II did not repudiate scholasticism. It was the system in which most of the bishops had been trained, and that which they knew best. Without explicitly mentioning scholasticism, the council at various points reaffirmed instructions from Pius XII and Paul VI favoring the method of Thomas Aquinas. The Declaration on Christian Education extolled the teaching of St. Thomas for showing how faith and reason can give harmonious witness to the unity of all truth (GE 10). The Decree on Priestly Formation recommended that students be taught according to "that philosophical heritage which is perennially valid," and in such a way that students "will be led to acquire a solid and coherent knowledge of humanity, the world, and God" (OT 15). Future priests should be made "conversant with contemporary philosophical investigations, especially those which have greater influence in their own country," but in studying such systems they should hold fast to principles that are demonstrably true, so as to be able to detect and refute errors (ibid.).

Postconciliar Pluralism

Since the council there has been a great diversification in Catholic theology. New methods and questions have been imported from literary criticism, sociology, psychology, and philosophy. The new pluralism in philosophy may here be illustrated by a brief, and necessarily impressionistic, overview of certain important trends in Protestant and Catholic thought.

Neo-scholastic Thomism in the vein of Etienne Gilson and Jacques Maritain is still a movement to be reckoned with. In fact it shows signs of reviving in conservative Catholic circles. But in theological speculation it has been overshadowed by the transcendental Thomism of Karl Rahner, Bernard Lonergan, and their disciples. This system, while it has a certain basis in Thomas himself, is heavily influenced by the transcendental idealism of Kant, if not by that of Fichte. Rahner's transcendental Thomism has affinities with Heidegger's existential phenomenology and also, I would judge, with Hegel's phenomenology of spirit.

More ancient philosophical options, such as patristic Platonism and medieval Augustinianism, remain operative in the thought of some Catholic theologians such as Henri de Lubac, Hans Urs von Balthasar, and Joseph Ratzinger. These authors, though keenly aware of current trends, are in some ways pre-Thomistic.

Hegel is perhaps the chief philosophical influence behind the work of several Protestant theologians, including Wolfhart Pannenberg and Jürgen Moltmann. Among contemporary Catholic theologians, Hans Küng is notable for having carried on a lifelong dialogue with Hegel, which has borne fruit in his lengthy volume on Christology.

Friedrich Schelling, who inspired a number of nineteenth-century Catholic theologians, was a primary source for Paul Tillich. Tillich also drew heavily on the thought of other philosophers, including Hegel and Heidegger. Among contemporary Catholics, Walter Kasper is noteworthy for his extensive use of Schelling in his own theology of revelation and of history.

Classical Marxism continues to have an impact on Latin American liberation theology. A few representatives of this movement, such as José Porfirio Miranda and Enrique Dussel, claim to be Christian Marxists. Others, such as Gustavo Gutiérrez and Juan Luis Segundo, are in lively dialogue with Marxism. The influence of dissident Marxists such as Ernst Bloch and Jürgen Habermas has carried over into the political theology of Johann Baptist Metz and Edward Schillebeeckx.

The phenomenology of Edmund Husserl, Max Scheler, and Maurice Merleau-Ponty has had a major impact on theologians of the stature of Edward Schillebeeckx (whose basic formation was Thomistic) and Bernhard Häring. It has also been a factor in the thinking of Karol Wojtyla, who has synthesized phenomenology with a kind of neo-Thomism. His social philosophy apparently owes a debt to the personalistic Thomism of Emmanuel Mounier. The American Protestant Edward Farley has developed a theology grounded in Husserl's phenomenology.

The existentialism of the early Heidegger has made a deep impression on Rudolf Bultmann, Gotthold Hasenhüttl, and the American Protestant Schubert Ogden. John Macquarrie, Gerhard Ebeling, Ernst Fuchs, and James M. Robinson have been influenced by the ontology of the later Heidegger.

The process philosophy of Alfred North Whitehead and Charles Hartshorne continues to be a ferment in the work of some American Protestants such as Langdon Gilkey, John Cobb, and Schubert

Ogden. A few Catholics such as Joseph A. Bracken have also been experimenting with process thought.

The linguistic analysis of Wittgenstein and his disciples has had a profound impact on Paul Holmer, Hans Frei, and a number of their colleagues at Yale, including George Lindbeck. Recent French studies in linguistics and semiotics, including the "discourse analysis" of Ricoeur and Lacan, have left their mark on the recent writing of the Catholic David Tracy, who has apparently abandoned the confident transcendental phenomenology of his early work *Blessed Rage for Order* (1975).[14] A few theologians are favorably impressed by the poststructuralism of Jacques Derrida.

In a more learned and protracted exposition it would be profitable to discuss additional philosophical influences such as Martin Buber, Eric Voegelin, Maurice Blondel, Michael Polanyi, Charles Peirce, William James, and John Dewey. Hasty though it be, this overview may suffice to show that contemporary theology, Catholic as well as Protestant, retains strong links with philosophy. Systematic theologians generally elaborate their positions on the basis of conscious philosophical options. The most vigorous currents in contemporary theology are sensitive to trends of philosophy that have arisen since Kant, but the classical heritage of Christian antiquity remains a powerful resource, especially for Catholics.

Merits of the Philosophical Tradition

There are many good reasons why Catholics should not be content today with scholastic theology as the sole instrument for systematic theology. Scholasticism is most at home in dealing with abstract concepts, propositions, and formal reasoning. Theology, however, is not exclusively or even primarily deductive. The theologian must be able to perceive the import of signs and symbols, to grasp what is merely suggested or evoked. Because of the historical character of biblical revelation, theology must be able to assess historical evidence and to interpret texts in their literary and historical context. Because conversion involves attitudinal changes, the theologian must have resources for probing human motivation and affectivity. Because faith involves personal relationships with God and with one's fellow believers, theology must be able to understand the nature and growth of interpersonal relations. Because living faith is inseparable from works, theology must be able to deal with praxis and with the logic of action. For all these dimensions of the theological task, philosophies other than scholasticism offer equal or greater resources.

The intent of Pope John XXIII and of the fathers at Vatican II that Catholic theology should be revitalized by contact with new and more modern philosophical sources has been successfully achieved in the past twenty-five years. As a result, Catholic theology has experienced a new ferment and has attracted favorable attention from thinkers who do not share the Catholic faith. These gains should not be underestimated, but at the same time it must be asked whether the full program of Vatican II has been realized. The directives of Vatican II quoted above seem to make it clear that the council was recommending that theology be based on the perennially valid philosophical heritage that comes down through Thomas Aquinas. This does not mean a rigid or servile adherence to scholasticism, but it does involve a serene confidence that the basic principles used for theological reasoning over the centuries have not lost their validity. Three main reasons may be given for cherishing the classical philosophical tradition as it survives in patristic and medieval thought.

Since the first ecumenical councils the Catholic Church, in its creedal and dogmatic utterances, has deliberately taken over the language of classical ontology. These doctrinal definitions, in my opinion, do not require under pain of heresy an acceptance of the technical terms and concepts that are employed,[15] but they do require those terms and concepts to be regarded as serviceable in the sense that they can illumine, and do not necessarily distort, the Christian message. To think with the Church about the nature of God, the Trinity, the Eucharist, grace, and eternal life, we must be receptive to these philosophical categories. We must be able to understand and affirm what the tradition has meant by statements that refer to nature, person, substance, accident, form and matter.

Besides using philosophical categories as vehicles for specifying the contents of revelation, church authorities have, in the second place, pronounced on certain philosophical questions that are intimately connected with faith. In continuity with the Christian philosophical tradition, the magisterium has taught, for instance, the freedom of the will, the immortality of the soul, the falsity of pantheism and emanationism, the knowability of God's existence, and the omnipotence and immutability of God. The Catholic philosopher, therefore, is not at liberty to adopt any system that denies these traditional positions.

Finally, for Catholic theology to grow in a healthy way, it must maintain contact with its own philosophical tradition. The fathers and early councils played a providential role in establishing guidelines for the proper understanding of faith. The medieval doctors must likewise be accepted as part of our own past. We are a part of their future. For the sake of progress the Church needs a relatively stable philosophical tradition. "Perennial philosophy," as it used to be called, should be cherished because it provides an intellectual home for Catholics who are conscious of their own philosophical roots.

The reclaiming of this ancient philosophical tradition will require some effort. Since Vatican II, many Catholic theologians, in their zeal to reach out to other intellectual families, have turned their back on the classical tradition. For the sake of acceptability many have felt compelled to impugn the Hellenistic patrimony, and scholasticism in particular, as a sterile intellectualism. This cavalier dismissal of an entire civilization is clearly unwarranted. The Greek philosophers, for all their supposed intellectualism, had great esteem not only for reason but for virtue and beauty. They were interested not only in knowing (*theoria*) but also in making (*poiesis*) and doing (*praxis*). They appreciated the power of metaphor and myth and were acutely conscious of the intrusion of the demonic into human affairs. They were also fascinated by the phenomenon of love. Patristic and medieval Christianity, building in part on the classical heritage, looked on God not only as being and truth but also as beauty and goodness, and indeed as subsistent love. The medieval scholastics engaged in a profound analysis of the will and the affections; they exalted charity as the supreme virtue. Those who spurn the alleged intellectualism of the scholastics often betray their own anti-intellectualism and their ignorance of the real teaching of the medieval doctors.

Perhaps, then, we have come full circle. It may be time to take a second look at *Humani Generis*. Without endorsing every detail in that controverted encyclical, we may put the questions: Could Pius XII have been correct in holding that philosophical systems such as immanentism, idealism, dialectical materialism, and existentialism in unamended form are incompatible with Catholic dogma? Was he far from the mark when he felt it necessary to defend the genuine validity of human knowledge and the mind's ability to attain certain and unchangeable truth?

Following in the footsteps of Pius XII, Paul VI in his encyclical *Mysterium Fidei* (1965) declared that the rules of language confirmed by the authority of councils ought not to be discarded at the pleasure of the individual, but should be religiously safeguarded. The integrity of the faith, he insisted, must be protected by a proper mode of expression "lest by the careless use of words we occasion the rise of false opinions regarding faith" (no. 23). While conceding that the dogmatic formulations used by ecumenical councils sometimes stand in need of clearer explanation, Paul VI maintained that the terms used by the councils for mysteries such as the Trinity and the Incarnation are not tied to a particular epoch or theological school, but "present that part of reality which necessary and universal experience permits the human mind to grasp" (no. 24).

These statements of Pius XII and Paul VI were further nuanced by the Congregation for the Doctrine of the Faith, which in 1973 admitted that "even though the truths which the Church intends to teach through her dogmatic formulas are distinct from the changeable conceptions of a given epoch, and can be expressed without them, nevertheless it can sometimes happen that these truths may be enunciated by the Sacred Magisterium in terms that bear traces of such conceptions."[16] In substance, however, the popes' insistence on the permanent validity of dogmatic statements is a needed bulwark against the philosophical relativism and historicism of the present day. Even though the interpretation of philosophical terms and concepts is somewhat affected by changing cultural contexts, such terms can express unchangeable truths in ways intelligible to later ages.

The Broadening Dialogue

It may seem that by recalling these affirmations of the abiding validity of traditional categories I am going against the spirit, if not against the letter, of Vatican II. Objections arising out of the intentions of John XXIII and the conduct of the council, as described above, must now be considered.

In its concern for pastoral relevance the council is often thought to have minimized the importance of abstract and speculative questions. Some consider that a pastoral attitude requires us to espouse some form of pragmatism or to place praxis ahead of theory. I do not regard this as a proper interpretation of the mind of John XXIII or the purposes of the council. The pope insisted that it was "necessary first of all that the Church should never depart from the sacred patrimony of truth received from the Fathers."[17] The world, he said, expected from the council "a step forward toward a doctrinal penetration and a formation of consciousness in faithful and perfect conformity to the authentic doctrine" and to the truth of the Lord, which remains forever.[18]

To this I would add that the pastoral may never be played off against the doctrinal. The mind requires truth in order to be fed. To accept anything as true, we must be able to understand what it means and to see its coherence. The Catholic Church has always had a high regard for reason and truth. In its message to intellectuals and scientists, Vatican II proclaimed: "Have confidence in faith, this great friend of intelligence. Enlighten yourselves with its light in order to take hold of truth, the whole truth."[19]

John XXIII wisely judged that it would be undesirable for the council to define new dogmas or anathematize new errors. He was speaking at a time when scholastic theology was in danger of turning in upon itself and seeking too much support from magisterial authority. But today the situation has almost reversed itself. The great need is to see the importance of the doctrines that are handed down. It is time for Catholic intellectuals not indeed to invoke the police power of the hierarchy but to argue strenuously for tenets that contribute to the right understanding of faith.

Fidelity to the heritage of ancient and medieval philosophy might seem to be an obstacle to the efforts of John XXIII and Vatican II to situate the Church in the modern world. If pursued in the spirit of antiquarianism, that might be the case. But a living tradition always renews itself. It becomes antiquated by disuse. Contemporary thinkers cannot limit themselves to medieval, baroque, or nineteenth-century scholasticism. They must reread Plato and Aristotle, Origen and Augustine, Aquinas and Bonaventure, in the context of our own day. But the classical and scholastic sources cannot be neglected without a loss of identity and direction. Progress is not achieved by always beginning again or by disruptive change. As John Henry Newman demonstrated at some length, authentic developments of Christian doctrine are recognizable by the continuity of their principles and by their conservative action on their own past.[20] The same, I suggest, is true of authentic philosophical developments.

They must support, extend, and refine the truth that was previously known.

Scholasticism could easily be seen as an obstacle to the ecumenism promoted by Vatican II. Ecumenism involves respectful dialogue and hence a readiness to listen and learn. But it also involves a readiness to give from the resources of one's own tradition. Catholics in dialogue are expected to be able to provide an intelligent account and a reasoned defense of conciliar and papal teaching. Familiarity with scholastic philosophy is an essential condition for penetrating the true meaning of the decrees of the medieval councils, Trent, and Vatican I. It is far more important for the Catholic ecumenist to be well trained in scholasticism than to be an authority on Luther, Kant, Kierkegaard, and Hegel.

Vatican II, as noted above, took cognizance of the fact that the Church was coming to maturity in parts of the world relatively unaffected by Western philosophical thought. It sought to restrain any kind of cultural imperialism and to encourage the young churches to develop forms of piety and expression suited to their own temperaments and traditions. But this should not be taken as implying a lack of confidence in the Western philosophical heritage, which has achieved insights of abiding validity.

An analogy from science can perhaps be helpful. It has been established beyond reasonable doubt that the earth is a sphere, that it revolves around the sun and that the solar system is millions of years old. These and similar truths have been discovered by methods used in Western science and expressed primarily in Western languages. But the methods and languages can, in the course of time, be made intelligible to non-Westerners. Possibly these others, drawing on their own gifts and cultural heritage, will find ways of further refining what has heretofore been expressed from a limited perspective. But that does not detract from the validity of the discoveries that have been made. So too, I would argue, respect for non-Western cultures should not be an occasion for doubting what the Church has definitively taught about the processions in the Trinity, the Incarnation, and the like.

It is highly improbable, if not impossible, that the great dogmas of Catholic Christianity can ever be formulated in language that owes nothing to the tradition of classical philosophy. Modern efforts to separate dogma from its official conciliar formulations have thus far proved unsuccessful. In the nineteenth century Anton Günther made one such attempt, but it was found deficient on various counts and was condemned by the Holy See in 1857.

A few decades ago several Dutch theologians tried to translate the doctrine of transubstantiation into modern dynamic categories such as "transignification" and "transfinalization." Paul VI, in his encyclical *Mysterium Fidei* (1965) reaffirmed the teaching of Trent on transubstantiation and repudiated those who speak only of what is called "transignification" or "transfinalization."[21]

Shortly after the council some attempted to rework the doctrine of the Trinity with the help of modern process philosophy. This experiment, which resulted in a denial of the coeternity of the divine persons and in effect reduced the processions to the missions, was repudiated in a 1972 declaration of the Congregation for the Doctrine of the Faith.[22]

Transcendental Thomism is perhaps the most auspicious of recent attempts to modernize Catholic theology. Insofar as it retains its Thomistic inspiration, it is unquestionably viable. But to the extent that it borrows from transcendental idealism, it remains contestable. It runs the risk of portraying God no longer as a real personal agent distinct from the world but rather as the dimension of transcendence of the evolving human spirit.

There is a lesson to be drawn, I think, from the experiments that have failed. For purposes of theological reflection, not all philosophical systems are equally valid. A system that was once used successfully to explicate the contents of revelation cannot simply be tossed aside and replaced by any other. It is necessary to challenge the nominalist supposition that abstract concepts and terms are mere conventions established for the sake of convenient communication. Theological experience suggests on the contrary that the ecclesiastically approved philosophical categories have been shaped by, and in some way correspond to, the structure of reality itself. They convey the wisdom of the past not only by their explicit content but also by their tacit implications. As Michael Polanyi remarks, "Words of great human significance accumulate through the centuries an unfathomable fund of subsidiarily known connotations, which we can bring into focus by reflecting on the use of such words."[23] Acceptance of this conceptual tradition is a singular asset for the better understanding of revelation. Sound theologies may take their departure from different philosophical perspectives but they must in the end converge toward a harmonious articulation of the meaning of revelation.

Catholic systematic theology can gain in vitality by entering into communication with a variety of modern philosophies, especially those that have appealed to committed Christian believers. Theology stands to gain from dialogue with idealism, dialectical materialism, pragmatism, process philosophy, and linguistic analysis. But as it grows through dialogue of this kind, theology must be mindful of its own philosophical heritage. The successful insights of the classical tradition must survive, or at least be subsumed in some recognizable form, in any future system. Historically, and I think providentially, Catholic faith has been linked with the metaphysical realism of classical thought, and has refined that realism in the light of revelation. Theology, therefore, will do well to preserve its links with that venerable philosophical tradition.

Dialogue with a variety of systems is consonant with the Catholic philosophical tradition, not least in its scholastic forms. Medieval scholasticism arose out of an attempt to find a hidden consensus among authorities who seemed to disagree. Philosophers, canon lawyers, and theologians such as Abelard, Gratian, and Peter Lombard sought to save the patristic authorities and find harmony within apparent discord. Thomas Aquinas in his philosophy and theology reached out to pagan, Muslim, and Jewish sources. The modern use of models can sustain a similar breadth of view. If it is true, as I have suggested in chapter 3, that diverse philosophical systems rest on different root metaphors, a method of models may be helpful for overcoming the lack of shared vocabulary and criteria. By attending to the symbolic and latent dimensions of meaning, this method can perhaps bring some order into the existing confusion of tongues. If the models are creatively used within a dynamic tradition, the method may be expected to do for our time what scholasticism in its several incarnations did for our forebears. It may serve to ground a new kind of unity and thus fill the gap created by the absence of any one dominant system.

9.

Theology and the Physical Sciences

Until early modern times the relations between theology and science were as harmonious as between theology and philosophy. Indeed, no sharp line of demarcation existed between philosophy and the natural sciences. As we have seen in the last chapter, systematic theology has retained, even to the present day, very close links with philosophy. The relations between theology and science have, however, been strained by a number of crises such as the Galileo affair in the early seventeenth century and the controversies about human evolution in the mid-nineteenth century. In our own century battles have continued to rage between fundamentalist Christians and scientists, as the Scopes "monkey trial" of 1925 and the court cases about "creation science" in the early 1980s bear witness. These conflicts direct our attention to the question of systematic theology's relation to the physical sciences.

Blondel on Faith and Science

Vatican I, without speaking directly of the physical sciences, laid down some general principles in its teaching on faith and reason. It affirmed that the two types of cognition can never be at odds and that they mutually support each other. Reason can assist faith by enabling it to construct apologetic arguments and theological systems. Faith assists reason by extending reason's sphere into the realm of supernatural mysteries and by delivering reason from errors, thanks to the surer light of revelation. Within its own proper sphere, the council declared, scientific reason enjoys a proper autonomy. Deriving from God, "the lord of the sciences," reason can, with the help of grace, lead people to God.

A generation after Vatican I, the French philosopher Maurice Blondel attempted to apply the teaching of the council to the academic situation of his own day. In the last two parts of a four-part article on faith, first published in 1906, he took up the linkage between faith and science.[1] The relationship can be variously conceived, he said, in correspondence with different conceptions of science. According to the classical concept of science, taken over by Thomas Aquinas from the ancient Greeks, the concepts and theories of science are controlled by their objects and are intended to reproduce the structures of external reality. In that case science could directly confirm, or directly collide with, philosophy and faith.

According to a second view, held by some of Blondel's contemporaries such as Pierre Duhem, science was a system of symbols or notations devised for the purpose of accomplishing certain practical tasks. Science in that case would make no metaphysical claims. The only criterion would be its fruitfulness. In that case science and faith could coexist in mutual indifference.

Blondel was dissatisfied with both theories. The first, demanding concordism, failed to give science its proper autonomy. The second theory, by divorcing science from the real, would eliminate the possibility of any interaction between science and faith. In Blondel's estimation, science was autonomous to the extent that it was concerned with formal coherence, logical force, and inner consistency. But insofar as science aims to serve the needs of human life, it must insert itself into the real order. Even though scientific discovery does not have directly metaphysical significance, it does refer to the real order. Its notations are not merely arbitrary or conventional. It yields an authentic, though limited, grasp of truth. Moral and religious thinkers must take account of certitudes acquired through science: for example, that the firmament is not a solid vault; that there are antipodes.

According to Vatican I, Blondel notes, science and faith must cooperate, even while following their distinct methods. Conflict can arise, as the council stated, either from a misunderstanding of faith or from false conclusions of reason. Faith gives rise to confusion when it is falsely reduced to exterior formulations or when people look for literal agreement with scientific statements, overlooking the different modes of discourse. Science can be responsible for conflicts when it usurps the competence of faith.

A measure of friction between science and faith, said Blondel, is inevitable. Such friction can lead to advances. When science operates rightly in its own proper sphere, its findings can help believers overcome their unconscious narrowness. By adjusting to the progress of geology, archaeology, and other sciences, faith gains in solidity. For the same God, as Vatican I declared, is the lord of science and of theology. God never contradicts himself.

Vatican II, in its Pastoral Constitution on the Church in the Modern World, extended the teaching of Vatican I along lines that Blondel would have welcomed. After affirming with Vatican I that the sciences have legitimate autonomy within their proper spheres of competence (GS 60), the Pastoral Constitution went on to admonish theologians to cooperate with experts in the various sciences and to propose the Church's teaching on God, humanity, and the world in ways that take advantage of recent scientific advances (GS 62).

Message of John Paul II

John Paul II, even before becoming pope, had a keen interest in the sciences; as pope he has maintained close relationships with leading scientists through instrumentalities such as the Pontifical Academy of Sciences. In 1983, at the 350th anniversary of the publication of Galileo's *Dialogues Concerning Two New Sciences*, John Paul II remarked that the Church's experience during and after the Galileo affair "has led to a more mature attitude and a more accurate grasp of the authority proper to her." He added: "It is only through humble and assiduous study that she learns to dissociate the essentials of faith from the scientific systems of a given age, especially when a culturally influenced reading of the Bible seemed to be linked to an obligatory cosmogony."[2] Already in 1979 the pope had established a commission to make a careful examination of the Galileo question. A member of the commission has interpreted the condemnations of 1616 and 1633 as having merely disciplinary, rather than doctrinal, force.[3]

A new phase in the development of the Catholic understanding of the relationship between religion and science was inaugurated by the Vatican-sponsored study week held at Castelgandolfo on September 21-26, 1987, to mark the 300th anniversary of the publication of Isaac Newton's *Philosophiae Naturalis principia mathematica*. In a message of June 1, 1988, reflecting on this conference, Pope John Paul II presented a very open, confident, and encouraging assessment of the relations between religion and science.[4] Ernan McMullin, an expert in the field, calls this message "without a doubt the most important and most specific papal statement on the relations between religion and science in recent times."[5] Without preempting the prerogatives of working theologians, philosophers, and scientists to make their own applications, the Holy Father proposes a program that appears to be feasible, valuable, and even necessary for the good of all concerned.

The general position taken by John Paul II may be indicated by reference to the standard typology of the relationships between religion and the sciences: conflict, separation, fusion, dialogue, and the like.[6]

Very clearly the pope rejects the position of conflict, in which it would be necessary to choose either science or religion to the exclusion of the other. This rejection can take either of two forms. One form is a "scientism" such as that of Thomas Henry Huxley, who asserted in a sermon in 1866: "There is but one kind of knowledge, and but one method of acquiring it," namely, science.[7] By the universal application of scientific method, positivists believed, it would be possible to dispel the dark clouds of dogma and inaugurate a bright new era of free assent to universally acknowledged truth. This triumphalist variety of scientism is not yet dead. The periodical *Free Inquiry*, for example, promotes science and reason as opposed to faith and religion.[8] The "scientistic" program tends to reduce quality to quantity and to emphasize the technological aspects of life. But it also makes room for a certain mystical exaltation of science, to the point where it becomes a pseudoreligion, involving what the pope in his message calls an "unconscious theology" (M 14). Jacques Monod and Carl Sagan are sometimes cited, though not by the pope, as examples of scientists who tend to extrapolate beyond the proper limits of their own discipline.

On the other hand, the pope no less firmly rejects the alternative possibility — the religionism of those who oppose science in the name of faith. In this framework theology becomes, as the pope warns, a pseudoscience (M 14). This may be judged to have occurred in the case of the "creation science" taught by some American fundamentalists. The "creationist" position, as Langdon Gilkey and others have shown, is in fact antiscientific.[9] According to the sounder view, held by the pope in his message, faith cannot do the work of science, nor can the Bible function as a textbook of astronomy or biology.

The second major position that the pope rejects may be called separationism. Some thoughtful Christians solve the problem by relegating religion and science to separate spheres. This kind of separation has become almost axiomatic in Protestant theology since Immanuel Kant, who confined the competence of theoretical reason to the order of phenomena and regarded religious beliefs as deliverances of practical reason. Not only liberal theologians, such as Albrecht Ritschl and Adolf Harnack, but neo-orthodox thinkers such as Karl Barth, Rudolf Bultmann, and Paul Tillich accepted this division into two spheres. In an extreme reaction against the excesses of Galileo's judges Tillich writes:

> Knowledge of revelation cannot interfere with ordinary knowledge. Likewise, ordinary knowledge cannot interfere with knowledge of revelation. There is no scientific theory which is more favorable to the truth of revelation than any other theory. It is disastrous for theology if theologians prefer one scientific view to others on theological grounds. And it was humiliating for theology when theologians were afraid of new theories for religious reasons, trying to resist them as long as possible, and finally giving in when resistance had become impossible. This ill-conceived resistance of theologians from the time of Galileo to the time of Darwin was one of the causes of the split between religion and secular culture in the past centuries.[10]

McMullin, in a recent article, notes that

> at the height of the 'creation-science' dispute in the U.S. some years ago, the National Academy of Sciences issued a declaration maintaining that religion and science are, in principle, entirely separate domains, one pertaining to faith and the other to reason, and hence of no possible relevance to one another. The new papal message takes issue with this convenient and popular way of avoiding the risks of conflict.[11]

In our own day philosophers and theologians influenced by Ludwig Wittgenstein frequently assert, as does Richard Braithwaite, that religious language is not intended to communicate cognitive truth but to recommend a way of life and to evoke a set of attitudes. In a somewhat similar vein, George Lindbeck maintains that doctrinal statements are "communally authoritative rules of discourse, attitude, and action."[12] In all these theories the dogmas of the Church, even though they may seem to describe objective realities, are reinterpreted as symbolic expressions either describing the inner experience of the speaker or regulating the conduct of the worshiping community.

Some philosophers of science regard science as directly informative about the real order. But others, as we have noted in our discussion of Blondel, hold that science has a purely pragmatic aim, and thus that it cannot deny any claims of revealed religion about objective reality. Thus they rule out the possibility of conflict from the side of science.

Peace between religion and science is achieved in these systems, but only at the price of depriving religion or science of its capacity to say anything true about the world of ordinary experience. Wisely in my judgment, John Paul II takes a position akin to that of Blondel. He refuses to settle for a world divided into two cultures, literary and scientific, as described by C. P. Snow in his classic essay.[13] Interaction, according to the pope, is necessary for the proper functioning of both religion and science. Without it science can become destructive and religion sterile (M 14).

For his program of unification the pope gives several arguments. The human mind, in its quest for understanding, inevitably seeks to unify and synthesize. By unifying many data we are able to make sense of the whole (M 9). Unity, likewise, is a demand of love. A fully inclusive human community is promoted to the extent that all the members are able to share, and profit from, one another's insights. Finally, the relational unity between science and religion is a demand of Christian faith, which sees all things as created in and for Christ (Col. 1:16–17) and as destined to be reconciled through him (Col. 1:20; Eph. 1:10). The pope attributes the founding of universities by the Church to this faith-conviction (M 10).

While repudiating separationism, which could be called a kind of methodological Nestorianism, John Paul II also rejects the opposite extreme of fusion, which might be compared with Monophysitism in Christology. Science, he warns, is not called to become theology nor is theology called to become science. Nor, finally, should both of them be swallowed up in some tertium quid that would be a higher integration of both. The pope wants each discipline to retain its own principles and its own identity while challenging and being challenged by the other (M 7). He does not envision a disciplinary unity between theology and science.

Interaction and Dialogue

Positively, then, the pope accepts a fourth position — that of dialogue and interaction. In this relationship neither science nor religion should either seek to dominate the other or submit uncritically to the deliverances of the other. Yet each discipline should profit from, and contribute to, the attainments of the other. In a memorable paragraph the pope explains:

> To be more specific, both religion and science must preserve their autonomy and their distinctiveness. Religion is not founded on science nor is science an extension of religion.... While each can and should support the other as distinct dimensions of a common human culture, neither ought to assume that it forms a necessary premise for the other. The unprecedented opportunity we have today is for a common interactive relationship in which each discipline retains its integrity and yet is radically open to the discoveries and insights of the other. (M 8–9)

To suggest what he has in mind John Paul II gives two historical examples. The early chapters of Genesis, he points out, borrow fruitfully from the cosmologies of the ancient Near East, which afforded concepts and images that, with the necessary purification, could well serve to communicate revealed truth. In the Middle Ages theologians borrowed from ancient Greek philosophy a whole panoply of technical concepts such as form and matter, substance and accident. Although the Church made use of such concepts, and further refined them, in exploring the sacraments and the hypostatic union, "this did not mean that the Church adjudicated the truth or falsity of the Aristotelian insight, since that is not her concern. It did mean that this was one of the rich insights offered by Greek culture, that it needed to be understood and taken seriously and tested for its value in illuminating various areas of theology" (M 11). This last statement has considerable theological importance, since Pope Pius XII has been understood as teaching that the Church did certify the truth of the principles of Aristotelian and scholastic metaphysics.[14]

Pope John Paul II then goes on to encourage contemporary theologians to appropriate insights from scientific methodology and from the philosophy of science. Without explicitly mentioning the particular system of Teilhard de Chardin, which some critics have judged to be deficient either on scientific or on theological grounds, the pope seems to put his blessing on the adventurous spirit that motivated the great French palaeontologist.

The type of program suggested by the pope is actually being pursued on a number of fronts. Several examples from the realm of cosmology may here be mentioned. Some are convinced that the "big bang" theory of cosmic origins provides a scientific confirmation of the Christian doctrine of creation — a view that the pope mentions with the warning that "uncritical and overhasty use" should not be made of the "big bang" theory for apologetic purposes (M 11–12).[15] Others ask whether the scientifically predicted "cold death" of the universe, through the operation of the laws of thermodynamics, has something to say to Christian eschatology. Then again, it may be asked whether the "anthropic principle," according to which the universe seems to have been "fine-tuned" from its origins to produce and support human life, gives new relevance to classical arguments from design. Some theologians, moreover, believe that the principle of indeterminacy in Werner Heisenberg's quantum physics can be helpful in overcoming the dilemmas of freedom and necessity and in showing how Providence can act without violating the established order of nature. A number of theologians, finally, hold that Niels Bohr's principle of complementarity, according to which light exhibits both wavelike and corpuscular characteristics, could suggest new ways of dealing with mystery and paradox in theology. Yves Congar, for instance, asks whether the Eastern and Western traditions in Trinitarian theology should be seen as irreducibly different but complementary articulations of a mystery too rich for any one conceptual system.[16]

It may be premature to give definitive answers to any of these questions. In the spirit of the pope's letter we may say that it is proper for theologians to state whether, and under what conditions, they could accept or welcome the new scientific hypotheses, and to explore the ways in which such hypotheses can provide new imagery and vocabulary for speaking about traditional Christian doctrines. Theologians should, however, be on guard against a facile concordism that would link the doctrines of faith too closely with fragile scientific hypotheses. Conversely, scientists, while they should refrain from proposing their theories as deductions from doctrines of Christian faith, may allow their religious faith to suggest lines of scientific investigation that would not otherwise have occurred to them. Scientists who are also believers will be reluctant to accept scientific hypotheses, such as Jacques Monod's doctrine of "chance and necessity," as long as these hypotheses seem incompatible with Christian faith.[17] In this connection it may be pertinent to recall that Pope Pius XII in 1950 asserted that the theory of polygenism, in certain forms, was unacceptable "since it is in no way apparent how such an opinion can be reconciled" with the biblical and ecclesiastical teaching about original sin.[18]

Methodological Convergence

One of the areas of dialogue suggested by the pope concerns methodology (M 11). Since early modern times it has been customary to accept a sharp contrast between the methods of science and theology. Blaise Pascal put the matter very strongly:

> Authority alone can enlighten us in these [historical] matters. But such authority has its principal force in theology, because there it is inseparable from truth, and truth is unobtainable in any other way. Thus, to give complete certitude concerning matters most incomprehensible to reason, it is sufficient to show that they are found in the sacred books; and to demonstrate the uncertainty of things that seem quite evident, it is enough to point out that they are not contained in Scripture. For the principles of theology are above both nature and reason. Since the mind of man is too feeble to attain them by its own efforts, it cannot achieve such lofty understanding unless it is borne by an almighty and supernatural force.

But in matters that lie within the scope of the senses and of reason, the situation is far different. Here authority is useless; reason alone is in a position to know them. The two types of knowledge have their separate prerogatives. In the former area authority has all the advantage; here reason reigns in its turn.[19]

Developments in twentieth-century science and theology have shown this contrast to be exaggerated. Science is not committed to reason alone nor faith to authority alone. Each discipline works with a subtle combination of faith and experience, intuition and reason, imagination and deduction, personal insight and communal wisdom.

The role of faith in science has been strongly emphasized by Max Planck, among others. In an interview he put the matter very strikingly: "Anybody who has been seriously engaged in scientific work of any kind realizes that over the gates of the temple of science are written the words: *Ye must have faith*. It is a quality which the scientist cannot dispense with."[20] Einstein, Eddington, Heisenberg, and Oppenheimer could easily be quoted to the same effect.[21] The scientist has to act on the premises that an external world exists, that it is orderly, and that the mind has the capacity to grasp the order that is there. Further acts of faith are demanded for anyone to become committed to the scientific enterprise, to learn the current state of the discipline, and to advance toward new discoveries. At each stage one must put one's trust in some idea or principle that could conceivably be false — in other words, one must make an act of natural or scientific faith. Thus faith, in a broad and generic sense, may be seen as a bond between science and theology.

Conversely, religious faith depends to some extent upon reason. Revelation could not be made except to a rational being, for a brute animal could not grasp the meaning or credibility of God's word. Theology, as a methodical inquiry into the significance and coherence of the revealed message, is eminently a work of reason.

Another link between science and religion is the authority of tradition in each discipline. Admittedly, many scientists since the Enlightenment have been in some ways hostile to authority and tradition. As Michael Polanyi reminds us, the founders of the Royal Society took as their device *Nullius in Verba*.[22] But historians of science have clearly shown that tradition plays an important role in science no less than in theology. In his little book *Tradition in Science* Werner Heisenberg points out that the scientist relies heavily on tradition to supply the state of the question, the problems to be solved, and the concepts, paradigms and methods that may be helpful for the solution.[23] In science, as in theology, development occurs gradually. Progress would not be possible if past achievements were not remembered and employed.

Just as continuity has its place in science, so, conversely, change is a factor in religious knowledge. The theologian cannot be content simply to repeat the words of venerated predecessors. New problems must be addressed with new information and new methods of inquiry. In theology, as in the natural sciences, there can be sudden breakthroughs or "scientific revolutions" in which whole areas are perceived from a radically new perspective.[24]

Theologians, quite evidently, operate within a community of faith. They receive their faith from the Church, carry on their reflections within the Church, and offer the results of their labors to the Church for appraisal. Scientists, similarly, do not work in isolated independence. Polanyi makes the point that neophytes in the sciences must join the scientific community and submit to a process of formation in which they learn by example and supervised performance. He writes:

> This assimilation of great systems of articulate lore by novices of various grades is made possible only by a *previous act of affiliation*, by which the novice accepts apprenticeship to a community which cultivates this lore, appreciates its values and strives to act by its standards. This affiliation begins with the fact that a child submits to education within a community, and is confirmed throughout life to the extent to which the adult continues to place exceptional confidence in the intellectual leaders of the same community.[25]

The scientific community is less formally organized than the Church. But it has, in its way, a hierarchy of leadership. Ecclesiastical officials control the transmission of Christian doctrine not only by direct teaching but also indirectly, by a variety of means such as the supervision of seminary appointments, ordinations, and theological publications. So, likewise, the leaders of the scientific community exercise a kind of doctrinal authority not only by their own utterances but also through their influence on the curriculum of instruction, the bestowal of honors and degrees, university appointments, fellowships, and the acceptance of articles for scholarly journals. The capacity "to grant or withhold opportunity for research, publication and teaching, to endorse or discredit contributions put forward by individuals" is, according to Polanyi, "indispensable for the continued existence of science." Without such controls the journals would be flooded with rubbish and valuable work would be banished to obscurity.[26]

These similarities, to be sure, are not identities. As John Paul II insists, science and theology do have distinct methods. Unlike religious faith, assent to scientific truth does not depend on divine grace. Science does not rest on an unalterable deposit of faith; it does not look back to unique, unrepeatable past events as its essential basis. Nor does the scientific community have a magisterium that claims to be divinely assisted and capable of rendering, on occasion, infallible judgments. Church doctrines, consequently, are not mere theories or hypotheses. Nevertheless, the analogies are sufficient so that it is possible, as the pope suggests, for theologians and scientists to learn from one another.[27]

The dialogue between faith and science can produce palpable benefits to both. For one thing, each discipline, by maintaining contact with the other, is protected from certain errors and excesses to which, by itself, it would be prone. On the one hand, theology is liberated from a naive or fundamentalist reading of Scripture, such as that which played a part in the condemnation of Galileo, and that which continues to thrive in "creation science." Through scientific education believers are able to overcome a superstitious or magical attitude that takes insufficient account of the established order of secondary causality. On the other hand, science is, as the pope also remarks, purified "from idolatry and false absolutes" (M 13). Pursued in isolation, the brilliant achievements of science can be destructive of higher values.

The mutual benefits flowing from dialogue are not only negative but also positive. This is apparent in the area of cosmology, on which the pope is chiefly commenting. The theological imagination has been immensely enlarged by the fresh vistas offered by contemporary physics and astronomy. Theologians no longer discuss the doctrines of creation and Providence in the narrow framework provided by ancient myths and philosophic systems. Creation means far more when understood in terms of the "infinite spaces" that made Pascal shudder with anxiety and awe.[28] Providence and salvation history take on a wholly new significance when seen against the background of the billions of years of cosmic existence postulated by contemporary science but undreamt of by Bishop Ussher and his contemporaries.

Scientific cosmology, if enriched by the study of theological method, can gain a deeper realization of its own reliance on faith, tradition, community, and authority. Science can better understand its own nature and history by viewing its achievements in the light of religious thought. As the pope remarks, science develops more successfully to the extent that "its concepts and conclusions are integrated into the broader human culture and its concerns for meaning and value" (M 13). Insights of religious thinkers of the stature of Newman, Tillich, Teilhard de Chardin, and Rahner can help scientists to insert their findings into this broader framework and thus direct their labors to the well-being of the human family. In opposition to the idolatry of science, a religious perspective can remind us that the progress of science and technology is not an absolute to be sought at any price.

Although the situation is still too fluid for solid syntheses to be achieved, the long warfare between science and theology may be coming to an end, and a new era of mutual friendship and collaboration may be at hand. According to the fathers of Vatican II, "Never perhaps, thank God, has there been so clear a possibility as today of a deep understanding between real science and real faith, mutual servants of one another in the one truth."[29] The message of John Paul II and the conference that occasioned that message give further encouragement to such hopes.

10.

University Theology in Service to the Church

University theology is not always considered a benefit to the Church. In the light of certain well publicized cases of recent memory some might be inclined to repeat the proposition: "Universities, with their programs of study, their colleges, their degrees, and their professorships, are products of vain heathenism; they are as much good to the Church as the devil is." This proposition, taken from the writings of John Wycliffe, was condemned by the Council of Constance in 1415.[1] The condemnation, approved by Pope Martin V in 1418, may be taken as evidence, at least indirect, for the Church's appreciation of universities and their theological faculties.

As more positive evidence of the Church's appreciation of university theology, one may cite the recent apostolic constitution of Pope John Paul II on Catholic universities. He writes:

> Theology plays a particularly important role in the search for a synthesis of knowledge as well as in the dialogue between faith and reason. It serves all other disciplines in their search for meaning, not only by helping them to investigate how their discoveries will affect individuals and society, but also by bringing a perspective and an orientation not contained within their own methodologies. In turn, interaction with these other disciplines and their discoveries enriches theology, offering it a better understanding of the world today and making theological research more relevant to current needs. Because of its specific importance among the academic disciplines, every

Catholic university should have a faculty, or at least a chair, of theology.[2]

No sharp opposition can be drawn between theology done at the university and that done in other forums, but theology does tend to take on different hues depending on the environment in which it is practiced. Patristic theology, for instance, had a particularly pastoral character since it was closely linked with the preaching of the bishops to their flocks. In the early Middle Ages theology, chiefly practiced in monasteries, became more contemplative; it was closely bound up with the pursuit of holiness and with prayerful reading of sacred texts, both biblical and patristic. In the High Middle Ages the universities emerged as the chief centers of theological productivity. Theology became more academic and scientific. Then, in early modern times, when the universities became secularized and nationalized, theology moved by preference to the seminaries; there it remained for the most part until about a generation ago. Seminary theology has usually been somewhat clerical and doctrinaire. Since the mid-1960s, there has been a notable shift back to the university but in a situation quite unlike the Middle Ages. As yet few theologians have reflected seriously on what should be expected from university theology as a service to the Church in our day. The answer to this question will depend in part on how one appraises the changing character of the university itself.

Catholic Universities and the Church

The golden age of university theology was no doubt the High Middle Ages.[3] The earliest medieval universities grew up spontaneously as expansions of preexisting schools, and were subsequently recognized by papal or royal charters. Later medieval universities were founded directly by popes or, in some cases, by kings and emperors. The university faculties of theology, especially at Paris and Oxford, produced the greatest speculative theology of the age, and perhaps of any age. Bonaventure, Albert the Great, Thomas Aquinas, and Duns Scotus composed philosophically sophisticated articulations of Christian doctrine that still remain vital elements in the heritage of Catholicism. When new problems have arisen in later centuries,

Catholics have found light and guidance in the work of the medieval masters.

It is not easy to summarize the manifold contributions of medieval universities to the life of the Church. Most obviously, they provided Europe with some learned clergy. In particular, many of the popes, cardinals, and bishops were former students or even professors of theology or canon law. Viewed in historical perspective, the intellectual probings of the medieval scholastics have given the Church of later ages an invaluable doctrinal resource. The theology of Thomas Aquinas guided the Council of Florence in its teaching on the Trinity and on the sacraments; it was used by the Council of Trent for its teaching on justification and the Eucharist, and again by Vatican I for its decrees on faith and reason and on papal primacy. Modern developments in Mariology, notably the doctrine of the Immaculate Conception, gained impetus from the speculations of Duns Scotus at Oxford and Pierre d'Ailly at the University of Paris. The theology of grace and of salvation history, as developed by many modern authors, is indebted to Bonaventure.

The medieval universities, especially from the fourteenth century on, cooperated with popes and bishops in the formulation of doctrine and maintenance of orthodoxy. The university theologians were considered to have quasi-hierarchical status as members of what was called the *ordo doctorum*. The decrees of the Council of Vienne (1311–12), by order of Pope Clement V, were not promulgated until they had been reviewed by the universities.[4] University theologians in great numbers attended councils such as those of Constance and Basel, and were entitled to a deliberative vote within their "nation" or "deputation" — a right of some importance because the *doctores* frequently outnumbered the bishops themselves. At Paris in the fourteenth century the theological faculty had an acknowledged privilege to pass judgment on its own members before any ecclesiastical authority could censure them for doctrinal deviations. When controversies arose, the theological faculties pronounced on questions of orthodoxy and heresy. Thus the University of Oxford condemned the eucharistic teaching of Wycliffe and the University of Prague censured certain errors of Jan Hus. The theological faculties of Cologne, Louvain, and Paris drew up lists of errors culled from Luther's writings, so that Rome had little more to do than ratify what the universities had previously done.

In certain crises the university faculties of theology were of direct assistance in matters of church governance. Robert N. Swanson in his *Universities, Academics, and the Great Schism*[5] has shown in some detail how the eyes of Europe turned to the universities, especially Paris, to provide a remedy for the constitutional problem created by the rivalry of two, and eventually three, claimants to the see of Peter at the end of the fourteenth century.

The medieval universities were able to make a unique contribution because the Catholic faith was dominant throughout Western Europe and because the modern national state had not yet arisen. Later the loss of Catholic faith in large sections of Europe and the subjection of the universities to kings and parliaments severely limited the value of the universities to the Catholic Church. But even after the Reformation and the rise of nationalism, Catholic universities continued to serve the cause of Catholic orthodoxy in regions known to us as Belgium, Spain, Portugal, Germany, Austria, and Italy. These universities, staffed principally by Dominicans, Jesuits, and Carmelites, produced updated syntheses of theology and philosophy, modeled on the great summas of the Middle Ages, and laid the groundwork for a vigorous proliferation of controversial literature, catechetical literature, and seminary handbooks. Besides responding to the new challenges of the Protestant Reformation, rationalism, and skepticism, the university theologians of the sixteenth and seventeenth centuries attempted to deal with social and moral problems arising from the modern nation-state and the colonial expansion. Spanish and Portuguese authors such as Francisco de Vitoria, Francisco Suárez, Juan de Lugo, and John of St. Thomas added luster to their age.

Crushed by the secular spirit of the Enlightenment and the oppressive tactics of absolutist monarchs, Catholic university theology suffered a severe decline in the eighteenth century, but began to revive by the middle of the nineteenth. The Gregorian University, in close alliance with the papacy, promoted a new vintage of scholasticism, which survived down to Vatican II. This theology, heavily apologetic in tone, became the basis of seminary textbooks and apologetic literature throughout the Catholic world. The German universities developed several creative strains of theology. The professors of Münster, Tübingen, and Munich entered into fruitful dialogue with German idealism and German historical scholarship, thus paving the way for major developments in the twentieth century.

With a few notable exceptions, such as Tübingen and Rome,

Catholic university faculties in the nineteenth century were relatively weak. In many parts of Europe they labored under laws that discriminated against Catholicism or even against all religion in higher education. In laicist France no Catholic university faculties survived, but some of the functions of university theology were performed by Catholic institutes of higher studies and by houses of formation in which religious orders educated their own members.

In the English-speaking world of the nineteenth century John Henry Newman thought it necessary to defend the very existence of theology as a university discipline. He argued, in summary, that since theology is a branch of knowledge, it ought to have a place in a university, since a university is a place in which universal knowledge is taught. When religion, or even revealed religion, is excluded, the other branches of knowledge tend to fill the vacuum. Cosmologists, philosophers, sociologists, psychologists, and historians seek to supply the answers that properly belong to the province of revealed religion. In so doing, these other disciplines exceed their proper competence. Thus the university suffers not only from the absence of a branch of knowledge that ought to be there, but from the distortion of other branches that seek to compensate for that absence. Newman developed his argument in four points, which he summarized as follows:

I have argued... first, from the consideration that, whereas it is the very profession of a University to teach all sciences, on this account it cannot exclude Theology without being untrue to its profession. Next, I have said that, all sciences being connected together, and having bearings one on another, it is impossible to teach them all thoroughly, unless they are all taken into account, and Theology among them. Moreover, I have insisted on the important influence, which Theology as a matter of fact does and must exercise over a great variety of sciences, completing and perfecting them; so that, granting it to be a real science occupied upon truth, it cannot be omitted without great prejudice to the teaching of the rest. And lastly, I have urged that, supposing Theology is not taught, its province will not simply be neglected, but will be actually usurped by other sciences, which will teach, without warrant, conclusions of their own in a subject-matter which needs its own proper principles for its due formation and disposition.[6]

In the United States it became possible for Catholics to erect their own colleges and universities, but until after World War II these institutions were small and poorly endowed. Graduate programs in theology, where they existed at all, were designed for clergy and religious. In the late 1940s a women's college, St. Mary's in Indiana, opened a school of theology for sisters and laywomen. In the 1960s doctoral programs in theology, offering civilly recognized degrees, came into existence at a number of Catholic universities, including Notre Dame (1961), Marquette (1963), Fordham (1967), and St. Louis (1969).[7] Catholic institutions also entered into joint theological programs such as the Graduate Theological Union at Berkeley, California. Today, therefore, there exist many doctoral programs in Catholic theology, some of them having a serious research component. A glance at the membership lists of theological associations, at publishers' catalogues, and at the tables of contents of learned journals strongly suggests that Catholic theological leadership has in recent years passed from the free-standing seminaries to the universities and graduate schools. A similar shift would seem to have taken place in many European countries. The Catholic university faculties of Germany, Belgium, and Holland have produced much of the most creative theology of the past few decades. The fact that a former university professor has been elected pope may be of more than symbolic significance.

Benefits of University Theology

In view of the contemporary preeminence of university theology, it becomes important to inquire what kind of benefits such theology can be expected to confer upon the Church in our day. The question can be approached by considering the typical characteristics of university theology as contrasted with seminary theology. The two would appear to be mutually complementary. The seminary, generally speaking, is oriented toward the formation of future clergy. For this reason it puts the accent on teaching rather than on pure research. The seminary professor can normally assume that the students are already convinced believers and adherents of the particular church or denomination in charge of the seminary. Seminary theology is specifically aimed to equip the students for the specific tasks of the ordained priesthood — especially preaching, counseling, and the ministry of the sacraments. Seminaries generally operate in comparative isolation, feeling little need to expose their students to intellectual challenges coming from other disciplines. The intent is to transmit safe and established doctrine. Proof frequently takes the form of an appeal to authoritative texts, such as Scripture, the councils, and papal utterances.

University theology, by contrast, is oriented more heavily toward research. In order to make new advances, it maintains, or should maintain, close contact with other disciplines, such as history, literary criticism, sociology, psychology, and philosophy. It makes use of reason not only deductively but also critically. It may address a widely diversified audience, including people who are adherents of different religious traditions, or even of no particular religion. It concentrates on open and unsolved questions that cannot be settled by a simple appeal to authority. For all these reasons university theology can become the seedbed of new and exciting developments.

The reentry of Catholic theology into the universities is no doubt providential. Since the Council of Trent theology had become too far removed from the modern world with its ebullient secularity. Skillfully as the traditional scholastic questions continued to be pursued, vibrant movements of the day were not addressed with sympathy and understanding. The Church confronted the secular world too much as a judge, too little as a participant. The kind of careful attention that Thomas Aquinas gave to Aristotle, Maimonides, and Averroes was rarely given to modern thinkers such as Newton, Kant, Hegel, and Heisenberg, all of whom were mentioned as adversaries but scarcely read in Catholic seminaries. The products of the seminary system, staffing the Roman congregations and other sensitive positions, maintained and defended the Catholic tradition but seemed ill at ease in the modern world. The new shift back to the university corresponds to the call of Vatican II for openness and dialogue. Reminding Catholic Christians of their involvement in the problems common to all humanity, the council strongly endorsed the teaching of theology in Catholic universities. It called for research in the sacred sciences so that the Church might make its presence felt in the enterprise of advancing higher culture and might form citizens capable of witnessing to their faith and shouldering social responsibilities in the world of our day.[8] These emphases reappear in *Ex Corde Ecclesiae*, the apostolic constitution on universities of Pope John Paul II.

The revival of university theology cannot make its expected contribution unless lessons are drawn from the past. Precisely because it encourages independent thinking, such theology can easily be a source of error. Many heresies since the twelfth century have been associated with university theology. One thinks in this connection of Wycliffe, Hus, and Luther; of Averroism, Conciliarism, Gallicanism, Jansenism, and various forms of rationalism.

Even when it escapes the trap of heresy, university theology exhibits certain weaknesses as compared with the typical seminary theology. It tends to become rather detached from the Church and from pastoral concerns. It easily adopts methods more appropriate to secular disciplines. It frequently becomes tinged with skepticism, positivism, historicism, relativism, and similar errors. Discouraged by the failure of the German universities to stand up against the Nazi ideology, Dietrich Bonhoeffer resigned from the University of Berlin in 1934 and in the following year founded a kind of religious community for seminarians and newly ordained ministers. In a letter to a friend he explained: "The whole ministerial education today belongs to the Church — monastic-like schools in which pure doctrine, the Sermon on the Mount, and the liturgy are taken seriously. In the university all three are not taken seriously, and it is impossible to do so under present circumstances."[9] Bonhoeffer, of course, was speaking of ministerial formation in state-controlled universities in Nazi Germany, but his words may be read as a warning to any university that undertakes to treat theology as an objective science independent of faith and ecclesiastical authority. If a faculty did not take the gospel, worship, and sound doctrine seriously, could it claim to be teaching theology at all?

A certain tension has always existed between the Church and scientific university theology, as may be seen from the struggles with the Averroists in the Middle Ages and with the Gallicans in early modern times. In a form that comes closer to home, the conflict broke out in Germany in the middle of the nineteenth century. In 1863 the Catholic historian Döllinger presided over a congress of Catholic scholars and intellectuals at Munich.[10] In his presidential address Döllinger questioned the adequacy of traditional scholastic theology and called for greater attention to biblical criticism and scientific history. True theology, he insisted, must not panic when scholarly inquiry threatens to demolish what had previously been regarded as unassailable truth. The received opinions of scholastic philosophy and theology, he maintained, should not be accorded the kind of authority that belongs to defined dogma alone.

Döllinger's address was widely interpreted as an effort to liberate Catholic scholars from the scholastic heritage and to exempt Catholic universities from the vigilant supervision of Roman congregations. Pius IX felt it necessary to react to this challenge. In a letter to the archbishop of Munich (December 21, 1863), he warned that Catholic scholars cannot regard themselves as entitled to contest whatever falls short of defined dogma. They are bound to accept the ordinary teaching of the magisterium throughout the world as a matter of faith. In addition, they must reverently submit to the doctrinal decisions of the Roman congregations and respect the authority of the scholastic theologians of previous centuries.[11]

The clash between the Munich Congress and Pius IX in the mid-nineteenth century is instructive because the issues then were much the same as in several contemporary collisions between the ecclesiastical magisterium and university theologians. The situation in the United States today is further complicated by two themes that have greatly developed since the nineteenth century — academic freedom and religious pluralism.

Supervisory Role of Magisterium

Vatican II asserted that the various branches of knowledge are to be pursued according to their own principles and methods, with appropriate freedom for scientific investigation.[12] The revised Code of Canon Law, following up on the council, recognizes that theologians must have freedom for competent research and for communicating their own ideas.[13] The recent apostolic constitution on Catholic universities recognizes that university professors of theology enjoy academic freedom so long as they are faithful to the principles and methods proper to their discipline.[14]

In the next chapter I shall discuss in some detail the nature of the academic freedom that is suitable to theology. For the present it may suffice to say that theology requires a living relationship to a community of faith and to the official leadership of that community. If academic freedom meant that theologians were entitled to teach as true whatever seemed to them to be suggested by purely rational methods of inquiry, without any deference to Scripture, tradition, or ecclesiastical authority,[15] theology would sacrifice its status as a reflection on the corporate faith of the Church and would cease to render the kind of service that the Church expects from it.

Since popes and bishops have an indispensable role in specifying the contents of Catholic faith, their authoritative proclamation has a positive and normative function for theology. Before such proclamation, theologians may by their study prepare the way for the judgment of the Church.[16] After the ecclesiastical magisterium has spoken, theologians have the tasks of interpreting the statements and fitting them into the total self-understanding of the Church. They may continue to raise questions arising from their personal study and reflection and in this way prepare for further refinements of the official teaching. But theologians cannot simply disregard the teaching of the pastors. They cannot responsibly substitute their own opinions for the official teaching. Pope John Paul II, speaking at New Orleans on September 12, 1987, summed up the matter in these words: "The bishops of the Church, as *magistri et doctores fidei* (teachers and doctors of the faith), should not be seen as external agents but as participants in the life of the Catholic university in its privileged role as protagonist in the encounter between faith and science and between revealed truth and culture."[17] The university status of a theologian, therefore, must not be understood as placing that theologian outside or above the Church.[18]

John Henry Newman in his lectures on *The Idea of a University* suggested that the university is related to the Church somewhat as reason to faith and nature to grace.[19] Because there can be no real contradiction between faith and reason, true progress in the academic realm is never a threat to the Church. New developments in the secular sciences may seem to conflict with faith, but in the long run it will appear either that the developments were unsound, or that there is no real conflict, or that the conflict is not with faith itself.[20] But to find out which of these answers is correct may take time and discussion. The magisterium of the Church should not be pressed into deciding the issues before the debate has matured.

Theology as an academic discipline gathers evidence, sifts it, frames hypotheses, and tests them. Often enough the hypotheses prove faulty and must be amended. To succeed by its own methods theology must be given its due measure of freedom. It cannot serve unless it is free to make its own specific contribution (*Non ancilla nisi libera*). Scholars who are striving to grasp some new truth often fall into error in matters of detail. Such was the case, Newman concedes, with Malebranche, Cardinal Noris, Bossuet, and Muratori. Yet the service of these thinkers to religion, Newman holds, was too great for them to be molested on account of their occasional deviations.[21]

In many cases the progress of science and scholarship has required painful revisions in the understanding of the faith. This was true in early modern times, when the Dionysian corpus, the Donation of Constantine, and the Isidorian Decretals were exposed as unauthentic. Then came the major shifts in astronomy, geology, and archaeology, followed by biblical criticism, which radically changed the previous state of church teaching with regard to the dating and authorship of the biblical books. All these discoveries, heralded by progressive university theologians, were initially disturbing to churchmen. But in the long run they proved acceptable, even beneficial to the understanding of the faith. Faith is solidified when it is liberated from time-conditioned human opinions that have attached themselves to it in the course of history.

Only where theologians operate in dialogue with other academic disciplines can there be a vital and stimulating interchange between faith and reason. Theology can be invigorated and purified by interaction with the human and natural sciences. The scientific community can profit from the comprehensive vision of theology and from theology's integration of truth with values. In his letter to George Coyne, S.J., Pope John Paul II has illustrated this interaction with regard to anthropology, Christology, eschatology, and cosmology.[22] Without such an exchange, he suggests, theology can profess a pseudoscience or science can become an unconscious theology.

While advocating restraint and tolerance on the part of church authorities, Newman laid down four conditions for scientific investigation.[23] Adapting these conditions to the subject matter of theology, we may paraphrase Newman's principles approximately as follows: it must not collide with dogma; it must not issue pronouncements on religious matters in competition with the official magisterium of the Church; it must not indulge in brilliant paradoxes but rather propound serious views; it must take care to avoid shocking the popular mind or unsettling the weak. If these four conditions had always been observed by university theologians, many bitter conflicts with ecclesiastical authority could have been avoided.

It is often imagined that popes and bishops are forever trying to shackle university theologians in their scholarly pursuits. In point of fact ecclesiastical authorities have often acted to restrain intolerant believers from recklessly accusing scholars of heresy. Increasingly, this seems to be a problem today. Many nontheologians who want simple and secure answers to every conceivable question are urging church authorities to clamp down on the freedom of theologians to raise uncomfortable questions. Good communications between the ecclesiastical magisterium and university theology can be of great assistance in resisting the assaults of anti-intellectual bigots. At New Orleans in 1987 Pope John Paul II called attention to the close relationship that has always existed between faith and the love of learning. He then added: "Religious faith itself calls for intellectual inquiry; and the confidence that there can be no contradiction between faith and reason is a distinctive feature of the Catholic humanistic tradition as it has existed in the past and as it exists in our own day."[24] Applied to the question of academic freedom, the Holy Father's words may be taken as meaning that Catholic faith is a powerful safeguard of the just liberty of responsible scholarship.

Context of Religious Pluralism

In addition to the problems arising from conflicting views of academic freedom, university theology in the United States is troubled by questions arising from religious pluralism. I shall touch on the problem only briefly and with specific reference to the nature of theology. Occasionally it is said that the pluralistic character of the society in which we live makes it impossible for theology to be taught in a university.[25] By its very nature, we are told, a university must avoid intruding into the sphere of faith, which is viewed as purely a private matter. If anything is to be taught about religion, therefore, this must be a matter of objective scientific study, free of value judgments. Departments of theology should consequently be dismantled in favor of departments of "scientific" religious studies.

Influenced by the secular pluralism of the American climate, most of the universities founded under Protestant auspices voluntarily abandoned their religious character well before the middle of the twentieth century. Harvard, Yale, Princeton, Columbia, Chicago, and most other originally Protestant universities no longer have any recognizable religious identity.[26] Except in divinity schools that are marginal to the university, theology is no longer taught in these great institutions of learning.

Since Vatican II many Catholic universities in the United States seem to be moving in the same direction. As an example one may cite the Land O'Lakes statement, adopted in 1967 by a number of prominent Catholic educators under the leadership of Theodore Hesburgh, then president of Notre Dame. In its opening paragraph that statement declared:

> The Catholic university today must be a university in the full modern sense of the word, with a strong commitment to and concern for academic excellence. To perform its teaching and research functions effectively, the Catholic university must have true autonomy and academic freedom in the face of author-ity of every kind, lay or clerical, external to the academic community itself. To say this is to assert that institutional au-tonomy and academic freedom are essential conditions of life and growth and indeed of survival for Catholic universities as of all universities.[27]

In this atmosphere it is not surprising that there has been a steady drift from course offerings that presupposed the authority of the Catholic sacred order, through courses of an ecumenical or inter-religious nature, to courses on religious phenomena in which the methodology and criteria appear to be taken over from secular dis-ciplines such as sociology or anthropology.[28] Prior to 1960 Catholic universities in their theology departments offered almost exclusively courses in subjects such as the triune God, Christology, ecclesiol-ogy, and sacraments, with course descriptions that reflected a clear acceptance of the Roman Catholic perspective. Ten years later the greatest number of course offerings fell in the ecumenical or inter-religious category and dealt with the encounter between different normative traditions or between belief and unbelief. By the mid-1980s the dominant category had become courses that subjected all supposedly sacred orders to secular methodologies. This shift can perhaps be defended in view of the large number of non-Catholic students in Catholic institutions. But even so, the question arises whether Catholic universities that have moved in this direction can still successfully represent the religious and theological heritage of the Church. Do university authorities look upon the support of faith and the service of the Church as important objectives? Is theology, in the traditional sense, a function of the university?

Since religious studies are not pursued in the light of faith and are not intended to contribute to the understanding of faith from within the believing community, the substitution of religious studies for theology on a large scale would notably impair the kind of service that the Church has traditionally received from university faculties. Without denying the legitimacy of religious studies, I would contend that theology still has a place on many campuses even in a pluralistic situation. Pluralism consists in the coexistence of several living faiths, no one of which can be well understood except from within its own framework. In a university which is Catholic by tradition and has a large proportion of Catholic students, courses should be offered in theology from a Catholic point of view. A Catholic university would fall short of its mission if it failed to present its students with the possibility of gaining a mature and sophisticated understanding of their faith, developed in proportion to the general state of their intellectual culture. Training in theology should make the students judicious and ecumenically sensitive. It should equip them with a free and honest commitment to values and beliefs tested by inquiry and reflection. Without exposure to university theology many students would never unite their faith with rigorous intellectual discipline.

In a pluralistic situation allowance must of course be made for faculty and students who do not profess the Catholic religion. Non-Catholics should presumably be offered options other than Catholic theology. Even in Catholic theology it would be inappropriate to demand a profession of faith from the student. Here again a certain difference appears between university theology and seminary instruction that is intended to qualify students for ordained ministry.

In these remarks I have in mind, first of all, private universities with a Catholic affiliation of some kind. Parenthetically, however, it may be noted that in many other religiously pluralistic countries, such as Germany, Holland, Australia, and Canada, there seems to be no difficulty about teaching Catholic and Protestant theology in publicly funded state universities.

In our own country the relationship of university theology faculties to the Church varies enormously from one institution to another.[29] Some universities have canonically established faculties that confer ecclesiastical degrees in courses of study approved by Roman congregations. Others confer civilly recognized degrees in

Catholic theology. It is possible also to have joint theological programs with faculty members from a variety of religious traditions. There is nothing in the nature of theology that precludes any one of these arrangements. The choice is to be made on pragmatic grounds: Which is the most feasible and best adapted to the needs of a given constituency?

The kind of service rendered to the Church varies according to the type of faculty and program. Ecclesiastical faculties, generally speaking, collaborate more directly with the Church's magisterium and enjoy a stronger ecclesiastical certification. But even a non-ecclesiastical faculty that is free of juridical controls by church authorities will ordinarily take pride in transmitting the Catholic tradition in its purity.

Past Progress and Present Needs

Catholic universities in the United States have already performed a signal service in forming several generations of theologically literate graduates. The relatively high degree of theological education enjoyed by many Catholic laity in this country has greatly enhanced the vitality of American Catholicism. Large numbers of clergy and religious in this country have benefited likewise from university programs in theology.

Until recently the focus of Catholic university theological education in the United States has been more on instruction than on research. The professors of theology were in many cases priests handing on simplified versions of their seminary course. In the past generation this situation has been rapidly changing. We are beginning to get respected graduate departments of theology that can hold their own in comparison with the renowned faculties of Western Europe. It must, however, be confessed that the Catholic universities in this country have not as yet produced the kind of creative scholarship associated with Rome, Strasbourg, Louvain, Innsbruck, Fribourg, Nijmegen, Tübingen, Münster, and Munich. But time is needed to develop a theological tradition. Many of our universities are still hampered by the lack of adequate funding.

While taking some legitimate pride in the quality of their teaching and in the loyalty of their graduates, our American theological faculties are today challenged to make further advances. In living dialogue with contemporary culture and technology, university theology must bring the full resources of Catholic tradition to bear on major questions regarding belief and conduct raised by other disciplines. These answers, inevitably somewhat tentative and exploratory, must ultimately be tested by the faith of the whole Church and by its official leaders. But theology alone has the responsibility to open up new lines of reflection and new styles of systematization. University theology, which has so ably served the Church in centuries past, is urgently needed in our day. It still has much to contribute to the renewal of Catholic intellectual life.

11.

The Teaching Mission of the Church and Academic Freedom

In the last chapter I promised a fuller discussion of academic freedom in theology, which has been a subject of sharp controversy in several recent incidents. In this chapter I shall try to cast further light on the question by concentrating on the relationship between university theology and the doctrinal mission of the Church. What does it mean to say that the Church teaches? Is the teaching of the Church a synonym for that of the hierarchical magisterium? How does the day-to-day teaching of parents, catechists, and theologians fit into the doctrinal activity of the Church? Can university theologians, in the name of academic freedom, claim the right to teach in opposition to the pope and the bishops? And if not, can they be said to have academic freedom at all? These questions must be taken up in relation to the principles on theological dissent set forth in Chapter 7.

The Teaching Office of the Church

According to a widely prevalent theological convention, endorsed by the documents of Vatican II, Jesus Christ had a threefold office as prophet, priest, and king. In his prophetic office he spoke to the world in the name of God. The term "prophet" in this context means one who speaks in the name of another — that is, God. In Greek the verb *pro-phemi* means to speak on behalf of; a *pro-phetes* is a spokesperson. As a prophet of God, Jesus announced the advent of the eschatological Kingdom. But he did more than deliver a bare announcement. He also instructed his disciples in the mysteries of the Kingdom. This authoritative instruction constitutes what we may call the prophetic teaching of Jesus. It is prophetic in the technical sense that Jesus spoke authoritatively as one sent by the Father.

The Church as a whole participates in the threefold office of Christ. As explained in Vatican II's dogmatic constitution *Lumen Gentium*, the Church, as prophet, has the task of announcing the good news, or of evangelizing. As an authoritative witness, it continues to proclaim the good news given in Christ. But it does more than proclaim. It has the task of offering precise and progressive instruction to its faithful so that they may to some extent understand the message they have received. This instruction may be called teaching.

Teaching may be attributed to the Church as a whole, but it is actually carried out by particular persons. The popes and bishops have an indispensable role in the total process, but they are not the sole educators of the faithful in matters of religion. Parents, according to Vatican II, are the first educators of their children.[1] Every Christian believer, by virtue of baptism and confirmation, has a vocation to be a witness to the gospel, and those who are reflective and educated in their faith have the capacity and the responsibility to instruct others.

The Church as a corporate body has the obligation to see to it that the faith is not corrupted or distorted in the process of transmission. For this reason certain controls are established. The entire process of transmission takes place under the supervision of the pope and the bishops, who are divinely appointed successors of the apostles in maintaining the correct understanding of the Christian message. The bishops have among their principal duties those of personally preaching the faith and instructing their people by sermons and pastoral letters. Their most effective teaching is often done when they associate others with themselves in the teaching apostolate. Priests and deacons, who are ordained to preach and to teach, are closely associated with the bishops. So also are a multitude of religious educators and catechists, some of whom function in Catholic schools, others in parishes and nonacademic situations.

It is helpful, therefore, to distinguish two ways in which the Church teaches — the official and the unofficial. It teaches officially through the pope and the bishops, who are by divine institution empowered to teach in the name of Christ. These office-holders speak in the name of the Church, in the sense that their official positions are those of the Church as a public institution. They have the right and duty to establish the doctrine of the Church as such. Without an official teaching organ, the Church would not be able to maintain a coherent body of teaching, and to that extent it would be deficient in carrying on the prophetic ministry of Christ. But the hierarchical office-holders are not the sole agents by whom the Church teaches. It teaches unofficially by means of those of its faithful who have sufficient knowledge to be able to bring others to a certain understanding of the faith. Religious instruction on the elementary level is called catechesis; on higher levels it takes the form of advanced courses in Christian doctrine and theology. The entire process of Christian education takes place under the supervision of the hierarchical magisterium. To assure the proper continuity between official magisterial teaching and day-to-day religious education, some teachers of religion are given an office or commission from the hierarchy.

Theologians as Teachers in the Church

All education in Christian doctrine involves a measure of reflective understanding of the Christian message and thus may be called, in some sense, theology. Theology has been defined in many ways, but it is difficult to improve on the phrase of Anselm, who spoke of "faith seeking understanding." Every believer who seeks to acquire or impart an understanding of the faith may be called, at least in a rudimentary way, a theologian or teacher of theology.

In modern times the term "theology" is usually restricted to scholarly reflection upon the faith by persons who have attained a high degree of competence, normally certified by advanced degrees or noteworthy publications. In their pondering of the faith, theologians commonly deal with questions such as these: What is the precise meaning of the accepted statements of faith? What is the basis of such statements in the sources of revealed knowledge? How can the credibility of such statements be shown? What is their inner coherence and intelligibility in relation to the total Christian message? What relevance do they have for the human quest? What are the theoretical and practical consequences of the things that Christians believe, or should believe? The theologian seeks to answer such questions by drawing on all the sources of knowledge that might prove helpful, but the most basic reference point for theology is the faith itself, authoritatively set forth in normative documents.

In recent years there has been some debate about whether the theologian has to be a believer. Normally theologians are believers, for there would be little point in attempting to explore the implications of a faith one did not accept. Furthermore, it may be doubted whether a nonbeliever could be a really competent theologian. One who simply looks at a religion from outside without sharing its beliefs will rarely be a good interpreter of the tenets and implications of that religion. We may conclude, then, that theology is a reflection upon faith from within the commitment of faith. Those who attempt a purely detached analysis may be engaged in some legitimate type of religious studies, but they generally remain at the surface level and fail to achieve the kind of penetration that is expected in theology.

What, then, must the theologian accept? To do Christian theology at all one has to acknowledge the existence of God, the fact of revelation, the centrality of Christ in God's saving plan, and the reliable transmission of the gospel through Scripture and the Church. In addition, Catholic theology is predicated upon the validity of the Catholic tradition and upon the guidance offered by the hierarchical magisterium. The Catholic theologian who wishes to remain a Catholic is bound to accept the definitive ("irreformable") teaching of the magisterium and must be favorably disposed to accept whatever the magisterium puts forth as obligatory doctrine.

There are limits, therefore, to the freedom of theology. Under pain of self-destruction it is prevented from denying its own foundations. This kind of limitation is by no means peculiar to theology. Every discipline is bound to admit the reality of its own object and the conditions of accessibility of that object. No geologist, while remaining a geologist, can take the position that the earth does not exist or that it is unknowable. Astronomy cannot deny the heavens, optics cannot deny the light, and medicine cannot deny the fact of disease. As a human being the theologian remains free to become an unbeliever, even an atheist, if so prompted by conscience. But in so doing one automatically ceases to be a theologian. Let it not be said, therefore, that the theologian, as theologian, can reject revelation or that the Catholic theologian can reject the canonical Scriptures and dogmas of the Church. To accept these things is not a limitation on theology but rather the charter of its existence and freedom to be itself. The more firmly theology is grounded in faith, the more capable, generally speaking, will it be of understanding the nature and contents of faith.

Although Catholic theology must, as I have just said, adhere to the word of God as it comes through Scripture, tradition, and the hierarchical magisterium, theology does not simply repeat what is in its sources. It reflects on the sources with a view to answering contemporary questions, questions not explicitly answered in the sources themselves. It seeks the intelligibility of the revelation in all the ways I have just indicated — through positive theology that probes the sources; through apologetics that seeks to establish credibility; through systematics that concerns itself with the inner coherence of the whole scheme of revelation; and through practical theology that ponders the implications of the revealed message for human conduct. Within its particular sphere of competence theology is free to reach whatever conclusions are indicated by a proper application of its own method. Popes and bishops have no mandate to tell the theologian how to do theology, beyond the negative mandate of seeing to it that theology does not undermine the life of faith itself. Theology, therefore, possesses a certain freedom over against even the hierarchical magisterium. Without that freedom it could not be theology, and hence it could not be of service to the Church. The medieval axiom *non ancilla nisi libera* holds for theology.

While emphasizing the fidelity of theology to the teaching of the hierarchical magisterium, I have not ruled out the possibility of critical questioning. I recognize that in certain cases, which I would take to be rare in view of the overall reliability of the magisterium, a given theologian may find the official doctrine unconvincing. A proper docility will move the theologian to seek reasons in favor of the teaching in question, but there comes a point where the will cannot compel the intellect to assent, and where the possibility of an error in noninfallible magisterial teaching must be reckoned with. The approved theological manuals have for many years taken account of this eventuality, and since Vatican II the United States bishops have put out guidelines for the public expression of dissenting positions in the Church.[2]

Dissent should neither be glorified nor be vilified. It is not necessarily an act of greater probity and courage to dissent than to assent. Whenever dissent is expressed, it tends to weaken the Church as a sign of unity. Nevertheless, dissent cannot be totally eliminated. It may be subjectively and even objectively justified. To deny its existence or to seek to suppress it would be more harmful than to acknowledge it and deal with it honestly.

Theology always stands under correction. The hierarchical magisterium has the power and the responsibility to approve or disapprove of theological teaching from the standpoint of orthodoxy. By approving of the works of the fathers and doctors of the Church, including saints such as Augustine and Thomas Aquinas, the Church has given them a quasi-official status, so that the faithful may be confident that the works of these authors are conducive to a better grasp of the faith. But the magisterium never has canonized, and, I think, never could canonize, the theology of any school or individual. Just as faith differs from any systematization of faith, so the doctrine of the magisterium differs in its object from theology. Even when popes and bishops approvingly quote the works of theologians, they do not make the theology of these authors binding on the faithful.

The magisterium can associate certain theologians very closely with itself. Some, for example, are members of, or consultors to, the Congregation for the Doctrine of the Faith. Some are asked to draft papal encyclicals or other official documents. Some are given a canonical mission by their bishops to teach in seminaries or other ecclesiastical faculties. According to the apostolic constitution *Sapientia Christiana*, published by Pope John Paul II in 1979, those who teach with canonical mission "do not teach by their own authority but on the strength of a mission received from the Church" (art. 27, no. 1).

Occasionally one hears it said that professors who have a canonical mission teach "in the name of the Church." The "Instruction on the Ecclesial Vocation of the Theologian," issued by the Congregation for the Doctrine of the Faith, speaks of the commitment of theologians "to teach in the name of the Church" (par. 37). The supporting references in the footnote given at this point are to the paragraph of *Sapientia Christiana* just quoted and to canon 812 of the Code of Canon Law. Neither of these documents, however, speaks explicitly of "teaching in the name of the Church." Although a proper interpretation can be given to this phrase, I prefer to avoid it, since it tends to obscure the distinction between the role of bishops, who can by their teaching publicly commit the Church, and that of theologians, who cannot. A theologian who has a *nihil obstat* from the Holy See or a canonical mission or mandate from the competent authority is able to exercise his or her functions with the added prestige that comes from these tokens of official trust. But the theologian is not thereby dispensed from having to proceed according to the proper methods of the theological disciplines and from being subject to criticism from peers for any failures of scholarship or reasoning.

Academic Freedom in Relation to Theology

Up to this point I have been attempting to clarify what is meant by the teaching of the Church. I have found it helpful to distinguish between the teaching *of* the Church, which is that of the hierarchy, and teaching *in* the Church, which is nonhierarchical. Both bishops and theologians teach, but they do so in different ways. Bishops teach with authority to bind in the name of Christ; theologians teach in an academic, nonauthoritative way. I have spoken of the sense in which theology is bound to the doctrine of the official magisterium, and of the senses in which it is free. It will now be possible for me to turn, in the remainder of this chapter, to the issue of academic freedom. Such freedom applies most obviously to teachers in the academy, that is to say, in institutions of higher learning that are committed to exacting standards of scholarship. Is the theologian or the professor of other sacred disciplines, such as biblical studies and canon law, entitled to academic freedom, and if so, in what sense?

There is no official or uncontested definition of academic freedom.[3] In current usage, at least in the United States, the term generally denotes the freedom of professionally qualified teachers, first, to pursue their scholarly investigations without interference; second, to publish the results of their research and reflection; and, third, to teach according to their own convictions, provided that they remain in the area of their competence and present the alternative positions with sufficient attention and fairness. Many statements on academic freedom add that in cases of dispute, the competence and professional conduct of the teacher should be assessed by experts chosen from among academic colleagues or peers.[4]

In the United States there is a strong tendency to maintain that academic freedom is essential to the very concept of a college or university. The American Association of University Professors (AAUP), in a series of statements since its inception in 1915, has promoted this position. Limitations on academic freedom are considered injurious to the academic standing of the institution and likely to imperil the accreditation of its degrees by professional associations.[5]

As the AAUP has recognized on several occasions, the concept of academic freedom raises delicate questions for church-related institutions. A Catholic college or university is not purely and simply an academy in the secular meaning of the term. It seeks to discharge a service toward the Church and toward the religious development of its students, especially those who are Catholics.[6]

It could be objected, of course, that any such practical orientation to goals that lie beyond the cultivation of rationally acquired knowledge is extraneous to the nature of the university. If so, theology, as I have explained it in this chapter, would have no place in the university curriculum. This solution, as drastic as it is simple, is unrealistic. It rests upon a purist concept of the university that neglects the relation of education to the world as it is and to human beings as they are. The Church and the Catholic people legitimately expect that some universities will provide an intellectual environment in which the meaning and implications of the faith can be studied in relation to the whole realm of human knowledge. Without Catholic university theology, the Church would be less able to relate to the culture of the day and to reflect on its faith with the instruments of contemporary knowledge. Catholic parents and students often choose church-related colleges and universities because such institutions provide a favorable situation in which to gain a mature, reflective understanding of the faith.

As I have shown in chapter 10 above, the opportunity for university study of Catholic theology may be considered a fundamental educational right of Catholic parents and students. If theology were expelled from the university, the Church would be deprived of an important resource for its mission. The university, too, would suffer because, as Newman pointed out, other disciplines would occupy, without adequate warrant or competence, the territory vacated by the departure of theology.[7] The larger society would stand to lose because in our pluralistic culture Catholic theological faculties provide valuable input from one of the major religious traditions of the nation.

It would be ironic indeed if university education, which arose in many parts of Europe under the sponsorship of the Church, and which frequently looked upon theology as its crowning discipline, were now to be defined in a way that excluded theology. It is an undeniable fact that many of the leading universities of the world, both in the past and in our own day, have flourished under ecclesiastical sponsorship and direction. It would be sheer ignorance to deny the quality of scholarship that emanates from some of the major Catholic universities and theological faculties in the United States and in many other countries. To define university education so as to exclude such institutions and faculties is evidence of a parochialism that is, in its own way, sectarian. If narrow-minded religious sectarianism is to be rejected — as indeed it should be — secular sectarianism should not be established in its place.

Supposing, then, that theology as a systematic reflection upon faith does have a right to exist, at least in some universities, we must inquire what kind of academic freedom is desirable to protect this discipline. It does need protection. History provides abundant cases in which civil and religious authorities have unjustly intervened to prevent theologians from publishing and teaching according to the canons of their own discipline. Several years after the death of Thomas Aquinas, a number of his positions in philosophy and theology were condemned by the bishop of Paris and the archbishop of Canterbury. Some of his faithful followers were severely punished for heresy. Before long, the condemnations were withdrawn, but the very occurrence of the error illustrates the likelihood that local episcopal authorities will be overzealous in seeking to enforce orthodoxy. In modern times the state has sometimes been even more oppressive than the Church in attempting to control theology. Consider, for example, the actions of the Parlement of Paris in requiring adherence to Gallican doctrine and those of the Emperor Joseph II of Austria in regulating university and seminary curricula, not to mention the excesses of Bismarck and many others. Clearly, then, theology stands to gain, as do other disciplines, from the protection of academic freedom. But academic freedom must be rightly understood.

The prevalent secular theories of academic freedom are not fully satisfactory. Among other difficulties, they seem to imply that academic freedom absolves the Christian or Catholic theologian from the obligation to teach in accordance with the Christian or Catholic faith. Some theorists contend that no professor can be required to adhere to any substantive teaching. To set limits to scholarly conclusions, it is argued, is to violate a basic principle of academic freedom.[8]

This view of the matter, in my opinion, embodies some confusions. No one can be coerced into personally holding the faith. Faith is by its very nature free. But a rejection of Catholic faith, even if merely private, would be detrimental to theology as a reflection upon faith. A nonbelieving professor would be ill suited to present the tradition of the Church from the point of view of faith or to assist the student to reflect upon the implications of faith. In teaching according to his or her own convictions, such a professor could not be teaching Catholic theology. Thus a person hired for the purpose of teaching Catholic theology might well be disqualified by a failure to hold and profess the Catholic faith.

The Methodist theologian Lonnie Kliever contends that the modern American university is committed to "methodological skepticism — the habit of mind that remains open to radical challenge and revolutionary changes." Charles Curran in a recent book vigorously disagrees. Kliever's view, he asserts, "would not be able to accept Catholic theology as a discipline, and many other disciplines would also be in jeopardy."[9] Curran gives a broad definition to competency, maintaining that it "requires that one be true to the presuppositions, source, and methods of the discipline.... Competency demands that a Catholic theologian theologize within the parameters of the Catholic faith. A Catholic theologian who does not believe in Jesus or does not accept a role for the pope in the church could rightly be judged to be incompetent."[10] Although I do not concur with Curran's inclusive concept of competence, I agree with him on the importance of religious belief for theology.

Further difficulties arise from the contention, frequently made, that academic freedom implies that alleged violations of the norms of Catholic theology should be judged only by colleagues, or "peers" as they are commonly called. It is not entirely clear who the peers of a Catholic theologian in a Catholic institution would be. Would they all be Catholics? Would they be theologians? If the question under dispute is whether a Catholic theologian has exceeded the bounds of orthodoxy, non-Catholics or nontheologians could hardly be qualified to reach a verdict. I would even doubt whether a group of Catholic theologians could be expected to render a truly objective judgment. Peer pressure would be too strong. According to a longstanding Catholic tradition, pastoral judgments concerning purity of doctrine are, in the last instance, the prerogative of the ecclesiastical magisterium.[11]

I deliberately insert the words "in the last instance." For reasons already indicated, when I spoke of the condemnations of Thomistic doctrine in France and England, I am apprehensive that bishops or their curial assistants, possibly aroused by one-sided letters of complaint, might pronounce overhastily upon technical questions in which they were not fully competent. They should make sure that they have correctly understood exactly what the theologian is saying and why. This will often require a familiarity with the state of the discipline and with the special meanings that certain terms have acquired in the literature of the field. Theologians need scope in which to develop tentative positions and to make hypothetical statements that could easily be misunderstood by nonspecialists. They are entitled to raise some legitimate questions about the current noninfallible teaching of the magisterium. They must of course be held to prudence in the ways in which they publicize their theories and hypotheses, but they cannot always be responsible for the uses that others make of statements quite proper in themselves.

To avoid perpetrating injustice, bishops may sometimes have the duty to enter into a dialogue process something like that suggested in the guidelines adopted by the United States bishops at their Seton Hall meeting in June 1989. According to that document, "In cases of dispute, the theologian has the right to expect access to a fair process, protecting both substantive and procedural rights."[12] In a university due process for its professors will normally be provided for by the statutes and the faculty manual.

Every theologian should enjoy academic freedom, in the sense of a right to inquire, publish, and teach according to the norms of the discipline.[13] But because theology is an essentially ecclesial discipline, the freedom of the theologian must not be absolutized over and against other elements in the community of faith. While the freedom of the professor as an individual scholar should be respected, it should be seen in the context of other values. One such value is the integrity of Catholic theology as a meditation on the shared faith of the whole Church. Whoever substitutes a purely individual or deviant faith forfeits any title to be called a Catholic theologian. Another such value is the maintenance of sound doctrine, even in matters that are not strictly of faith. Although sound doctrine is a particular responsibility of the hierarchical magisterium, it is of crucial importance for theology itself. In the interests of their own profession, theologians should support the magisterium as it seeks to safeguard the apostolic heritage, whether by way of positively encouraging sound developments or by way of administering, on occasion, a word of caution or correction. The rights of the theologian as an academician become real only when situated in this ecclesial framework.

Bishops have an important role in overseeing the faithful transmission of Catholic doctrine in university situations, as elsewhere, but that role does not necessarily give them the power to intervene in the internal affairs of the university. Even when they do not enter directly into the internal governance of the university, however, bishops will do well to maintain close personal and pastoral relationships of cooperation and dialogue with university theologians and administrators.[14] Questions concerning the implementation of the pastoral judgments of the hierarchy within the university have to be answered in different ways for universities of different types. In each case the charter and statutes of the university must be considered, as well as the terms of the contract entered into between the university and the faculty member in question. Unless the statutes so provide, I do not see how the Holy See or the bishops could intervene directly in the working of a civilly chartered university by dismissing a professor or preventing a course from being taught. Whether the officers or trustees could dismiss a professor whom the hierarchy judged to be lacking in orthodoxy would depend upon the variables just mentioned.

A given university might by its statutes engage itself publicly to hire in its department of theology only professors who have received some kind of license or mission from ecclesiastical authorities. In the United States, however, this type of arrangement would presumably be rare, and would normally be accompanied by provisions to assure due process. Such an arrangement would not be detrimental to university theology. Here as in other countries, ecclesiastical control can be, has been, and is fully compatible with a high level of theological research. Theologians of the stature of Rahner and Lonergan regularly taught, I believe, with a canonical mission or its equivalent.

I conclude, therefore, that the prevailing secular model of academic freedom, as described by standard authorities, requires some modification before being applied to Catholic or other church-related institutions. The model shows signs of having been constructed with a laudable but one-sided purpose of protecting university professors from incompetent outside authorities, who might unjustly seek to impose their own ideas. This model overlooks the responsibility of theology to the community of faith and the mandate of the ecclesiastical magisterium to assure the doctrinal soundness of theology.

The secular model, moreover, is somewhat narrowly based on a theory of knowledge more suited to the empirical sciences than to theology, which rests primarily on divine revelation. The dogmas of faith do not have the same status in theology as currently accepted theories have for secular science. Those who practice theology with the conviction that revealed truth exists and is reliably transmitted by authoritative sources will see the need to work out a properly theological concept of academic freedom. Such an adapted version will protect authentic theology but will not separate theologians from the body of the Church; it will not set them in opposition to the community of faith or its pastoral leadership. Theologians and bishops, in spite of their different roles in the Church, are fundamentally allies because they are alike committed to maintain and explore the unfathomable riches of Christ, in whom alone is given the truth that makes us free.

12.

Method in Ecumenical Theology

As late as a few decades ago, Catholics frequently spoke as though faith did not exist beyond the confines of their own Church, but today they generally recognize that divine and salvific faith exists among members of other Christian communities, among adherents of non-Christian religions, and even among people who are not formally religious. The Second Vatican Council, in several important texts, encouraged this new tendency. In its Decree on Ecumenism it stated that faith, hope, and charity "can exist outside the visible boundaries of the Catholic Church."[1] In its Decree on the Church's Missionary Activity it declared that "God, in ways known to himself, can lead people who through no fault of their own are ignorant of the gospel, to that faith without which it is impossible to please him."[2] Since the council, Catholics such as Raimundo Panikkar have argued that faith is a "constitutive dimension of man,"[3] while Protestants such as Wilfred Cantwell Smith contend that faith is "generically human" and "constitutive of man as human."[4]

Method in Interreligious Theology

If theology is understood as faith seeking understanding, it may be judged to exist wherever faith is found, even without Christian or biblical revelation. The theological enterprise, in some sense of that term, is open to all who wish to converse seriously about questions of ultimate truth and meaning on the basis of an existential concern. A generic or analogous commonality in theology does not neces-

179

sarily presuppose a common creed, common scriptures, or common ecclesiastical authorities. Rather, the articulation of creeds, the canonization of scriptures, and the recognition of magisterial authorities result, in part, from theological reflection on the historic experience of peoples.

Notwithstanding the tension among rival faiths, which shows no sign of abating, the coming decades, I suspect, will witness the maturation of an interreligious or broadly ecumenical theology in which adherents of different religions, confessions, and ideologies can fruitfully collaborate. Such a theology would be a shared reflection, from different perspectives, on life and reality in light of the all-embracing transcendent mystery — a mystery that Christians identify with the God who has revealed himself definitively in Jesus Christ. All who find themselves caught up in the quest for transcendence could profitably meditate together on what is implied in phenomena such as petitionary prayer, worship, thanksgiving, repentance, atonement, self-sacrifice for ideals, altruistic love, obedience to conscience, and hope in the face of inevitable death. Thus far Christian theologians have generally addressed these questions within the relatively narrow confines of their own traditions. If we wish to take advantage of the theological resources that are available in our day, we shall be well advised to widen our horizons so as to approach universal human questions within horizons that are equally universal.

Hans Küng, among others, has recognized this characteristic of our age. In a recent work he writes:

> Despite all the obvious obstacles and difficulties, we seem to be witnessing the slow *awakening of global ecumenical consciousness* and the beginning of a serious religious dialogue between leading experts and broad-based representatives. This is possibly one of the most important phenomena of the twentieth century, though its consequences will likely not make themselves felt until the twenty-first century — should humanity live to see it. And so we have less reason than ever today for understanding ecumenism in a narrow, constricted, ecclesiocentric fashion: Ecumenism should not be limited to the *community of the Christian churches*; it must include the *community of the great religions*, if ecumenism — in accordance with the original meaning of *oikumene* — is to refer to the whole "inhabited world."[5]

Interreligious theology may of course be carried out on a more modest scale, and with the expectation of more concrete results, by adherents of different faiths linked to each other by close historic ties. Jews and Christians, for example, can profitably engage in a joint theological reflection on the ways in which they find access to the living God through the religious heritage of ancient Israel. Christians taking part in such a joint reflection, while finding no need to disguise their distinctive convictions, need not insist that Christ be taken as the thematic center and starting point of this particular theological enterprise. If they did, the dialogue could not even begin.

The method of shared reflection on different religious commitments, based on different encounters with the transcendent, still remains to be worked out in practice. Initially we may assert with Wolfhart Pannenberg that such a reflection should not be a mere psychology, sociology, or phenomenology of religion, but rather a theology in the sense of being preoccupied with the truth about God and God's self-communication.[6] Writing as a Christian, Pannenberg is convinced that "the alien religions cannot be adequately interpreted as mere fabrications of man's strivings after the true God. Ultimately, they have to do with the same divine reality as the message of Jesus."[7]

In recent years Wilfred Cantwell Smith, a scholar with exceptional competence in Islam and other living faiths, has set forth a very ambitious proposal for what he calls a "world theology." Such a theology, he maintains, "will not displace but subsume its erstwhile sectional parts," that is, the particular theologies of the distinct religions.[8] In this new theology, as he envisages it, there should no longer be any talk of "we" and "they"; no barrier should stand between insiders and outsiders. Adherents of different religions will strive to speak about their own faith only in ways that members of other religious communities "can rationally approve of (or, at the very least, rationally understand)."[9]

Smith's advocacy of world theology rests in part on his understanding of the nature of faith, set forth more fully in the earlier work already mentioned, *Faith and Belief*. Faith, for him, is an absolute that cuts across all religious boundaries. There is no such thing as Jewish faith, Christian faith, or Muslim faith. For the classical theological tradition, Smith maintains, "faith is not the sort of thing of which there is more than one kind."[10] Since faith is a human response to God or the transcendent, theology may be seen as talk about God or, to speak more generically, talk about "the transcendent dimension of human life and the universe to which the history of religion bears witness."[11]

I can agree with Smith up to a point. With him I would hold that faith can exist among people who are not Christian, and indeed among those who have never had historical contact with the biblical religions. The Christian theologian should listen empathetically to what such people say about their own religious life, and seek to discern how their statements are rooted in their own experience and history. Conversely, Christians should strive to set forth their own faith in such a way that well-disposed members of other communities might be able to make sense of it. But I would express reservations about the claims of any common "world theology" to subsume or supersede the specific content of each particular religion. Christians, since they believe in the three-personed God and in Jesus Christ as the incarnation of the second divine person, will not be content to do theology as though the doctrines of the Trinity and the Incarnation were not true. I see no reason for forbidding Christians to mention aspects of their own faith that cannot be "rationally approved" apart from Christian revelation. Based on God's special revelation in Christ, Christian theology continues to differ from that of all other religions. No one could admit the truth of the Trinity or the Incarnation (with the meaning these doctrines have for Christians) without being converted to Christianity.

My difference with Smith is rooted in his concept of faith. For Christians of the classical tradition, faith and belief are correlatives, if not synonyms. To have faith is always to believe something as well as someone. Responding to Smith's interpretation of Thomas Aquinas, Frederick Crosson shows that for the Angelic Doctor faith necessarily involved a content, a material object, which was communicable, at least in some measure, by teaching or doctrine.[12] For Catholics (and, I would think, for most Protestants) faith continues to have a definite content. In the Christian act of faith Jesus Christ plays an indispensable role. Jesus, moreover, is believed and confessed to be the Son of God, the risen Savior, according to the Scriptures and the creeds. This doctrinal content, inseparable from Christian faith, cannot be subsumed or left behind in some new "world theology."

Whether different species of faith exist is a complex question that need not be settled here. Patristic and medieval theologians tended to hold that all faith is implicitly Trinitarian and Christological insofar as it is directed to the God who is in fact triune and who redeems humanity through the incarnation of the Son. But faith develops as this content is clarified by progressive revelation. Explicitly Christian faith differs qualitatively from faith that does not rest on Christ and the gospel. Its formal object is God as revealed in Christ and as attested by Scripture and the Church.[13]

Because it rests on a faith that is qualitatively different, the theology of Christians must have special characteristics. To be sure, Christians can and should concern themselves with the religious life of all peoples, and with God's redemptive presence to them. But it is normal and proper for Christians to try to understand non-Christian religions in the light of Christ. Küng, in contrast to Smith, disavows an approach in which the theologian would be "giving an account of the familiar history of Christianity and its traditional teaching, without professing any commitment to Christian faith and life."[14] He expects Christians in interreligious dialogue to affirm their own commitment to Christ. Members of other religions, conversely, will try to understand Christianity from their own perspective.

In the dialogue, therefore, all the participants will seek to communicate a better understanding of their own heritage, with the hope of achieving convergence. In the course of the discussion they may gain unexpected insights that may lead them to revise some of their previous positions. For purposes of the conversation, the distinctive tenets of each religion are neither presumed to be true nor excluded as false. The supposition is that all the parties enter the dialogue with a commitment to the traditions and confessional positions of their own communities and that they are eager to learn more about the other parties.

The proper spirit of interreligious dialogue has been well described by Pope John Paul II in his recent encyclical on missionary activity, *Redemptoris Missio:*

> Those engaged in this dialogue must be consistent with their own religious traditions and convictions, and be open to understanding those of the other party without pretense or closed-mindedness, but with truth, humility, and frankness, knowing that dialogue can enrich each side. There must be no abandonment of principles nor false irenicism, but instead a witness given and received for mutual advancement on the road of

religious inquiry and experience, and at the same time for the elimination of prejudice, intolerance, and misunderstandings. Dialogue leads to inner purification and conversion which, if pursued with docility to the Holy Spirit, will be spiritually fruitful.[15]

It is of course possible to explore shared aspects of faith jointly with adherents of other religions. But in the present state of relative estrangement these common aspects are still too slender to serve as the basis of a very rewarding dialogue. Conversation can be far more fruitful if the participants feel free to speak of matters on which they do not as yet agree.

Method in Ecumenical Theology

In intra-Christian ecumenism similar questions of method arise. Some theologians have contended that Christians of different churches and communities should abandon their distinctive approaches and accept a common ecumenical method, based on agreed positions. Hans Küng, although his principles for interreligious dialogue are opposed to those of Wilfred Smith, proposes for intra-Christian dialogue a confessionally neutral theology analogous to Smith's "world theology." He writes, for example:

> In view of the manifold political, economic, and military threats to the one world and to the common future of humanity the *transition from particularist to universal thinking,* from a *"theology of controversy"* to an *"ecumenical theology"* is an absolutely necessary desideratum. Denominational Christian traditions are not to be perpetuated, but to be received with a view toward what they contribute to an ecumenical community of all Christians. An ecumenical style of thinking is called for, in which particular-denominational elements can be understood not as a realization of the whole, comprehensive Christian truth, but as a part of it.[16]

Küng's method, while Christocentric, seeks to transcend the denominational differences. Thus he proposes:

The basic norm of a critical ecumenical theology is the Christian message — which arises out of Jewish tradition — the *Gospel of Jesus Christ.* This primal and fundamental Christian testimony, as expressed in the Old and New Testament, is wholly focused on the living Jesus of history, who is also the norm and criterion of my quite personal Christian faith.[17]

Küng is aware, of course, that the Christian message has been variously constructed in different schools of interpretation and even in the New Testament itself. For this reason he goes back not simply to Scripture but to the original Christian message. He asserts, for instance:

> The criterion determining all other criteria of Christian theology can never again be some ecclesiastical or theological tradition or institution, but only the Gospel, the original Christian message itself. Thus, theology must everywhere be oriented toward the biblical findings analyzed by historical-critical analysis.[18]

Commentators have found it difficult to understand exactly what Küng means by the "original Christian message" and why he regards it as supremely normative.[19] Where is the original message to be found? What is the privileged moment characterized as "original"? Is it the preaching of Jesus, as reconstructed by biblical scholars? Is it the earliest testimonies to the risen Christ, the kerygma of the post-Easter community, or the earliest parts of the New Testament? Is Paul sufficiently original to be included? If so, must one put the later Pauline epistles (and those attributed to Paul's disciples) on a lower plane than the earlier? It is hard to see why the Church could not have achieved a better grasp of its own message as it grew in experience and reflection with the aid of the Holy Spirit. As Peter Chirico has said, historians in most fields agree that initial interpretations tend to be narrow and limited, whereas later interpretations often reflect a more comprehensive perspective. Accordingly, it seems unreasonable to subject later interpretations to an initial interpretation as the standard to which they must conform.[20]

Another possibility is to use as the primary norm for ecumenical theology the teaching of the New Testament, analyzed and synthesized with the help of historical-critical scholarship. As noted in an earlier chapter, Raymond E. Brown has written on the value for ecumenism of "historical biblical criticism," which he understands to be primarily concerned with establishing "what the biblical author conveyed to his readers in the text that he wrote."[21] This method has in fact been employed with some success in several volumes of biblical studies commissioned or executed by the Lutheran-Catholic dialogue in the United States.[22] These volumes have not only examined the individual texts but have attempted a synthesis in terms of the "trajectories" of development, pointing to possible further developments beyond the biblical testimonies themselves.

Catholics and Protestants can agree on the fundamental importance of the New Testament testimony for Christian faith. It is the original and canonically recognized record of the decisive events and interpretations on which the Church is founded. As an inspired record, the Bible may be called the word of God in written form.[23] Scripture is the only normative objectification of the faith of the foundational period to which we have access. For this reason Karl Rahner and several other theologians of our time have felt authorized to say that there is a Catholic *sola scriptura*.[24] The classical Lutheran view of the Bible as the definitive norm, the *norma normans*, can be defended by Catholics on the ground that no tradition can be authentically Christian unless it harmonizes with God's word in Scripture. So rich and profound is Holy Scripture that it may be recognized as "the soul of sacred theology."[25] If it is the soul of Catholic theology in general, why should it not be the soul of ecumenical theology?

In the chapter on tradition, however, we have seen some reasons that militate against calling the Bible the *norma normans*, and against speaking of a Catholic *sola scriptura*. These terms have to be carefully explained lest they seem to imply that Scripture and tradition are two separable quantities, the second of which must be measured by the first. This dualism between Scripture and tradition was repudiated by the Fourth World Conference on Faith and Order at Montreal in 1963 and by Vatican II in its *Dei Verbum*. According to a commission report received at Montreal, the exclusive sufficiency of Scripture is indefensible in the face of "the historical actuality of *Scriptura nunquam sola!* Scripture is nowhere by itself alone."[26] Vatican II insisted that Scripture and tradition, "flowing from the same divine wellspring, in a certain way merge into a unity and tend toward the same end."[27] Taken apart from the tradition in which it comes to the faithful, the Bible would no longer deserve to be called the word of God.

As the Montreal conference recognized, tradition does not exist concretely except in the form of particular traditions. Different churches have developed divergent traditions, which are in some cases incompatible. Granted that Scripture must be read in light of tradition, tradition itself (considered as a divinely authoritative medium) has to be distilled from the traditions. Particular traditions do not necessarily give the apostolic tradition in pure and undistorted form.

According to Catholic doctrine Christ has equipped the Church with a teaching office, a magisterium, which has the task of judging disputes about the interpretation of Scripture and about the authenticity of particular traditions. Vatican II therefore maintained that the criterion of sound doctrine involves three elements: Scripture, tradition, and magisterium. Although the magisterium is not above the word of God but stands at its service, it has authority to identify and interpret God's word in Scripture and tradition. "Thus it is clear that, by God's wise design, tradition, Scripture and the Church's magisterium are so connected and associated that no one of them stands without the others, and all together, each in its own way, under the action of the one Holy Spirit, contribute effectively to the salvation of souls."[28]

In the last analysis, then, Catholics, like other Christians seriously committed to a particular church or communion, will not be satisfied with an approach to theological truth that neglects the authority of tradition and of the official teaching. They will not be content to subject the creeds and dogmas of the Church to a higher magisterium of scholars purporting to have found the original Christian message by means of historical-critical scrutiny. For purposes of some particular project it may be acceptable to use Scripture as a purely historical source, putting tradition and dogma provisionally in brackets, but when Catholics speak their convictions honestly, they will have to reckon with these other voices. They will not restrict themselves to a confessionally neutral historical method. They will insist that any given question be approached, in the end, with all the tools that may be useful. To oblige them to disregard the tradition of their own church in the name of ecumenicity would be to deprive them of what they quite properly esteem as a precious instrument in their quest for truth. In this connection one recalls Cardinal Newman's objections to Paley's evidential method in apologetics. These rules of evidence, for Newman, were too confining:

> Rules of court are dictated by what is expedient on the whole and in the long run; but they incur the risk of being unjust to the claims of particular cases. Why am I to begin by taking up a position not my own, and unclothing my mind of that large outfit of existing thoughts, principles, likings, desires, and hopes, which make me what I am?[29]

It could be objected, of course, that to adhere to a confessional tradition is arbitrary and subjective. This objection, however, ignores the role of authority in the quest for knowledge. To use church tradition as a *locus theologicus* is no more authoritarian than to accept the historical Jesus or the canonical Scriptures as normative. Whatever may be the case with Christians of other affiliations, the Catholic is committed by the very fact of church membership to accept the teaching authority of the ecclesiastical magisterium. This need not be a matter of "ecclesiastical opportunism" or subservience to the "ecclesiastical system" (Küng's phrases); it may be a means of better attaining the truth of revelation. To depart without solid reasons from the doctrinal norms of the ecclesial body to which one belongs, far from being scholarly and scientific, would be subjective, arbitrary, and even self-contradictory.

I conclude, then, that Küng's proposals for intra-Christian ecumenism are subject to many of the same objections that are made against Wilfred Cantwell Smith's case for a world theology. Each proposal may be adopted to establish ground rules for a particular report or conversation, but both would be inadequate and impoverishing if made mandatory for all ecumenical or interreligious studies. Preferable to either of these proposals, I believe, is the method of dialogue set forth in the documents of Vatican II, and particularly in the passage on "dialogue between competent experts" in the Decree on Ecumenism:

> At these meetings, which are organized in a religious spirit, all parties explain the teachings of their communion in greater depth and bring out clearly its distinctive features. In such dialogue, everyone gains a truer knowledge and more just appreciation of the teaching and life of each communion. In

addition, the way is prepared for fuller cooperation between them in undertakings for the common good of humanity that are demanded by every Christian conscience; and, whenever this is allowed, prayer is offered in common. Finally, all are led to examine their own faithfulness to Christ's will for the Church and, as may be needed, to undertake with vigor the task of renewal and reform.[30]

The idea of dialogue, as it has developed in modern theology, implies a mutual exchange of views between diverse parties who do not fully agree but who respect and are prepared to learn from one another. Reuel Howe, an Episcopalian expert on pastoral theology, gives an excellent description of such two-way communication. "Dialogue," he writes, "is a reciprocal relationship in which each party 'experiences the other side' so that their communication becomes a true address and response in which each informs and learns." In such dialogue, Howe explains, each regards "the other as a partner, someone to be taken seriously, whose point of view must be understood and whose meanings must be examined; both are aware of the possibility that the meanings of one may cause those of the other to be revised."[31]

Ecumenical Agreements and Their Limits

With the added participation of the Catholic Church, there has been an extraordinary flowering of intra-Christian ecumenical dialogue since Vatican II. The bilateral conversations among Lutherans, Anglicans, Orthodox, and Roman Catholics on the national and international levels have been particularly rich in theological substance. The results of these dialogues have fed into multilateral statements such as those sponsored by the Groupe des Dombes in France and others held under the auspices of the Faith and Order Commission of the World Council of Churches. The Faith and Order paper "Baptism, Eucharist, and Ministry" adopted at Lima in 1982 was characterized by the Vatican Secretariat for Promoting the Unity of Christians as "perhaps the most significant result of the [Faith and Order] Movement so far."[32]

In the twenty-five years since the council, the dialogues have moved beyond the stage at which the various churches and communities were discovering one another and experiencing surprise at how much substantive Christianity existed outside their own traditions. The churches have seen and expressed the unity that already exists in their basic Christian beliefs and practices. Now that the easy agreements have been achieved, it becomes necessary to face the hard questions. Thus far none of the dialogues has been able to come up with a striking convergence, let alone a consensus, on thorny issues such as papal primacy of jurisdiction, the Mass as propitiatory sacrifice, purgatory, the Immaculate Conception of Mary, the invocation of saints, or the ordination of women to the ministerial priesthood. To an increasing extent the dialogues are running up against hardcore differences on which the theologians of each side do not feel authorized or even inclined to change the established positions of their churches.[33]

It is not altogether easy to separate the agreements from the disagreements. Just as the dialogues, in their first phase, were able to surface hidden agreements in their previous disagreements, so now, in their second phase, they are exposing hidden disagreements in their previous agreements. Some examples may be given from the Lutheran-Catholic dialogue in this country. The teams in 1965 reported agreement on the Nicene dogma of the divinity of Christ, but the solidity of the agreement was weakened by a difference of opinion about what constituted dogma. Was it an infallible decision of the Church or a generally accepted but reformable interpretation of Scripture? It was also unclear what the two parties meant by the divinity of Christ: Did it involve an ontological understanding of Christ as possessor of a divine nature, or could it be interpreted in merely functional terms as meaning that Jesus makes God present to us as Savior?

Or again, to turn to a different area, how fully do Catholics and Lutherans in the United States agree about the real presence of Christ in the Eucharist, as was claimed in 1967, if one group finds Christ present only in the actual administration of the sacrament while the other is committed to a real presence that persists after the eucharistic service is concluded? Do we agree about ministry, as the 1970 statement on the subject seemed to suggest, if one group looks upon ordination as a sacrament, effectively conferring radically new powers, while the other is perhaps content to view it as a community authorization to perform certain acts that can, in principle, be performed by any lay person? And with reference to the 1983 statement on justification by faith, how complete is the agreement if one group maintains that justification consists in faith alone whereas the other holds that faith does not justify unless it is animated by charity and fruitful in good works? And finally, to touch on a question that was asked in the most recent dialogue, can the two parties really agree about Christ as the sole mediator of salvation if they disagree about whether the invocation of saints and of Mary detracts from the sole mediatorship of Christ? The agreements are frail, and are in danger of coming unraveled when the contentious questions are raised. If they do become unraveled, we could easily fall back into the polemics of the past.

Suggested New Strategies

Difficulties such as those just mentioned suggest that the ecumenical period inaugurated for Catholics by Vatican II may be coming to an end. The programs set forth in the Decree on Ecumenism have borne excellent fruits, but some reassessment of the agenda may now be in order. Possibly we stand on the verge of a new "ecumenical moment" in which we shall have to generate new strategies. Although the choice of the right course still remains to be determined, I shall take the risk of offering several suggestions.

1. *The primacy of truth.* In order to meet popular and journalistic expectations, the churches are under enormous pressure to bury their academic scruples and come up with dramatic new consensus statements. The prevailing intellectual climate, deeply infected by relativism and agnosticism, increases this pressure and makes ecumenism appear as a mere exercise of diplomacy. Differences among the churches and even among the religions tend to be written off as mere matters of taste, culture, or historical conditioning. The danger is that a unity purchased at the expense of deeply held convictions may turn out to be illusory. By seeking to accommodate all points of view we cheapen the value of communion itself.

Many theologians involved in ecumenical dialogue are coming to distrust this easy relativism. The dialogues, they find, have shown the continuing importance of the traditional doctrinal issues. After working for a generation to build up mutual confidence and friendship, the dialogues have matured to the point at which divisive issues may now be squarely faced. The theologians are today eager to explore the most neuralgic issues with a frank recognition that the prospects of full agreement are minimal. The differences turn out not to be merely cultural and linguistic, nor always peripheral, but in some cases substantive and important. The dialogues can usefully clarify the issues; they are not asked to produce ambiguous compromises that paper over real disagreements. If faith is, as we believe, a matter of fidelity to a sacred trust, unity must not be purchased at the expense of honest conviction.

It follows, then, that we should not be in too great haste to overcome our diversities. In order to act responsibly we must first of all get possession of ourselves. The Methodist Stanley Hauerwas has a word for Catholics on the importance of fidelity to their own tradition: "I want you to be Catholics. I also believe that there is nothing more important for the future unity of the Church than for you to be Catholic. . . . You have been so anxious to be like us that you have failed in your ecumenical task to help us to see what it means for any of us to be faithful to the Gospel on which our unity depends."[34]

2. *Mutual enrichment.* Vatican II, in its Decree on Ecumenism, maintained that for the sake of unity "one must 'impose no burden beyond what is indispensable' (Acts 15:28)" (UR 18). But the same decree warned against a "false conciliatory approach" that would fail to present Catholic doctrine in its entirety (UR 11). While we may be grateful that many Christian communities agree on the basic doctrines of the Trinity and the Incarnation, we cannot settle for these fundamental articles as a sufficient basis for unity. No church seeking to promote ecumenism should jettison its own distinctive heritage, which may well contain elements needed to enrich the whole Christian world. What could be more useless than a giant supermarket Church that stands for nothing in particular while offering something to everybody? Much of the hostility and suspicion encountered by the ecumenical movement comes from the fear that it aims at such a debasement.

My own involvement in ecumenism over the past forty years has led me to cherish other values. I have acquired a deeper realization of how much the Catholic Church has to contribute from the wealth of its own heritage. At the same time I have gained an enormous respect for the other churches that have venerable traditions of their own. The Orthodox, I have found, possess an immensely rich heritage of Trinitarian and sacramental piety handed down from the Eastern fathers. They have a sense of spiritual communion (or *koinonia*) that supplements and partly corrects the more legalistic approach characteristic of the West. From Lutherans and other Protestants I have learned the spiritual power of a theology of the word of God that is capable of completing and balancing the more sacramental vision of the Catholic and Orthodox churches. The task of ecumenism, as I see it, is not to choose between legalism, sacramentalism, and evangelical faith, but to discover ways of harmoniously integrating these values, without loss of their respective strengths, into a plenitude that is, in the best sense of the word, Catholic.

Too often the ecumenist is perceived as asking how little we need to accept in order to be Christian. In the perspective I am proposing the question is rather: How much can the various churches give to, and accept from, one another? Authentic ecumenism is not a matter of whittling away from one's heritage in order to get back to some supposed primitive simplicity. More appropriately, it is a matter of sharing from our own riches while seeking to receive as much as we responsibly can from others. In their joint declaration of October 2, 1989, Pope John Paul II and Archbishop Robert Runcie of Canterbury put the matter very succinctly: "The ecumenical journey is not only about the removal of obstacles, but also about the sharing of gifts."[35]

3. *New alignments.* Hitherto the principal participants in ecumenism have been the more liberal churches, those with the least demanding doctrinal and liturgical heritage. Churches with firm doctrinal standards and stable traditions were considered at best dubiously ecumenical. In an ecumenism of mutual enrichment, such as I am here recommending, the priorities are reversed. The churches that have held most steadfastly to the deposit of biblical and patristic faith, and those that have best resisted the allurements of modernity, may have most to offer to an age that is surfeited with the lax and the ephemeral. The time is ripe to welcome the more traditional and conservative churches into the dialogue. For the Catholic Church it may not prove easy to reach a consensus with either the Orthodox or the conservative evangelicals, but these churches and communities may have more to offer than some others because they have dared to be different. Catholics have the right and duty to challenge the adequacy of some of their positions, but they should be invited to challenge Catholics in their turn.

Through earnest dialogue among communities that hold fast to their own heritage of faith, it may be possible to effect a new kind of fellowship, very valuable in its own way. A community of witnessing dialogue, cutting across denominational barriers, is one of the finest fruits of ecumenism. In such a community each church can profit from listening to clear and unambiguous presentations of the others' points of view; it stands to gain from hearing its own doctrines criticized from the perspective of outsiders. In this way individual believers may achieve a deeper realization of the ecclesial character of their own faith-commitments; the churches can learn to formulate their distinctive doctrines more circumspectly, and all can acquire a deeper appreciation of other Christian traditions. As a result, the participating churches may be able to find a path toward deeper convergence in the truth.

4. *Spiritual renewal.* With our characteristically Western bias toward activity and measurable results, we Americans are often guilty of excessive reliance on our own abilities and projects. Our ecumenical experience of recent years, with its difficulties and setbacks, has taught us to respect the teaching of the Decree on Ecumenism to the effect that the goal of the ecumenical movement "transcends human energies and capacities" (UR 24). The Church must constantly place all its hope in Christ's prayer for unity and in the ability of the Holy Spirit to bring about what lies beyond merely human powers. According to the decree the soul of the entire ecumenical movement is spiritual ecumenism, which consists in a "change of heart and holiness of life, along with public and private prayer for the unity of Christians" (UR 8).

Theological ecumenism, therefore, can succeed only within the larger framework of ecclesial spirituality. "Every renewal of the Church," according to the Decree on Ecumenism, "consists essentially in an increase of fidelity to her own calling" (UR 5). The decree thus confirmed on an official level what the great French ecumenist Yves Congar had said to Catholics in 1943:

I believe more than ever that the essential ecumenical activity of the Catholic Church should be to live its own life more fully and genuinely; to purify itself as far as possible, to grow in faithfulness, in good works, in depth of prayer and in union with God. In being fully herself, in the full strength of her vigor, she will develop her ecumenical power.[36]

To advance ecumenically, theologians must have a vivid sense of the realities signified by the biblical and traditional formulations. Unless they are united with God through their prayer, worship, and practice of the faith, they can have no adequate grasp of the tacit or symbolic significance. They will be unable to converse ecumenically because they will not see beyond the explicit and surface meanings of the formulations.

A generation ago colleges and seminaries were busily introducing courses on ecumenism to supplement the existing theological curriculum. The assumption seemed to be that there were two different kinds of theology, denominational and ecumenical. With the passage of time the two methods have converged. If ecumenical theology does not require its practitioners to put their own confessional stance in brackets, and if denominational theology stands to gain from attention to other traditions, the two types of theology tend to merge. They differ in degree rather than in kind.

All good theology, I have contended, must take its stand in a given confessional tradition and must at the same time be eager to escape from unconscious narrowness. Christian theology must always keep its primary focus on God and on Jesus Christ as the great revelation of God. It must be biblically rooted, ecclesially responsible, open to criticism, and sensitive to the present leading of the Holy Spirit. The rules for ecumenical theology, then, do not differ essentially from the prescriptions for any good theology. And the warrants for ecumenism in theology are as strong as the warrants for theology itself.

13.

Theology and Worship

Chapter 12 concludes with a recognition of the importance of prayer and worship for ecumenical progress. It thereby picks up a theme already broached in chapter 1, in which the liturgy was recognized as a prime theological source. If theology relies on symbolic communication as heavily as I have maintained in my second chapter, situations of worship in which the word of God is reverently heard, and in which the faithful participate in sacramental worship, deserve fuller treatment than I have given to them thus far. In the present chapter I propose to look more closely into this theme, retaining, as I do so, the ecumenical perspective of the immediately preceding chapter.

The Priestly Office of Christ and the Church

According to a common theological schematization often attributed to John Calvin, and accepted in many other traditions, Christ exercises a threefold office as prophet, priest, and king. In his prophetic role he teaches in the name of God. In his priestly capacity he offers sacrifice, intercedes for sinners, and communicates God's favor and grace. In his royal function, he inaugurates the kingdom of God and brings it to completion. The three offices overlap and interpenetrate, but for some purposes they may usefully be distinguished.

All three of these titles are predicated of Christ in the New Testament, but the priestly role bears most directly on Christ's activity as savior and is the function most intimately connected with worship. Worship, as I understand it, is the basic human response to God as holy presence. It is an attitude of total and loving submission to God's sovereign wisdom, goodness, and power. Worship expresses itself in a great variety of acts, such as adoration, praise, thanksgiving, contrition, sacrifice, and obedience.

Worship can be either private or public. Individuals and voluntary groups can worship God when and as they feel moved to do so. Christians are able to offer public worship to God when the Church, the body of Christ, gathers to celebrate the liturgy. Worship in the broad sense includes all acts of religion, but in a narrower sense it is verified in ritual activity, especially that of the Church as an organized community.

The New Testament frequently attributes priestly functions to Christ. It portrays him as the great high priest who offered prayers and supplications to God (Heb. 5:7) and surrendered himself once for all as a spotless victim (Heb. 9:12–14). Having humbled himself, becoming obedient even to the point of death, he was exalted, so that every knee should bend to him and every tongue confess that he is Lord (Phil. 2:8–11; cf. Heb. 5:8). His death on the Cross is considered the fulfillment of the sacrifices of ancient Israel (Heb. 9:1–28), especially the Paschal Lamb (1 Cor. 5:7). Through his blood Jesus mediates the new covenant (Heb. 12:24) and expiates the sins of the whole world (1 John 2:2; Rom. 3:25). Raised to heavenly glory, Jesus continues to make intercession for sinners (Heb. 7:25; 1 John 2:1). All of these ministries pertain to the category of worship.

Christ delivered himself up for the Church as his bride, to sanctify her and make her without spot or blemish (Eph. 5:25–27). He commissioned the Church to perpetuate on earth, with his promised help, the threefold ministry of making disciples, teaching his way of life, and baptizing (Matt. 28:19–20). In its prophetic capacity it must teach the revelation of Christ; in its royal function it must advance the reign of God, and in its priestly role it must free people from the bondage of sin and bring forth fruits of holiness.

The New Testament depicts the Christian community as a holy priesthood called to offer spiritual sacrifices (1 Pet. 2:5). Through Christ it offers God a continual sacrifice of praise (Heb. 13:15). The members of the Church are constituted as a kingdom of priests (Rev. 1:6; cf. 5:10). They are to announce the praise of Christ, who has called them to eternal life (1 Pet. 2:9). Not content to offer praise with their lips, they are to offer their bodies as a living sacrifice (Rom. 12:1), giving themselves up to death for the sake of Jesus (2 Cor. 4:11) and thus making themselves a fragrant incense (2 Cor.2:15). Setting an example for his followers, Paul allows his life to be poured out as a libation (Phil. 2:17; 2 Tim. 4:6).

In its formal worship the Church anticipates the heavenly liturgy. It addresses God gratefully in psalms, hymns, and spiritual songs (Col. 3:16; cf. Eph. 5:19) and thereby joins in the eternal worship offered by the saints and angels before the throne of the Lamb (Rev. 4:4–5:14). Built on the foundation of the apostles and prophets, the Church grows into a temple sacred to the Lord, a dwelling place for God in the Spirit (Eph. 2:20–22). It looks forward to the day when the whole Church in glory will adore God and "the Lamb who was slain" (Rev. 5:12; 22:3).

The entire Church is called to prayer and sacramental worship. Already in baptism the Christian is conformed to Christ's death and raised up with him to a life of invisible union with God (Rom. 6:3–4; Eph. 2:6; Col. 2:12). Sanctified and cleansed "by the washing of water with the word" (Eph. 5:26), Christians are called to partake of the sufferings of Christ and by this means to find the way to share in his glory (Rom. 8:17; Col. 1:24; 2 Tim. 2:11; 1 Pet. 4:13).

Through the Eucharist the Christian becomes still more deeply incorporated into the body of Christ (1 Cor.10:17). In the Eucharistic memorial (*anamnesis*), which shows forth the death of the Lord until he comes, the faithful receive the body and blood of Christ and are obliged to discern it in faith lest they partake unworthily, to their own judgment (1 Cor.11:23–29). The community of the disciples after Pentecost devotes itself steadfastly "to the apostles' teaching and fellowship, to the breaking of bread and the prayers" (Acts 2:42). Essentially, then, it is a community of worship.

Lex Orandi/Lex Credendi

I think it important to recognize that there is a certain reciprocity between the priestly and the prophetic, with the result that prayer and belief mutually assist each other. In elucidating this relationship I hope to cast some light on a common source of misunderstanding between Protestants and Catholics. Protestants tend to certify their beliefs by appeal to Scripture, which they frequently read with the help of historical-critical method, and to reject doctrines that cannot be established from this source. Catholics, conversely, treat the Scriptures as an irreplaceable record of the faith of the early Church, but not as an exclusive font of doctrine. They expect that the Church, as it prays, worships, and reflects on its faith in new and changing circumstances, will gain insights that go beyond what is explicit in the biblical texts. They are content if the doctrine of the Church does not contradict the Scriptures and can be seen as a development from what is seminally in the inspired record.

This difference of perspectives may be seen as involving different attitudes toward the ancient maxim *lex orandi/lex credendi.* It will be instructive, I believe, to inquire how that maxim came into being and functioned at various points in the history of the Church. Is there a strict mutuality between faith and prayer, or does the one have precedence in time or dignity over the other? If so, which enjoys the priority? What precisely is the "prayer" that can constitute a law even for believing?

The key reference in this discussion is the famous *Indiculus gratiae* of Pope Celestine I (422–32). This document consists of a letter of the pope followed by a number of "chapters," as they are called. The chapters are today attributed to the lay monk Prosper of Aquitaine, a moderate disciple of Augustine. They affirm a basically Augustinian position on grace and free will against the views then held by some theologians whom we would today call Semi-Pelagians.

The first seven chapters of the *Indiculus* summarize the decrees of the Holy See against Pelagius and his followers. They teach that the initial impulse toward faith, further progress in the Christian life, and final perseverance are all attributable to the grace of Christ. Then in chapter 8 the document continues:

Besides these decrees, let us also examine the sacred words of the prayers the priests say. Let us examine these sacred words that were handed down from the apostles throughout the world and are uniformly used in every Catholic church, so that the law of supplication may establish the law of believing (*ut legem credendi lex statuat supplicandi*). For when the leaders of the holy people perform the functions of the office entrusted to them, they plead the cause of the human race before the tribunal of the divine mercy. And with the whole Church earnestly praying along with them, they beg and entreat that faith may be given to infidels, that idolaters may be freed from the errors of their ungodliness, that the veil may be removed from the hearts of the

Jews and that the light of truth may shine on them, that heretics may come to their senses and accept the Catholic faith, that schismatics may receive the spirit of renewed charity, that sinners may be given the healing powers of repentance and, finally, that catechumens may be brought to the sacrament of regeneration and that the heavenly court of mercy may be opened to them. That these requests to the Lord are not just perfunctory or useless is shown by the actual course of events. For God, indeed, deigns to draw many from errors of every description, having rescued them from the power of darkness and transferred them into the kingdom of his beloved Son.[1]

As most Catholics (and some members of other traditions) will recognize, Prosper is here referring to the intercessions in the Good Friday liturgy on behalf of infidels, Jews, heretics, schismatics, lapsed Catholics, and catechumens. These prayers, according to Prosper, are in full agreement with the teaching of the Holy See on grace, which he has previously summarized. The prayers themselves rest on apostolic authority and are uniformly celebrated in all Catholic churches throughout the world. Because the law of supplication is so solidly founded, it serves to establish or confirm the law of belief.

When Prosper speaks of the "law of supplication" he does not simply mean the Church's practice in praying. Rather, he means the way the Church is required to pray in view of the teaching of the apostles found in Scripture. In a parallel passage from his *The Call of All Nations* Prosper makes it clear that he has in mind the precept given in 1 Timothy 2:1–4:

The Apostle commands — rather the Lord speaking through the Apostle commands through him — *that supplications and intercessions, thanksgivings be made for all men, for kings and for all that are in high station.* All priests and all the faithful adhere unanimously to this norm of supplication in their devotions. There is no part of the world in which Christian peoples do not offer up these prayers.[2]

Prosper, therefore, is saying that the requirements of faith can be inferred from the requirements for proper worship. In instructing the Church how to pray the apostle is implicitly teaching what it should believe. In this instance the requirements of prayer are laid down in Scripture, to which Prosper appeals as his primary authoritative source.

In recalling Prosper's argument against the Pelagians of his day, I am not introducing some recondite point, some idiosyncratic theory of an obscure theologian. On the contrary, I am giving a classic illustration of the kind of process that has been regularly at work when the Church has attempted to impart its doctrine to new members and to defend that doctrine against heretical deviations.

The close bond between prayer and doctrine can already be noted in the New Testament. The divinity of Christ gradually emerged as an article of the Church's faith because the community in its prayer had from the beginning called upon Jesus as Lord. Jesus was addressed as *kyrios* or, in Aramaic, *mar.*

One of the earliest prayers of the Church is surely the petition *maranatha,* meaning "Come, Lord Jesus!" (1 Cor. 16:22; cf. Rev. 22:20). This prayer attests to the Church's faith in the present lordship of the risen Christ as well as its expectation that he would return in glory to establish his definitive reign. Seeking to give an account of what the Christians believed, Pliny the Younger in his letter to the Emperor Trajan (about A.D. 112) perceptively focused on their worship. The Christians, he reported, sang hymns to Christ as to a god (*Christo quasi deo*).

The divinity of Christ is proclaimed in a number of New Testament hymns that presumably antedate both the Pauline epistles and the Gospels.[3] A clear example is the hymn of Phil. 2:5–11, which proclaims that every knee must bow to him who has received the Name above all names. But there are many other examples, such as the heavenly liturgy described in the Book of Revelation:

> Worthy is the Lamb who was slain, to receive power and wealth and wisdom and might and honor and glory and blessing! . . . To him who sits upon the throne and to the Lamb be blessing and honor and glory and might for ever and ever! (Rev. 5:12–13)

By teaching Christians how to pray, the biblical authors taught them what they should believe.

The influence of the baptismal and eucharistic liturgy on other aspects of Christian doctrine is not difficult to trace.[4] The clearest trinitarian text in the entire New Testament is contained in Matthew 28:20, which presumably reproduces a formula used in the baptismal ritual. Paul's teaching on original and baptismal regeneration is worked out through his reflections on the baptismal rite, which calls for a symbolic immersion in water and a reemergence in a purified state. The Church's teaching on the Eucharist likewise grows out of the liturgy. The "institution narratives" in the Synoptic Gospels and in 1 Corinthians, chapter 11, are generally held by New Testament scholars to include borrowings from liturgical formulas.

In the early centuries the instruction of catechumens and neophytes was centered about the sacraments of initiation. The baptismal interrogations and responses are the seedbed of the earliest creeds. The bishop was expected to impart the fundamental doctrines of the faith by explaining to the neophytes the meaning of the initiatory sacraments. Examples have come down to us in the mystagogical catechesis of bishops such as Cyril of Jerusalem, Ambrose of Milan, John Chrysostom, and Theodore of Mopsuestia.[5]

In its struggle against heresy the Church defined the orthodox teaching, to a great extent, by drawing out the implications of the approved liturgy. The official prayer of the Church served as a norm for the articulation of its faith. Some examples from the patristic age should suffice to establish this point beyond doubt.

— Ignatius of Antioch refutes the Docetists on the ground that their disparagement of the body contradicts the truth conveyed by Christ's real and bodily presence in the Eucharist.

— Irenaeus uses the materiality of the Eucharist as evidence that cosmic matter is not evil and that it was created by the same God whom Christians worship as the Father of Jesus Christ, both of which points were denied by the Gnostics.

— Tertullian appeals to the sacraments to demonstrate against the Gnostics that Christ saves the body as well as the soul. "The flesh," he wrote, "is the hinge of salvation" (*caro salutis est cardo*).[6]

— In his debate with Cyprian about the validity of baptism by heretics, Pope Stephen rests his case for validity on the tradition of the Roman church, which laid on hands but did not rebaptize Christians coming from heresy into the unity of the Catholic fold. In defending the Roman practice he enunciates the famous principle, "Let nothing be innovated beyond what has been handed down."[7]

— Ambrose warns his hearers against the subordinationism of the Arians by calling their attention to the fact that the neophytes, at baptism, confessed their faith in each of the three divine persons in identical terms ("I believe in....").

— Optatus and Augustine, in their debates with the Donatists, argue that the practice of the universal Church, in its toleration of sinful ministers, cannot be at fault. Even priests, they point out, are expected to pray daily to the Father, "Forgive us our sins."

— In his anti-Pelagian works, Augustine argues repeatedly from the liturgy, anticipating some of the arguments we have already found in his disciple Prosper of Aquitaine. To establish that all are born in a state of original sin, Augustine mentions not only the Church's prayers for unbelievers but the practice of infant baptism, together with the exorcisms and exsufflations that accompanied the baptism.

— Augustine, again, argues for the existence of Purgatory from the practice of the Church in praying for the dead.

— In the East the divinity of the Holy Spirit was affirmed indirectly in the creed of Constantinople by reference to the liturgical practice of the Church. Without directly calling the Holy Spirit God, the creed says simply that the Holy Spirit is "adored and glorified" together with the Father and the Son. The faithful were expected to come to a recognition that the Spirit was God from the way in which they prayed.

— The practice of the Church was directly at issue in the Iconoclastic Controversy. The Second Council of Nicaea (A.D. 787), in approving the veneration of images, resoundingly reaffirmed the constant usage of the Church at prayer.

Furthermore, in the Middle Ages theologians regularly argued not only from the words but from the gestures and actions of the liturgy to establish doctrinal points. St. Bernard and St. Thomas Aquinas both maintain that because the Church has a feast of the birth of Mary, Mary could not have been born in a state of original sin.[8] In discussing whether the transubstantiation of the host takes place before the consecration of the chalice, St. Thomas argues that it does, because the host is elevated and adored before the words of consecration are spoken over the chalice.[9]

Because the liturgy has always been a major source for the instruction of priests and faithful, the Church has been solicitous to protect it from unauthorized tampering. Heretics have continually sought to alter the words and gestures of the Church by introducing compositions of their own. Cyprian complained that the Novatians had introduced illicit words into the Eucharistic liturgy. The Ebionites, Valentinus, Paul of Samosata, Arius, and other heretics made improper innovations. In the sixteenth century, Lutherans, Calvinists, and Anglicans expunged major portions from the liturgy of the Mass and the other sacraments. In doing so, they were reforming the liturgy to reflect their own understanding of the word of God. This was in effect a reversal, but not precisely a denial, of the principle of Prosper that the law of prayer establishes the law of belief. The very recognition that the liturgy needed to be changed was an implicit recognition that the prayer of the Church has a powerful impact on the beliefs of the faithful.

Influence of Belief on Forms of Worship

Although initially the law of supplication was seen as grounding the law of belief, it gradually became common, even in the Catholic Church, for the law of belief to be used to modify the law of prayer. In the Latin Church from the fifth century onward, many collects were introduced that have a strong anti-Pelagian tenor. Josef A. Jungmann showed how the medieval liturgy, especially in the East, was modified in an anti-Arian direction. In place of prayers and doxologies addressed to the Father *through* the Son, formulas glorifying the Father *together with* the Son and the Holy Spirit were preferred.[10]

In the Modernist period, George Tyrrell made much of the axiom *lex orandi/lex credendi,* but he interpreted it as though it meant that popular devotions were normative for belief. This was a new principle quite different from anything intended by Prosper of Aquitaine and the classical tradition. Tyrrell was, in fact, a kind of religious empiricist. Theology and official teaching, he maintained, should let themselves be governed by the "facts" of the spiritual life. He believed that the faithful, when they pray, experience the presence of the Spirit, though he also recognized that popular devotions sometimes tended to get out of hand. Church authority may then intervene, he conceded, but only by "applying and enforcing the original *lex orandi.*"[11]

From the sixteenth century until well into the twentieth, the magisterium has taken on a progressively greater role in shaping the liturgy of the Catholic Church. Reacting to some degree against the Modernists, Pius XII in his encyclical on the liturgy, *Mediator Dei* (1947), treated the *lex orandi* axiom with great reserve. While acknowledging that liturgy has been used to provide important indications for deciding certain doctrinal questions, he declared that, speaking in absolute and general terms, the law of belief should determine the law of worship, for the liturgy is subject to the supreme teaching authority of the Church (§48). Although Prosper of Aquitaine, with his great veneration for the teaching authority of Rome, would not have contradicted Pius XII, a certain change of perspective is palpable. For Prosper the liturgy was still seen to be an independent stream of tradition, coming down from the apostles and reflecting the faith as held throughout the Catholic Church. Precisely because of its relative independence it had, he believed, a capacity to confirm the teaching of the Roman see. For Pius XII the liturgy was valuable because it presumably reflected the teaching of the Roman magisterium, which had authorized it.

The *Lex Orandi* and the Development of Marian Dogma

Mariology is one area in which popular devotion has had a significant impact on the development of dogma. Already at Ephesus in A.D. 431 the intense devotion of the Egyptian monks played a role in obtaining the Council's approval of the title *theotokos* (God-bearer). Devotion, however, did not have exclusive sway. The title was also justified by theological arguments. Cyril of Alexandria and others expounded the principles for applying the attributes of Christ's human nature to him as a divine person. By virtue of the interchange of predicates (*communicatio idiomatum*), they held, it was legitimate to speak of the incarnate Son, divine though he was, as having a human mother, and conversely of the mother as having brought forth God the Son.

In the Middle Ages popular devotion to Mary ran somewhat ahead of both dogma and liturgy. Although the feast of Mary's birth was celebrated from early times, the feast of her conception was resisted by important theologians and was actually suppressed for a while in England under William the Conqueror (1066–87). But enthusiasm for the feast was rekindled in England, France, and elsewhere in the twelfth century. Only by the fourteenth century did theologians begin to work out a theory to explain how the Immaculate Conception of Mary could be reconciled with the dogma of original sin. From the fifteenth century to the nineteenth, the papal magisterium took an increasingly benign attitude toward the feast, gradually extending it, in response to numerous petitions, to the universal Church.

In defining the Immaculate Conception in 1854, Pius IX alluded to the *lex orandi,* interpreting it in accordance with his own authoritarian outlook as a vehicle of papal teaching. "Our Predecessors, indeed, by virtue of their apostolic authority, gloried in instituting the feast of the Conception, with its own office and its own Mass, in the Roman Church. . . . Finally, . . . they were pleased to grant, with the greatest satisfaction, permission to proclaim the Immaculate Conception in the Litany of Loreto and in the Preface of that Mass, so that the rule of prayer might thus serve to establish the rule of belief."[12]

The dogma of the Assumption is in many ways a parallel case. As a belief, it antedates the Immaculate Conception and is traceable to several seventh-century Byzantine theologians. The Assumption or Dormition of Mary was celebrated in certain Eastern liturgies as early as the sixth century. The belief never encountered the kind of resistance that the dogma of the Immaculate Conception did. It was unanimously held, at least as a "pious belief," by the great Scholastic *doctores,* including Bonaventure and Thomas Aquinas, and has encountered practically no opposition from Catholic theologians since their day. When defining the dogma in 1950, Pius XII used the liturgical argument, among others. Referring to what he himself had said in *Mediator Dei,* he appealed to the liturgical offices in the East and West commemorating the Dormition or Assumption. But he added this caution:

> However, since the liturgy of the Church does not engender the Catholic faith, but rather springs from it, in such a way that the practices of the sacred worship proceed from the faith as the fruit comes from the tree, it follows that the holy fathers and the great doctors, in the homilies and sermons they gave the people on this feast day, did not draw their teaching from the feast itself as from a primary source, but rather they spoke of this doctrine as something already known and accepted by Christ's faithful.[13]

We may conclude, then, that the *lex orandi* played a real but modest part in bringing about the Catholic dogmas of the Immaculate Conception and the Assumption. Many centuries before their definition, these beliefs were expressed in the prayer and devotion of the people and in the writings of certain spiritual teachers; they came to be celebrated in local liturgies. Only subsequently did the doctrines come to be held by numerous and important theologians, who appraised the popular beliefs by subjecting them to theological reasoning. When this stage was achieved, the popes permitted the feasts to be publicly celebrated in the universal Church. In authorizing the feasts, with their proper offices and Mass texts, the popes were, perhaps unconsciously, preparing the ground for the ultimate definition of the dogmas. The *lex orandi*, while in some respects preceding the *lex credendi*, was confirmed and regulated by the latter. The existence of local feasts in patristic and medieval times offered some positive, independent confirmation for the more recent papal teaching.

Ecumenical Implications

Whether the law of prayer governs the law of believing, or vice versa, it appears from all the cases here surveyed that the two finally coalesce and support one another. As the Church prays, so it believes; as it believes, so too it prays. It would be too simple, however, to imagine that the language of prayer and that of dogma totally coincide. In worship, the Church appeals more to the imagination and the emotions; it has more ready recourse to metaphor. Dogma tends to be framed in a more conceptually precise, and frequently philosophical, vocabulary. Hence a certain bridge has to be crossed from the figurative language of devotion to the prose of dogmatic statement. Some of the titles conferred on Our Lady in the Litany of Loreto, such as "Mystical Rose" and "Tower of Ivory," do not easily lend themselves to dogmatic transcription.

The Lutheran theologian Edmund Schlink, in a famous essay on "The Structure of Dogmatic Statements as an Ecumenical Problem," called attention to the differences between doxology and teaching.[14] He noted that in ecumenical circles the churches find it far easier to pray and confess together than to make common dogmatic declarations. In praying and confessing their faith, Schlink believed, Christians remain relatively close to the experience of the encounter with God. Such language is therefore primary. While dogmatic statements may at times be necessary, they should be recognized as secondary and derivative. In modern ecumenism, he proposed, some scope could be accorded for variety in dogmatic statements as expressions of one and the same faith. This seminal essay of Schlink has been extremely fruitful in ecumenical dialogues, and its promise, in my opinion, has not yet been exhausted.

The Catholic theologian Yves Congar, seeking a way of overcoming the doctrinal impasses between the Orthodox and Catholic Churches on the procession of the Holy Spirit, suggests that ecumenists should see how the differing formulas actually function in the worship of the churches:

> The confessing community lives out its faith by celebrating it. It is no coincidence that in Scripture the doxologies are the best expression of the dogmatic content of faith. The church prays, sings, and celebrates its faith. Dogma is only a landmark, holy though it may be, in the church's experience of the fullness of its faith which it attains by celebrating it. There is nothing more profound and decisive than faith lived out, expressed in spiritual life and prayer. Now despite the difference in dogmatic formulae, that faith is the same, and it is lived and prayed out similarly in both West and East.[15]

Under the impact of a variety of influences, including linguistic philosophy, some contemporary theologians make a sharper opposition between worship and belief. Prayer, they assert, uses the language of love; dogma, that of fact. Theologians such as Maurice Wiles and Paul Knitter believe that we can achieve more harmonious relations among the religions if we recognize that our worship-language must not be taken literally. Members of each religion, they contend, should feel free to call upon their own savior figures and confess what they owe to these figures, but no one should make unfavorable judgments regarding other religions. As Knitter puts it: "We are persuaded by those who speak with deep conviction of what their savior has done for them. We are not persuaded by those who tell us, with deep conviction, 'my savior is bigger than yours.' "[16]

If there were no such thing as dogma, the positions of Wiles and Knitter might have a certain plausibility. But the Church has meditated on the meanings of the biblical and liturgical formulations and has seen fit to affirm in clear prose that Jesus Christ is the one and only incarnation of God and that he is the center and goal of all human and cosmic history. According to the Christian faith, as defined by several councils, Jesus is the savior of the whole world. Pope John Paul II in his encyclical *Redemptoris missio* (1990) emphatically teaches that Christ alone is the one mediator of all salvation (§§4–6). A distinction between the language of dogma and that of worship is no help here, because both worship and dogma make the same claims. As the Church prays, so she believes.

It is imperative not to let the links between worship and dogma be dissolved. The maxim *lex orandi/lex credendi* needs to be put to work in both directions. We must interpret the liturgy in the light of the declared faith of the Church, and we must contemplate the dogmatic inheritance as an outgrowth of the Church's corporate worship. Without renouncing essential points of their faith, Christians cannot deny that God the Son became incarnate in Jesus of Nazareth, and in him alone. If it is to make its distinctive contribution to the world, Christianity must zealously protect the essentials of its faith.

A difficulty in our time is that Christians lack the solidarity in prayer and worship that was characteristic of the early centuries. As Prosper and his contemporaries recognized, the united prayer of the Church all over the world is a powerful bastion against schism and heresy. More perhaps than any other agency, the liturgy gathers God's people into unity. It cuts across all divisions of class, race, gender, and age, and establishes them in a communion that knows no bounds of time or space.

If the positions of this chapter have any validity, it may be hoped that by placing greater emphasis on worship and attending more closely to the logic of prayer and devotion, the churches will find themselves on a path of convergence. In worship the Church does not simply act on its own initiative. It submits to the present lordship of Christ and invokes his Spirit to be its guide. For this reason, perhaps, the prayers and hymns of the various churches have wider ecumenical currency than their doctrinal formulations. Worship itself, moreover, "releases the urge to make visible the congregation of all believers in Christ."[17] To a remarkable degree the hymns of Lutherans, Anglicans, Methodists, Catholics, and Orthodox are in ecumenical currency. Reading the same Scriptures, celebrating the sacraments as signs of Christian unity, and observing together the major feasts of the Christian year, the churches may hope to find ways of achieving greater consensus in matters of doctrine.

14.

Historical Method and the Reality of Christ

After a period of relative quiescence, the quest of the historical Jesus has again become lively. The revival was marked by the appearance of two major contributions — John P. Meier's *A Marginal Jew*[1] and John Dominic Crossan's *The Historical Jesus*[2] — both of which were published just before Christmas 1991. The criticisms and countercriticisms of these and similar books have focused primarily on issues of method. The current interest in these questions calls for a more ample discussion of the relations between faith and biblical history, treated rather summarily under the rubric of "historical reconstruction" in chapter 5 above.

The quest of the historical Jesus is not an idle pastime. It began in the eighteenth century as a fierce attack on the Christ of faith. Throughout the nineteenth century its aim was to establish another Christ to replace the Christ of dogma. In the words of Albert Schweitzer, who wrote the classic history of the early quest, "The dogma had first to be shattered before men could once more go out in quest of the historical Jesus, before they could even grasp the thought of his existence."[3] The assault on orthodox belief has not died out. Many historians of the present day share the same animus.

Can believers be indifferent to the historical quest? Can they keep their faith intact while letting historians do what they please with the Jesus of flesh and blood? Can they let go of the historical grounds that have heretofore sustained Christians in their belief? These questions raise difficult and fundamental issues about what faith is, what history is, and how the two are related.

For purposes of this chapter faith will be understood as a firm adherence to a total vision of reality in the light of God's revealing word. For Christians that word comes to us preeminently in Christ, as he is known through the canonical Scriptures and the teaching of the Church. Faith involves a free, reasonable assent made possible by the grace of God, which enables us to discern and confidently embrace God's revealing word.

The Concept of History

The concept of history is complex and controverted. In the broadest sense the term includes all past events, especially those concerned with humankind. In a more specific, but still broad, sense, it means a narrative of such past events. A "history" in this sense can recount anything we know, or think we know, about the human past, whether based on faith, on vague general impressions, or on methodical investigation.

In a narrower sense "history" is knowledge derived by means of a recognized method devised to provide reliable access to the human past. The method involves a kind of detective work by which we critically use the available sources, including documents that testify to past events. Applied to Christian origins, historical method will seek to ferret out the earliest and most reliable reports about Jesus and, from them, to reconstruct the sayings and deeds that may most plausibly be attributed to Jesus and his circle.

There are no rules that automatically determine what accounts are to be accepted as accurate. Historians generally rely on rules of thumb.[4] For instance, they prefer accounts that can be traced to early witnesses and those that are attested by several independent sources. They are also inclined to credit reports that present Jesus as saying and doing what the Jews of his day would have avoided and assertions that would be embarrassing to the early Church. This "principle of discontinuity" (as it is often called) does not presuppose that Jesus was never in agreement with the Jews of his day or that his character and doctrine were generally out of phase with the teaching of the early Church, but rests on the premise that the early tradition or the New Testament authors would probably not have imputed to Jesus actions or statements that were at odds with their own expectations about him.

To give more precision to their method, some historians make assumptions of a philosophical character. According to a positivist view that was widely accepted fifty or a hundred years ago, history is a science analogous to physics or chemistry. It proceeds on the assumption that the world is a closed system in which causes and effects are connected by strict necessity. History, in that view, leaves no place for the unique, the exceptional, and especially not for events brought about by God's direct activity. On positivist grounds many historians wrote off the Gospels as unreliable, insofar as they portrayed Jesus as a utterly unique figure, conscious of a special relationship to God, and working miracles by divine power.

This positivist view is not convincing. The historian cannot antecedently rule out the possibility that something unique and unparalleled might happen, especially if God were to act freely in the world. If positivist rules were adopted, history and faith would be on a collision course from the beginning.

Does the possibility of miraculous or supernatural events introduce a surd and thereby destroy the intelligibility of history? This might be the case if God frequently interposed his action without any plan or reason. In the view of theology, however, God respects the order of created causality that he himself has established. If he intervenes, he does so rarely and according to a rationale that has its own intelligibility. Where serious grounds exist for suspecting that God has acted in a direct, supernatural way, historians cannot dismiss the evidence in the name of historical integrity. They are invited to look higher and to enter into dialogue with theologians. Such dialogue is necessary for the sake of history itself. The theological intelligibility of the alleged event, as an integral part of God's redemptive plan, should enter into the assessment of the credibility of the reports. History, therefore, can profit from associating itself with theology.

In their quest for the historical Jesus, scholars have adopted four different basic approaches, which illustrate different ways of treating the relationship between history and faith. In what follows each approach will be briefly expounded and evaluated from a theological point of view.

First Approach: History against Faith

According to the first position, history is antithetical to faith. The quest of the historical Jesus, as I have said, arose from hostility to dogma. In the works of Hermann Samuel Reimarus, David Friedrich Strauss, Ernest Renan, and others, efforts were made to substitute a purely human Jesus of history for the Christ of faith and dogma. This effort still goes on in our day, as may be seen from the works of John Allegro, Rudolf Augstein, Morton Smith, Thomas Sheehan, and A. N. Wilson. Another partisan of this effort, Paul Hollenbach, asserts that the Jesus of history is to be sought "in order to overthrow, not simply correct, [what José Porfirio Miranda calls] 'the mistake called Christianity.' " The mistake, according to Hollenbach, was the "divinization of Jesus as Son of David, Christ, Son of God, Second Person in the Trinity, etc."[5]

This use of history is of course unacceptable to Christian believers. They reply that antidogmatic historians are dogmatic in their own way, since they antecedently rule out the unique and the transcendent. Their approach ruptures the continuity between Jesus and the community of his followers. It does violence to the sources by expunging sayings and deeds of Jesus that are attested by what, according to the standard criteria, must be regarded as early and reliable traditions. Having reduced Jesus to the stature of a common rabbi, prophet, or wonder worker, this approach has difficulty in accounting for the passionate loyalty of Jesus' followers, for the bitter hostility of his adversaries, and for the rapid emergence of Christianity as a distinct religious faith.

Crossan's book *The Historical Jesus* in some ways resembles the first approach just described. Setting out from a rather eccentric reconstruction of the earliest Christian sources, he portrays Jesus as a "peasant Jewish Cynic," whose conception of the kingdom of God involved "a religious and economic egalitarianism that negated alike and at once the hierarchical and patronal normalcies of Jewish religion and Roman power" (421–22). Crossan describes Jesus as a magician bent on subverting the existing social structures. He denies the historicity of the Last Supper, including the institution of the Eucharist. He likewise rejects the stories about the burial of Jesus and the discovery of the empty tomb. The earliest accounts, he believes, saw no need for resurrection appearances between the departure of Jesus and his now imminent return in glory. But Crossan does not portray himself as opposing the Christ of dogma. In fact, he defends the assertion that Jesus was wholly God and wholly man. "I find, therefore, no contradiction between the historical Jesus and the defined Christ, no betrayal whatsoever in the move from Jesus to Christ" (424).

Unlike many representatives of the first approach, Crossan is not opposed to Christologies that go beyond the historically reconstructed Jesus. In the Epilogue to his *The Historical Jesus* and even more clearly in a later volume, *Jesus: A Revolutionary Biography*,[6] he speaks of a dialectic between the historical Jesus and the confessional Christ. The two are not identical but are interrelated. The Christologies of the past, he maintains, must be continually updated in the light of changing judgments about the Jesus of history. Relying on modern investigation, he characterizes the New Testament accounts of the Nativity and Easter and the nature miracles of Jesus as historicized myths conveying a symbolic message. In requiring dogma to be revised to conform to the latest historical conjectures, he gives his own peculiar brand of academic history the upper hand over faith.

Second Approach: Separation between History and Faith

The second approach may be called separationist. It maintains that history and faith, if each keeps within proper bounds, can neither confirm nor contradict one another. History deals with empirical facts of the human past that are accessible to any rational person who uses historical method. Faith, on the other hand, deals with transcendent realities that are known only by revelation, freely accepted by religious believers thanks to the grace of God. The Jesus who lived and died in Palestine belongs to history; the living, risen Christ belongs to faith. This, roughly speaking, was the position of the dialectical theologians between the First and Second World Wars, particularly Rudolf Bultmann and Paul Tillich.

To judge from the first volume of his *A Marginal Jew*, the Catholic exegete John P. Meier is not far removed from this second position. Since his views are subject to clarification and modification in future volumes, one can speak only tentatively at this point. It is also uncertain whether his method reflects his personal preferences or his desire to reach out to a wider audience, including non-Christians. In any case he keeps the Christ of faith well insulated from historical scrutiny, so that as a historian he can let the chips fall where they may. Agreeing with Bultmann and his school that "the Jesus of history is not and cannot be the object of Christian faith," he writes:

> In the historical-critical framework, the "real" has been defined — and has to be defined — in terms of what exists within this world of time and space, what can be experienced in principle by any observer, and what can be reasonably deduced or

inferred from such experience. Faith and Christian theology, however, affirm ultimate realities beyond what is merely empirical or provable by reason: e.g., the triune God and the risen Jesus. (197)

A little later Meier writes: "In the realm of faith and theology the 'real Jesus,' the only Jesus existing here and now, is this risen Lord, to whom access is given only in faith" (198).

Meier admits that there must be some continuity between the Jesus of history and the Christ of faith (5), since the risen Jesus was previously the man from Nazareth. But he leaves it unclear whether any particular assertions about the earthly career of Jesus are required by faith. His discussion of the virginal conception of Jesus, the "brothers and sisters" of Jesus, and Jesus' resurrection may be used as examples.

Having postulated that the historian cannot affirm the miraculous, Meier is faced with a serious problem in dealing with the biblical accounts of the conception of Jesus. He makes a great deal of the position of some radical Catholic exegetes such as Rudolf Pesch, for whom the virginal conception is not a matter of faith. These authors, Meier notes, call the virginal conception a *theologoumenon* (220, 244–45) — a term generally meaning "a theological narrative that does not represent a historical event."[7] While giving special prominence to this opinion in order "to indicate that my own position is not predetermined by confessional concerns" (245), he does point out in a footnote that some more conservative theologians such as Rahner and Kasper refuse to consider the virginal conception an open question. As a believer Meier presumably accepts the virginal conception, but it is difficult to discern this belief from his book. Since the infancy narratives deny that Jesus was the biological son of Joseph, Meier can give only a weak response to the charge that Jesus was an illegitimate child.

The same methodological difficulty underlies Meier's treatment of the abiding virginity of Mary. After explaining that he is prescinding from what is known by faith and later Church teaching, Meier goes on to maintain that, on purely historical grounds, it is more likely than not that the "brothers and sisters" of Jesus mentioned in the New Testament were true siblings (331). He vigorously attacks several modern Catholic exegetes who have tried to interpret the New Testament in accord with the Catholic doctrine of the perpetual virginity of Mary. When asserting that Jesus was survived by Mary his mother, Meier observes: "If it be granted that she would have been about fourteen years old when Jesus was born, and if it be granted that she was robust enough to bear at least six other children, there is nothing improbable about Mary's surviving Jesus" (318). It is hard for the reader to think that Meier looks upon Mary as "ever virgin."

Although Meier's first volume does not go beyond the childhood of Jesus, he announces in the Introduction that he will omit the resurrection in Part Four because it lies beyond the scope of a historical study and "can be affirmed only by fath" (13). To this it could be answered that even if the resurrection in its full reality transcends the grasp of history, it has a historical aspect. Historical research, conducted without false presuppositions, can help to establish the fact that Jesus did rise from the dead. If the resurrection was something that happened to Jesus, and not simply to the community, its occurrence would seem to be pertinent to the history of Jesus. The event of the resurrection casts a whole new light on the previous career of Jesus and gives credibility to sayings and deeds that might otherwise be dismissed as legend.

Meier repeatedly reminds his readers that he is not denying faith and revelation, only putting them in brackets. To judge from early reviews, non-Christians may find that Meier's attitude toward Jesus is not as neutral as he declares it to be. Christian believers, on the other hand, will wonder whether Meier the believer would disagree with Meier the historian. What would he say about the career of Jesus if he took his faith out of brackets? Perhaps in some other work, or in his promised Epilogue, he will find an occasion to say how his account of the history of Jesus would differ if he were to avail himself of faith.

This second approach has a degree of prima facie plausibility because as Christians we do assent to transcendent realities not knowable apart from faith in God's word. The eternal divine Sonship of Jesus and his life of glory are beyond the reach of history as a specialized discipline. But no total separation between history and faith is feasible. Catholic Christians consider themselves committed as believers to profess various facts about the earthly Jesus. While no official list is available, a good case can be made for including items such as the virginal conception of Jesus, his being Mary's only son, his consciousness of his own divinity, his miraculous and prophetic powers, his institution of the Eucharist and the apostolic ministry, his redemptive death on the cross, his empty tomb, and his bodily resurrection. If facts such as these were disproved, the faith of Catholics would be seriously affected.

Recognizing the importance of these matters for faith, the Church has considered itself obliged to defend the historical value of the Gospels. Vatican Council II, following up on several earlier pronouncements, taught that the Gospels, "whose historical character the Church unhesitatingly asserts, faithfully hand on what Jesus the Son of God, while living among men, really did and taught" (*Dei Verbum,* 19). The second approach, by severing the links between faith and history, tends to deliver the entire earthly career of Jesus to the vicissitudes of historical research, and thereby imperils the integrity of Catholic faith.

Third Approach: History as Ground of Faith

According to a third group of scholars history is the ground of faith. That is to say, historical investigation established rational foundations for the commitment of Christian faith. This position has been developed in at least three different forms.

The first is exemplified by many apologists of the early twentieth century, including Hilarin Felder and Louis Claude Fillion, who belong to the "countercritical" movement described above in chapter 1. Taking up the challenge of the rationalists, they argued that the Gospels, viewed as strictly historical sources, could provide conclusive proofs that Jesus claimed to be, and in fact was, the only-begotten Son of God.[8]

These authors used a rather naive approach, ignoring what most scholars of our own day hold about the authorship, date, and literary form of the Gospels. As a result the work of these apologists is no longer convincing. More recent apologists, such as Joachim Jeremias, take a much more sophisticated approach to the Gospels and therefore make more modest claims. Jeremias argues persuasively that Jesus was conscious of having a relationship of singular intimacy with God as his Father.[9] But it is hard to say that his arguments give more than a high probability that could be upset by further research. Few Christians would want their faith to depend on scholarly hypotheses such as these.

The second form of the view that history is the ground of faith is the so-called "new quest of the historical Jesus," instituted in the late 1950s. Several former students of Bultmann, rebelling against his divorce between faith and history, made use of a kind of existential history and tried to recreate an experience of encounter with Jesus on the basis of the earliest Gospel traditions. The works of Günther Bornkamm, Heinz Zahrnt, and James M. Robinson, representative of this school, may still be read with profit.

These works succeed, in my opinion, in achieving an impressive picture of Jesus based on the texts that have good claims to historical reliability. The members of this school, however, limit their quest to Jesus as he presented himself in his public life. They do not incorporate the further light given to the community by the events of Easter and Pentecost. Their work, like that of Jeremias, must be regarded as a helpful beginning that can put the reader on the road toward eventually accepting the Christ of faith.

The third form of this approach is represented by Wolfhart Pannenberg. For him history is the only mode of access to the reality of the past; faith gives no information in addition to history. But he defines history in a very comprehensive sense, so that it is capable of discerning the action of God. Pannenberg finds that the event of Jesus Christ, when interpreted in its own historical context, must be seen as the work of God himself, ushering in the final age of the world. Because the resurrection of Jesus is a historical fact, says Pannenberg, historical reasoning can exhibit Jesus as the self-revelation of God.[10]

Pannenberg avoids the simplistic arguments of earlier apologists. He takes a highly sophisticated approach to the Gospels and does not admit the historicity of the virginal conception. But he does affirm the historicity of the empty tomb and at least of some post-resurrection appearances. Thus he arrives at a more complete Christology than is obtainable by the existential history of the "new quest."

Some difficulties may nevertheless be raised. Pannenberg's comprehensive concept of history is so broad that it deprives history of its character as a special discipline. But even in this inclusive sense, history does not seem to terminate in a firm intellectual commitment, higher than the fluctuating judgments of probability. The historical arguments for the divinity of Jesus do not provide the full assurance of faith except for those who submit to the attraction and illumination of divine grace within the Church, to which the authoritative interpretation of the Bible has been entrusted. Pannenberg's argumentation, however, is not without value, especially for purposes of apologetics.

Fourth Approach: The Gospels as Interpreted History

Finally there is a fourth approach, the most satisfactory. It holds that Christian faith does not normally arise from, or rest upon, a critical examination of the New Testament evidence concerning the Jesus of history. Rather, it comes from God's revealing word as conveyed by the testimony of the Church. But since the word of God tells us something about past events, faith and history cannot be cleanly separated. The content of faith includes certain events that are historical in the broad sense of the term explained above.

Although they are historical in their own way, the Gospels are not merely or primarily works of history. Above all else they are Gospels — that is to say, proclamations of the good news of God's saving action in Jesus Christ. They are religious testimonies, composed for the sake of arousing and strengthening the life of faith. Richly charged with theological interpretation, they give us much deeper insight into the real meaning of Jesus than stenographic reports about him could ever do.

Because they are written with a kerygmatic and pastoral concern, the Gospels should not be judged as though they were intended to be merely factual reports. The believer cannot say a priori that every Gospel narrative is an exact account of the event. The story of Jesus has been reworked in the light of the Church's Easter faith and then further adapted to meet the needs of the particular communities for which our four Gospels were written. According to the 1964 Instruction of the Biblical Commission, modern scholarship makes it evident that "the doctrine and life of Jesus were not simply reported for the sole purpose of being remembered, but were 'preached' so as to offer the Church a basis of faith and morals." The biblical interpreter, says the Instruction, must seek to explain why the different evangelists narrated the life and words of Jesus in different ways.[11]

If they had been intended simply as historical works, the Gospels could be judged deficient. They do not satisfy our curiosity about many points. For example, they give us no description of Jesus and no exact chronology of his life. They recast many of his sayings, rearrange them into continuous discourses, combine distinct events into a single story, and take other liberties that would be unacceptable in academic history.

It is therefore legitimate and possible to probe behind the Gospels and try to reconstruct a more accurate and detailed account of the career of Jesus. For Christian believers, the intention of the quest will not be to correct the teaching of the New Testament or the established doctrines of the Church (which do not depend on positive historical verification for their validity), but rather to provide additional data and thereby give a better understanding of Christ and the Gospels.

In this further probing into the history of Jesus, the Christian believer will use many of the same procedures as the neutral or hostile historiographer. Catholic and Protestant scholars, without prejudice to their faith, make use of textual criticism, source criticism, form criticism, redaction criticism, literary criticism, and historical criticism. It is important to obtain reliable texts, to identify their literary genre, and to single out the more primitive strata of material. The properly historical phase comes with the movement from the texts, considered as data, to the words and deeds to which they refer. Applying criteria such as early attestation, multiple attestation, and discontinuity from late Judaism and from early Christianity, the historian can make more or less probable judgments about the reliability of the accounts.

It must be recognized, however, that judgments of historicity depend in great part upon antecedent presumptions. Even those who try to bracket their faith have to use some presuppositions about the kinds of reports that are to be viewed as credible. Because of differing a prioris, some historians will admit, and others will discount, revelation and miracles. In the area of religion, presuppositions make all the difference. Believers who want to recover the full truth about Jesus will wish to take advantage of the light that faith can supply. They will not assume, even for purposes of the argument, that Jesus was less than faith declares him to be. To adopt such artificial restrictions would seriously prejudice the results. Newman's critique of Paley's apologetics, quoted above, merits repetition here:

> Rules of court are dictated by what is expedient on the whole and in the long run; but they run the risk of being unjust to the claims of particular cases. Why am I to begin with taking up a position not my own, and unclothing my mind of that large outfit of existing thoughts, principles, likings, desires, and hopes, which make me what I am?[12]

Christians, convinced that Jesus was an utterly singular person, the incarnate Son of God, will be prepared to credit testimony that God acted in him in a totally unprecedented way. Faith is an advantage because it alerts us to the particular strand of history in which God has acted decisively for our salvation. But faith does not make scholarly inquiry superfluous. Certain kerygmatic and theological ingredients have to be filtered out by the critic who wishes to reconstruct, as reliably as one can, what was actually said and done by Jesus in his earthly career.

Historical method, when applied to the Gospel materials, has achieved only modest results. It has not yet led to a broad or striking consensus. Most historians can agree about a few general features of the public ministry of Jesus and the fact of his execution by the Roman authorities. But the different perspectives on the relationship between history and faith will lead to radically different views on matters of doctrinal significance, such as the filial consciousness of Jesus, his miracles, and his resurrection. Even historians who share the same faith disagree about many factual details, such as the time and place at which Jesus was born, the duration of his public ministry, his messianic or divine claims, his intent to establish a Church, the dates of his Last Supper and of the crucifixion. Different historians will provide different theories and argue for them as best they can.

Of what use, then, is this historical investigation, conducted in the light of faith? Four main values come to mind.

First, on many points qualified historians will be able to supplement the information that could be gathered from faith and Church teaching without reliance on scientific historiography. They can give us probable answers to many questions that are not settled, one way or the other, by faith and theology. For example, they may be able to tell us whether the Matthean or the Lukan form of the Beatitudes or the Lord's Prayer is closer to the actual words of Jesus and whether it is likely that the Last Supper was celebrated as a Paschal meal. History may be able to clarify Jesus' attitudes on social and political questions such as war and revolution, the rights of women and the poor. On these and many other debatable questions historical investigation provides probable answers that are of interest.

Second, by identifying certain elements in the Gospel as historically factual, the historian can on some points confirm the faith of believers. Solid arguments can be made for holding that Jesus understood himself as bringing in the final age of salvation, that he chose apostles to share in his ministry during and after his own life, that he placed Peter at the head of the apostles, that he understood himself as having a singular intimacy with his heavenly Father, that he regarded his own death as redemptive, and that he was convinced that the Father would raise him from the dead. The figure of Jesus reconstructed by technical history, incomplete and tentative though it be, can be helpful to people who are inquiring into the credibility of the Christian religion.

Third, critical study of the Gospels enables us to distinguish more clearly between the respective competences of faith and history. In some cases historical investigation stands in tension with the teaching of the Church. For example, some serious scholars, including Catholics, think that the strictly historical evidence does not favor the virginal conception of Jesus or the perpetual virginity of Mary. Even if these scholars are correct in their estimate of what "pure history" can establish (a concession that should not be too readily made), the difficulties that they raise can be taken in stride. Critical historical method does not have the last word. Faith does not rest on historical research but on the word of God authoritatively proclaimed by Scripture and tradition. As Newman said, no doctrine of the Church can be rigorously proved by history. In some cases the historical evidence may seem to favor, and in other cases to point away from, Catholic doctrines. "In all cases," Newman concluded, "there is a margin left for faith in the word of the Church. He who believes the dogmas of the Church only because he has reasoned them out of History, is scarcely a Catholic."[13]

Fourth, historical study of the New Testament may contribute to the better understanding of faith and assist in the development of Christian doctrine. According to Vatican II, the work of exegetes is one of the means through which the judgment of the Church comes to maturity (*Dei Verbum,* 12). An instance of this may be the case of Jesus' knowledge and self-consciousness. Theologians of earlier centuries often spoke of Jesus' infused knowledge in such a way as to suggest that he did not need to learn from other people, from books, or from experience. Modern biblical scholarship has helped to correct this view, and has enabled us to make the psychology of Jesus more intelligible.[14]

Anxious to take advantage of modern historical research, many thoughtful Christians look to authorized biblical commentaries to show how new findings in this area cohere with the faith and teaching of their Church. In some cases they are fortunate in finding scholarly works that bridge the gap between exegesis and theology. But their expectations are disappointed when exegetes pursue their scientific investigations with a professional narrowness that takes no account of faith and pastoral prudence.[15] Has the gap between theology and biblical scholarship become so wide that each must be pursued without reference to the other? I am confident that faith and intelligence, dogma and history, can and must be integrated. Historical scholarship, if it erects itself into a purely positive discipline independent of philosophy and faith, can only widen the gap. But, conducted in dialogue with philosophy and theology, the historical quest can contribute to a better understanding of the reality of Christ.

In our fourteen chapters we have come full circle. Our explorations have confirmed the thesis regarding postcritical theology enunciated in the first chapter. The living Christ of faith encounters us as we listen to the gospel and take part in the living community of faith. The postcritical approach does not turn its back on critical inquiry. It does not rule out the legitimacy of efforts to reconstruct the person and teaching of Jesus by "presuppositionless" methods acceptable to nonbelievers. The resulting pictures of the "historical" Jesus are always intriguing and sometimes useful in illuminating aspects of the life and personality of the Redeemer. But in no case does the method provide a religiously adequate portrait, one that can take the place of Jesus Christ as proclaimed by the Church and received in faith.

God did not intend the faith of Christians to depend on the tentative and fluctuating results of historical-critical investigation. From the earliest years the faith of the saints has been nourished by the inspired preaching of the apostles, distilled and expounded for us in the inspired pages of the New Testament. The living voice of the gospel continues to resound in and through the Church, the community of faith, where the deeper meaning of the Scriptures comes to light. Those who prayerfully meditate on the Scriptures, dwelling within the Church and its tradition, can bring forth new riches pertinent to new situations. Ceaselessly building on the foundations that have been laid, theology, like other ministries, contributes to the increase in faith of the People of God. It helps to build up the body of Christ "until we all attain to the unity of the faith and of the knowledge of the Son of God, to mature manhood, to the measure of the stature of the fullness of Christ" (Eph 4:13).

Notes

Chapter 1: Toward a Postcritical Theology

1. Four varieties of postmodern theology (revisionary, deconstructive, liberationist, and restorationist) are distinguished in David R. Griffin et al., *Varieties of Postmodern Theology* (Albany, N.Y.: State University of New York Press, 1989). This work shows a preference for revisionary theologies of the Whiteheadian, Teilhardian, and "new-age" varieties. More oriented toward a hermeneutical retrieval of the past are the contributions to the collection edited by Frederic B. Burnham, *Postmodern Theology: Christian Faith in a Pluralist World* (San Francisco: Harper & Row, 1989). A third set of essays, edited by Hans Küng and David Tracy, bears the title *Paradigm Change in Theology* (Edinburgh: T. & T. Clark, 1989). This last collection reflects the influence of the philosopher of science Thomas S. Kuhn, especially his *The Structure of Scientific Revolutions*, 2d ed. (Chicago: University of Chicago Press, 1970).

2. Hilarin Felder, *Christ and the Critics*, 2 vols. (London: Burns, Oates and Washbourne, 1924), 1:99.

3. Ibid., 1:116.

4. Michael Polanyi formulates the general principle: "Tacit knowing is more fundamental than explicit knowing: *we can know more than we can tell and we can tell nothing without relying on our awareness of things we may not be able to tell*" (*Personal Knowledge: Towards a Post-Critical Philosophy* [New York: Harper Torchbooks, 1964], x).

5. At this point I broach certain themes that will be developed below in chapter 2, "Theology and Symbolic Communication."

6. Johann Adam Möhler, *Symbolism, or Exposition of the Doctrinal Differences between Catholics and Protestants* (London: Gibbings & Co., 1906), 277.

7. John Henry Newman, *On Consulting the Faithful in Matters of Doctrine* (Kansas City, Mo.: Sheed and Ward, 1985), 73.

8. The nature of tradition is more fully explored below in chapter 6, "Tradition as a Theological Source."

9. Maurice Blondel, *History and Dogma* (New York: Holt, Rinehart and Winston, 1965), 268.

10. See further what will be said below in chapter 5, "The Uses of Scripture in Theology."

11. Albert C. Outler, "Toward a Postliberal Hermeneutics," *Theology Today* 42 (1985): 281–91, quotation from 286.

12. Michael Polanyi, "The Creative Imagination," *Chemical and Engineering News* 44 (April 25, 1966): 85–92, quotation from 88.

13. Hans Urs von Balthasar, in the introduction to his *The Glory of the Lord: A Theological Aesthetics. 1. Seeing the Form* (San Francisco: Ignatius, 1982), especially 119–24, proposes the radiance of the incarnate Word as a theological norm.

14. In the next few paragraphs I touch on questions that will be more fully discussed in later chapters, especially chapter 7, "The Magisterium and Theological Dissent."

15. The status of apologetics will be examined more thoroughly in chapter 4 below, "Fundamental Theology and the Dynamics of Conversion."

Chapter 2: Theology and Symbolic Communication

1. George A. Lindbeck, *The Nature of Doctrine* (Philadelphia: Westminster, 1984).

2. Friedrich Schleiermacher, *The Christian Faith*, 2 vols. (New York: Harper Torchbooks, 1963), 1:76, no. 15.

3. Lindbeck, *The Nature of Doctrine*, 35.

4. Ibid., 16.

5. Avery Dulles, *Models of Revelation* (Garden City, N.Y.: Doubleday, 1983), 136.

6. Avery Dulles, *The Communication of Faith and Its Content* (Washington, D.C.: National Catholic Educational Association, 1985), 6–7.

7. Vatican II, *Dei Verbum*, no. 2.

8. Geoffrey Wainwright, *Doxology: The Praise of God in Worship, Doctrine and Life* (New York: Oxford University Press, 1980), 20–21.

9. On this style of theology, see Charles A. Bernard, *Théologie symbolique* (Paris: Téqui, 1978), especially 111–35.

10. Karl Rahner, "The Theology of the Symbol," *Theological Investigations* 4 (Baltimore: Helicon, 1966), 221–52, quotation from 224.

11. Ibid., 234.

12. Karl Rahner, "Theology. I. Nature," *Encyclopedia of Theology* (New York: Seabury/Crossroad, 1975), 1686–95.

13. I have dealt with these questions to some degree in other places, e.g., "The Church and Communications: Vatican II and Beyond," in Avery Dulles, *The Reshaping of Catholicism* (San Francisco: Harper & Row, 1988), 110–31. For an overview of current literature on the theme, see Paul A. Soukop, *Communication and Theology* (London: World Association for Christian Communication, 1983).

14. For a fuller explanation of the points compressed into this paragraph, see my *Models of Revelation*, chapter 9.

15. Karl Bühler, *Sprachtheorie* (Jena: G. Fischer, 1934), summarized by René Latourelle, *Theology of Revelation* (Staten Island, N.Y.: Alba House, 1966), 316.

16. On this subject, see Karl Rahner, *Inspiration in the Bible*, rev. trans. (New York: Herder and Herder, 1964).

17. See *Dei Verbum*, nos. 8 and 21. I have dealt with Scripture and revelation in *Models of Revelation*, chapter 12. In chapters 5 and 6 below, the uses of Scripture and tradition in theology will be examined in greater detail.

18. Bernard Lonergan, *Method in Theology* (New York: Herder and Herder, 1971), 355–56, referring to the *Handbuch der Pastoraltheologie*, ed. F. X. Arnold et al. (Freiburg: Herder, 1964–69).

19. See Vatican II, *Dignitatis Humanae*, nos. 3 and 10.

20. Bernhard Häring, *Free and Faithful in Christ*, 2 vols. (New York: Seabury/Crossroad, 1979), 2:40.

21. Pontifical Commission for the Means of Social Communication, *"Communio et Progressio," Pastoral Instruction for the Application of the Decree of the Second Vatican Council on the Means of Social Communication* (Washington, D.C.: United States Catholic Conference, 1971), nos. 11, 126. See also Häring, *Free and Faithful in Christ*, 2:153–54.

22. Karl Rahner, "The Theology of the Symbol," *Theological Investigations*, 4:237.

23. Paul Ricoeur, *The Symbolism of Evil* (Boston: Beacon, 1969), 15.

24. Vatican II, *Lumen Gentium*, no. 8.

25. Karl Rahner, "On the Theology of the Incarnation," *Theological Investigations*, 4:115.

26. "For the one who understands them, miracles have their own tongue. For since Christ himself is the Word of God, every action of the Word is also a word that speaks to us" (Augustine, *In Ioh.*, tract. 24:6; PL 35:1953).

27. Karl Rahner, "Salvation. IV. Theology," *Encyclopedia of Theology*, 1527.

28. See Jörg Splett, "Symbol," *Encyclopedia of Theology*, 1654–57, especially 1657.

29. Augustine, *Confessions* X.6.

30. Jean Daniélou, *God and the Ways of Knowing* (New York: Meridian, 1957), 23.

31. Ibid., 23–28.

32. See Avery Dulles, "Revelation and Discovery," in William J. Kelly, ed., *Theology and Discovery* (Milwaukee, Wis.: Marquette University Press, 1980), 1–29.

33. See Karl Rahner, *Hominization* (New York: Herder and Herder, 1963).

34. See Michael Polanyi, "The Creative Imagination," *Chemical and Engineering News* 44 (April 25, 1966): 85–92; also Michael Polanyi and Harry Prosch, *Meaning* (Chicago: University of Chicago Press, 1975).

35. Vatican II, *Gaudium et Spes*, no. 22. The first encyclical of John Paul II, *Redemptor Hominis* (1979), is practically a commentary on this text.

36. See Karl Rahner, "Man (Anthropology). III. Theological," *Encyclopedia of Theology*, 887–93, at 893.

37. Ricoeur, *The Symbolism of Evil*, passim.

38. See Piet Schoonenberg, *Man and Sin* (Notre Dame, Ind.: University of Notre Dame Press, 1965), 106–11.

39. See Jürgen Habermas, *Theory of Communicative Action* 1 (Boston: Beacon, 1983); also Gibson Winter, "The Ministry of Communication," chapter 4 of his *The New Creation as Metropolis* (New York: Macmillan, 1963), especially 99–113.

40. Häring, *Free and Faithful in Christ*, 2:157.

41. Peter Fransen, *The New Life of Grace* (New York: Desclee, 1969), 346.

42. Schoonenberg, *Man and Sin*, 119.

43. Henri Bergson, *The Two Sources of Morality and Religion* (Garden City, N.Y.: Doubleday Anchor, n.d.), 233–40.

44. "The Church and the Sacraments," in Karl Rahner, *Inquiries* (New York: Herder and Herder, 1964), 191–299, at 221.

45. "In the institution of the Holy Eucharist, Christ gave us the most perfect, most intimate form of communion between God and man possible in this life, and, out of this, the deepest possible unity between men" (*"Communio et Progressio,"* no. 11).

46. Edward J. Kilmartin, *Christian Liturgy* (Kansas City, Mo.: Sheed and Ward, 1988), 47.

47. Alexandre Ganoczy, *Introduction to Catholic Sacramental Theology* (New York: Paulist, 1984), 156; cf. Kilmartin, *Christian Liturgy*, 45.

48. The Protestant theologian Gerhard Ebeling has well said: "The phrase 'communication of faith' therefore does not mean mere communication about faith, instruction about the intellectual content of faith, but it is intended to express the communication of faith as an event of speech" (*The Nature of Faith* [Philadelphia: Fortress, 1967], 87).

49. Karl Rahner, "The Word and the Eucharist," *Theological Investigations*, 4:253–68.

50. Otto Semmelroth, *The Preaching Word* (New York: Herder and Herder, 1965), 226.

51. My own views on this subject are more fully set forth in my article, "Models for Ministerial Priesthood," *Origins* 20 (October 11, 1990): 284–89.

52. John Navone and Thomas Cooper, *Tellers of the Word* (New York: Le Jacq, 1981), 262.

53. *"Communio et Progressio,"* nos. 116, 120.

54. Paul VI, *Ecclesiam Suam* (Glen Rock, N.J.: Paulist, 1964), especially part 3, "Dialogue."

55. Vatican II, *Lumen Gentium*, no. 8.

56. Karl Rahner, "The Concept of Mystery in Catholic Theology," *Theological Investigations*, 4:36–73, especially 41–42 and 54–55.

57. See Juan Alfaro, "Cristo glorioso, revelador del Padre," *Gregorianum* 39 (1958): 222–70. See also Karl Rahner, "On the Eternal Significance of the Humanity of Jesus for Our Relationship with God," *Theological Investigations* 3 (Baltimore: Helicon, 1967), 35–46.

58. Karl Rahner, "Dogmatic Questions on Easter," *Theological Investigations*, 4:121–33, at 131.

59. Ibid., 132.

60. Karl Rahner, "The Theology of the Symbol," *Theological Investigations,* 4:236.

61. George H. Tavard, *The Vision of the Trinity* (Washington, D.C.: University Press of America, 1981), 126.

62. Häring, *Free and Faithful in Christ,* 2:155.

Chapter 3: The Problem of Method: From Scholasticism to Models

1. Sallie McFague, *Models of God* (Philadelphia: Fortress, 1987).

2. John F. O'Grady, *Models of Jesus* (Garden City, N.Y.: Doubleday, 1981).

3. Raymond F. Collins, *Models of Theological Reflection* (Lanham, Md.: University Press of America, 1984).

4. Avery Dulles, *Models of the Church* (Garden City, N.Y.: Doubleday, 1974; expanded edition, 1987).

5. Avery Dulles, *Models of Revelation* (Garden City, N.Y.: Doubleday, 1983).

6. Avery Dulles, *Revelation Theology: A History* (New York: Herder and Herder, 1969), 177–80.

7. Friedrich von Hügel, *The Mystical Element in Religion as Studied in Saint Catherine of Genoa and Her Friends,* 2 vols. (London: J. M. Dent, 1923).

8. Stephen Pepper, *World Hypotheses: A Study in Evidence* (Berkeley, Calif.: University of California Press, 1942).

9. Avery Dulles, *A Church to Believe In* (New York: Crossroad, 1982).

Chapter 4: Fundamental Theology and the Dynamics of Conversion

1. Bernard J. F. Lonergan, "Theology in Its New Context," *A Second Collection* (Philadelphia: Westminster, 1974), 55–67.

2. Elsewhere Lonergan states: "As conversion is basic to Christian living, so an objectification of conversion provides theology with its foundations" (*Method in Theology* [New York: Herder and Herder, 1972], 130).

3. Karl Rahner, *Foundations of Christian Faith* (New York: Seabury, 1978), 8–14. See also his article, "Formale und fundamentale Theologie," LTK[2] 4:205–6.

4. John Henry Newman, *Essay in Aid of a Grammar of Assent,* ch. 9, §3 (Garden City, N.Y.: Doubleday Image, 1955), 296–97.

5. Lonergan, "Theology in its New Context," 66.

6. Michael Polanyi, *Personal Knowledge: Towards a Post-Critical Philosophy* (New York: Harper Torchbooks, 1964), 150–51.

7. Cf. Thomas S. Kuhn, *The Structure of Scientific Revolutions,* 2d ed. (Chicago: University of Chicago Press, 1970).

8. "De l'apologétique à la théologie fondamentale," *Dieu connu en Jesus Christ. Les Quatre Fleuves* 1 (Paris: Ed. du Seuil, 1973), 57–70, at 69.

9. Polanyi, *Personal Knowledge,* 266 and passim.

10. Cf. Lonergan, "Theology in Its New Context," 66.

11. Michael Polanyi and Harry Prosch, *Meaning* (Chicago: University of Chicago Press, 1975), 180.

Chapter 5: The Uses of Scripture in Theology

1. For a concise survey, see Raymond E. Brown and Thomas Aquinas Collins, "Church Pronouncements," in *The New Jerome Biblical Commentary* (Englewood Cliffs, N.J.: Prentice-Hall, 1990), 1166–74.

2. *In rebus fidei et morum*, DS 1507. The word *morum* can also be translated "of customs" and is so translated in Norman P. Tanner, ed., *Decrees of the Ecumenical Councils* (Washington, D.C.: Georgetown University Press, 1990), 664.

3. The numerals stand for the paragraph numbers in EB. For English translations, see *Rome and the Study of Scripture*, 7th ed. (St. Meinrad, Ind.: Grail Publications, 1962) and James J. Megivern, ed., *Official Catholic Teachings: Bible Interpretation* (Wilmington, N.C.: McGrath, 1978).

4. See Joseph A. Fitzmyer, *Scripture and Christology: A Statement of the Biblical Commission with Commentary* (New York: Paulist, 1986).

5. These methodologies may be roughly designated as follows: (1) The classical approach based on dogmatic texts and sources; (2) revisionist approaches based on historical consciousness; (3) efforts to reconstruct the life and teaching of Jesus through historical probing; (4) a refinement of this latter approach with data from the history of religions; (5) study of Jesus in light of Palestinian Judaism; (6) approaches through salvation history; (7) a variety of anthropological approaches; (8) existentialist interpretations; (9) sociological and liberationist perspectives; (10) constructive systematic approaches; (11) further refinements of these constructive approaches in Christologies "from above" and "from below."

Some of these approaches are strictly exegetical; others involve larger hermeneutical programs.

6. Thorleif Boman, *Hebrew Thought Compared with Greek* (London: SCM, 1960).

7. Oscar Cullmann, *Christ and Time* (Philadelphia: Westminster, 1950).

8. Louis Bouyer, "Liturgie et exégèse spirituelle," *La Maison-Dieu* 7 (1946): 30. Cf. Henri de Lubac, *Sources of Revelation* (New York: Herder and Herder, 1968), 73.

9. de Lubac, *Sources of Revelation*, 27–28.

10. Ibid., 12 and 49.

11. Célestin Charlier, *The Christian Approach to the Bible* (Westminster, Md: Newman, 1958), 255–63; cf. de Lubac, *Sources of Revelation*, 13.

12. Hans Urs von Balthasar, "The Word, Scripture, and Tradition," in *Word and Revelation: Essays in Theology* 1 (New York: Herder and Herder, 1964), 9–30, quotation from 26–27.

13. Yves M.-J. Congar, *Tradition and Traditions: An Historical and a Theological Essay* (New York: Macmillan, 1967).

14. Karl Barth, *Church Dogmatics* 1/1 (Edinburgh: T. & T. Clark, 1956), 183.

See Thomas E. Provence, "The Sovereign Subject Matter: Hermeneutics in the *Church Dogmatics*," in *A Guide to Contemporary Hermeneutics*, ed. Donald K. McKim (Grand Rapids, Mich.: Eerdmans, 1986), 241–62, at 251; also Mark I. Wallace, "Karl Barth's Hermeneutic: A Way beyond the Impasse," *Journal of Religion* 68 (1988): 396–410, at 408.

15. For a compact account of Barth's use of Scripture, see, in addition to the articles already cited, David H. Kelsey, *The Uses of Scripture in Recent Theology* (Philadelphia: Fortress, 1975), 39–55. Kelsey finds in Barth a "narrative theology" similar to that of Kelsey's Yale colleague Hans W. Frei which I shall take up in my ninth category.

16. In these paragraphs I summarize a longer exposition and critique in my article, "Hermeneutical Theology" in *Communio: International Catholic Review* 6 (1979): 16–37. See also Anthony C. Thistleton, "The New Hermeneutic," in McKim, *Guide to Contemporary Hermeneutics*, 78–107, and Joseph Cardinal Ratzinger, "Biblical Interpretation in Crisis: On the Question of the Foundations and Approaches of Exegesis Today," in *Biblical Interpretation in Crisis: The Ratzinger Conference on Bible and Church*, ed. Richard John Neuhaus (Grand Rapids, Mich.: Eerdmans, 1989), 1–23.

17. George A. Lindbeck, *The Nature of Doctrine* (Philadelphia: Westminster, 1984), 16, 31–32, and passim.

18. "Theology in the New Testament," in Karl Rahner, *Theological Investigations* 5 (Baltimore: Helicon, 1966), 37–38.

19. Karl Rahner, *Foundations of Christian Faith* (New York: Crossroad, 1978), 370.

20. Ibid., 17.

21. Gregory Baum, "The Bible as Norm," *The Ecumenist* 9 (July–August 1971): 75.

22. David Tracy, *The Analogical Imagination* (New York: Crossroad, 1981), 108.

23. Ibid., 248. Even in this work, which attempts to give suitable authority to Scripture and tradition, Tracy attributes paramount importance to a "heightened awareness of the reality of what Otto named the 'numinous'" (169). To that extent he may be considered to exemplify Lindbeck's experiential-expressive type, as he is said to do by Garrett Green in *Imagining God: Theology and the Religious Imagination* (San Francisco: Harper & Row, 1989), 120. But Tracy has replied to his critics in "Lindbeck's New Program for Theology," *Thomist* 49 (1985): 460–72 and in "On Reading the Scriptures Theologically," in *Theology and Dialogue*, ed. Bruce D. Marshall (Notre Dame, Ind.: University of Notre Dame, 1990), 35–68.

24. Edward Schillebeeckx, *Jesus: An Experiment in Christology* (New York: Seabury/Crossroad, 1979).

25. "Jesus' original *Abba*-experience, source and secret of his being, message, and manner of life" (ibid., 256).

26. Ibid., 379–97.

27. For criticism, see George A. Lindbeck in his "Scripture, Consensus and Community," in Neuhaus, *Biblical Interpretation in Crisis*, 74–101, especially 87–88; also Garrett Green, *Imagining God*, 119–23.

28. See Raymond E. Brown, "The Contribution of Historical Biblical Criticism to Ecumenical Church Discussion," in Neuhaus, *Biblical Interpretation in Crisis*, 24–49; Joseph A. Fitzmyer, "Historical Criticism: Its Role in Biblical Interpretation and Church Life," *Theological Studies* 50 (1989): 244–59.

29. Raymond E. Brown et al., eds., *Peter in the New Testament: A Collaborative Assessment by Protestant and Roman Catholic Scholars* (Minneapolis: Augsburg; New York: Paulist, 1973); Raymond E. Brown et al., eds., *Mary in the New Testament: A Collaborative Assessment by Protestant and Roman Catholic Scholars* (Philadelphia: Fortress; New York: Paulist, 1978); John Reumann, *"Righteousness" in the New Testament*, with responses by Joseph A. Fitzmyer and Jerome D. Quinn (Philadelphia: Fortress; New York: Paulist, 1982).

30. Brown, "Contribution," 28–29.

31. Wolfhart Pannenberg, "The Crisis of the Scripture Principle," in his *Basic Questions in Theology* 1 (Philadelphia: Fortress, 1970), 7.

32. Wolfhart Pannenberg, *Faith and Reality* (Philadelphia: Westminster, 1977), 70–71.

33. Hans Küng, *Theology for the Third Millennium* (New York: Doubleday, 1988), 85.

34. Ibid., 98. Küng's italics.

35. Ibid., 111. Cf. 205: "The *norma normans* of any Christian theology cannot, once again, be any churchly or theological tradition or institution, but only the Gospel, the original Christian message itself: a theology everywhere oriented to the historico-critically analyzed facts of the Bible."

36. Ibid., 112.

37. Johann Baptist Metz, *Faith in History and Society* (New York: Seabury/ Crossroad 1980), 212.

38. Ibid., 213.

39. See Hans W. Frei, *The Identity of Jesus Christ: The Hermeneutical Bases of Dogmatic Theology* (Philadelphia: Fortress, 1975), "Preface," vi–xviii; also Frei's earlier work, *The Eclipse of Biblical Narrative* (New Haven, Conn.: Yale University Press, 1974). In a later essay, "The 'Literal Reading' of Biblical Narrative in the Christian Tradition: Does It Stretch or Will It Break?" Frei criticizes Tracy's approach through general hermeneutical theory, and differentiates his own position from the "new criticism." This essay is published in *The Bible and the Narrative Tradition*, ed. Frank McConnell (New York: Oxford University Press, 1986), 36–77.

40. Lindbeck, *The Nature of Doctrine*, 119.

41. Ibid., 117.

42. Ibid., 122.

43. Ronald F. Thiemann, *Revelation and Theology: The Gospel as Narrated Promise* (Notre Dame, Ind.: University of Notre Dame Press, 1985), 83.

44. Ibid., 84. Thiemann explains more fully how God's identity is conveyed by the biblical stories in "Radiance and Obscurity in Biblical Narrative," in *Scriptural Authority and Narrative Interpretation*, ed. Garrett Green (Philadelphia: Fortress, 1987), 21–41.

45. "Crisis in Jerusalem? Narrative Criticism in New Testament Studies," *Theological Studies* 50 (1989): 296–313, quotation from 312–13.

46. Lindbeck himself concedes this in *The Nature of Doctrine,* 117.

47. Juan Luis Segundo, *The Liberation of Theology* (Maryknoll, N.Y.: Orbis, 1976), 110.

48. An excellent example is Elisabeth Schüssler Fiorenza's *In Memory of Her: A Feminist Theological Reconstruction of Christian Origins* (New York: Crossroad, 1986). See also her *Bread Not Stone: The Challenge of Feminist Biblical Interpretation* (Boston: Beacon, 1984). For a helpful survey of the various trends, see Phyllis Trible, "Five Loaves and Two Fishes: Feminist Hermeneutics and Biblical Theology," *Theological Studies* 50 (1989): 279–95.

49. "The Theological Method of Segundo's *The Liberation of Theology,*" in *Proceedings of the Catholic Theological Society of America* 32 (1977): 120–24. Other reservations concerning Segundo's hermeneutical circle are articulated in Anthony J. Tambasco, "Segundo's Biblical Hermeneutics: An Appraisal" in *Readings in Moral Theology No. 4: The Use of Scripture in Moral Theology,* ed. Charles E. Curran and Richard A. McCormick (New York: Paulist, 1984), 321–36.

50. Congregation for the Doctrine of the Faith, "Instruction on Certain Aspects of the 'Theology of Liberation,'" *Origins* 14 (September 13, 1984): 193–204.

Chapter 6: Tradition as a Theological Source

1. These schools and their representatives are described by George Tavard in his *Holy Writ or Holy Church* (New York: Harper, 1959). See also Yves M.-J. Congar, *Tradition and Traditions* (New York: Macmillan, 1967).

2. Trent is treated by Tavard, *Holy Writ,* 195–209. Another valuable commentary is Joseph Ratzinger, "On the Interpretation of the Tridentine Decree on Tradition" in Karl Rahner and Joseph Ratzinger, *Revelation and Tradition* (New York: Herder and Herder, 1966), 50–68, 73–78.

3. Basil in *De Spiritu Sancto* 27:66 (PG 32:188) wrote of the teaching of Scripture and apostolic tradition that both have equal value for piety (*haper amphotera tēn autēn ischyn echei pros tēn eusebeian*). The exact meaning of *eusebeian* is debated. Congar (*Tradition and Traditions,* 163) suggests: "a welcoming acceptance full of respect and trust."

4. For Newman's doctrine of tradition, see Günter Biemer, *Newman on Tradition* (London: Burns & Oates, 1967); also Pierre Gauthier, *Newman et Blondel: Tradition et développement du dogme* (Paris: Cerf, 1988.)

5. *Certain Difficulties Felt by Anglicans in Catholic Teaching Considered,* 2 vols. (Westminster, Md: Christian Classics, 1969), 2:11–12.

6. On some of these theologians, see Walter Kasper, *Die Lehre von der Tradition in der römischen Schule* (Freiburg: Herder, 1962). On Franzelin, see James P. Mackey, *The Modern Theology of Tradition* (New York: Herder and Herder, 1963), especially chapter 1.

7. Blondel's doctrine of tradition may be found especially in his *History and Dogma* (New York: Holt, Rinehart, and Winston, 1964); for discussion,

see Gauthier, *Newman et Blondel*; also Congar, *Tradition and Traditions*, 215–17, 359–68.

8. See Josef Rupert Geiselmann, "Scripture, Tradition, and the Church: An Ecumenical Problem," in *Christianity Divided: Protestant and Roman Catholic Theological Issues*, ed. Daniel J. Callahan and others et al. (New York: Sheed and Ward, 1961), 39–72, with references to Geiselmann's earlier articles. Geiselmann's contention that in dropping the *partim . . . partim* the fathers at Trent intended to change the meaning of the decree has been contested by Heinrich Lennerz, Johannes Beumer, and others, on whom see Congar, *Tradition and Traditions*, 166–69.

9. The texts of these two unofficial schemas are given in *Le Révélation divine*, 2 vols., ed. Bernard-Dominique Dupuy (Paris: Cerf, 1968), 2:577–87 and 588–98.

10. A valuable commentary is provided by Joseph Ratzinger in *Commentary on the Documents of Vatican II*, 5 vols., ed. Herbert Vorgrimler (New York: Herder and Herder, 1969), 3:181–98. Further information on the history of the text can be gleaned from Dupuy, ed., *La Révélation divine* 1; volume 2 includes several commentaries from Protestant and Orthodox perspectives. See also Walter Kasper, "Schrift — Tradition — Verkündigung," in his *Glaube und Geschichte* (Mainz: Matthias Grünewald, 1970); Avery Dulles, "Vatican II and the Recovery of Tradition," in his *The Reshaping of Catholicism* (San Francisco: Harper & Row, 1988).

11. The only exception is in the quotation from Scripture (2 Thess 2:15) in *Dei Verbum*, no. 8. Throughout this and following chapters, letters abbreviated in parentheses identify the conciliar texts by abbreviated Latin title and paragraph number.

12. See the *relatio* to Text F distributed November 20, 1964, p. 19; reprinted in *Acta synodalia* 4:1, p. 353.

13. See Ratzinger's contribution to Vorgrimler *Commentary*, 3:185.

14. See Ratzinger, ibid., 3:186–87.

15. See Ratzinger, ibid., 3:188–89.

16. *Relatio* to Text E, July 3, 1964, p. 23; reprinted in *Acta synodalia* 3:3, pp. 86–87.

17. The term "authentic" is a technical term that conveys the idea of authority exercised in the name of Christ.

18. See, for instance, Robert P. Imbelli, "Vatican II — Twenty Years Later," *Commonweal* 109 (October 9, 1982): 78. In this section I shall repeat some observations made in my article "The Role of Tradition in Catholic Christianity," *Emmanuel* 96 (January–February 1990): 4–13, 21, 28–29.

19. See, for instance, Jean-Louis Leuba, "La Tradition à Montréal et à Vatican II: Convergences et Questions," in Dupuy, ed., *La Révélation divine*, 2:475–97.

20. The numbers in parentheses refer to sections in *The Fourth World Conference on Faith and Order, Montreal 1963*, Faith and Order papers 42, ed. Patrick C. Rodger and Lukas Vischer (London: SCM; New York: Association, 1964).

21. Quoted in Yves M.-J. Congar, *Challenge to the Church: The Case of Arch-*

bishop Lefebvre (Huntington, Ind.: Our Sunday Visitor, 1976), 78; translation modified in light of French original *La Crise dans l'Eglise et Mgr. Lefebvre* (Paris: Cerf, 1976), 96.

22. Paul VI, "Tradition Explains the Old and the New," General Audience, August 7, *L'Osservatore Romano* [English weekly edition], 15 August 1974, 1. A section of this address is quoted in another translation from the Italian by George Tavard in his "Tradition in Theology: A Methodological Approach," in *Perspectives on Scripture and Tradition*, ed. Joseph F. Kelly (Notre Dame, Ind.: Fides, 1976), 114.

Chapter 7: The Magisterium and Theological Dissent

1. This twofold dynamism in theology is affirmed in the "Instruction on the Ecclesial Vocation of the Theologian" issued by the Congregation for the Doctrine of the Faith, May 24, 1990; *Origins* 20 (July 5, 1990): 117–26, no. 7, p. 119. The numbers in parentheses throughout this chapter will refer to sections of this CDF Instruction.

2. "On the Interpretation of Dogmas," C.III.3; *Origins* 20 (May 17, 1990): 1–16, quotation from 12.

3. Ibid., C.III.1; *Origins*, 12.

4. Ibid., B.III.4; *Origins*, 10.

5. "Theologie und Lehramt," *L'Osservatore Romano* [German-language edition], 12 October 1990, 6.

6. *Pastor Aeternus*, chapter 4; DS 3074.

7. *Acta synodalia* 3:1, p. 251; cf. *Lumen Gentium*, no. 25. For commentary, see Francis A. Sullivan, *Magisterium: Teaching Authority in the Church* (New York: Paulist, 1983), 129–31. As Sullivan goes on to observe (133–34), the Congregation for the Doctrine of the Faith, in its declaration *Mysterium Ecclesiae* (1973), gave a similar explanation of the extension of the infallible magisterium.

8. In paragraph 16, the instruction refers to Vatican I, *Dei Filius* (DS 3005), as its authority; but this text says nothing explicitly about moral norms; it refers only to the fact that some revealed truths are also naturally knowable.

9. Umberto Betti in *L'Osservatore Romano*, 25 February 1989, 6, quoted by Francis A. Sullivan, "Some Observations on the New Formula for the Profession of Faith," *Gregorianum* 70 (1989): 553–54.

10. Ibid.

11. "The Theologian's Ecclesial Vocation and the 1990 CDF Instruction," *Theological Studies* 52 (1991): 51–68, at 55–58.

12. Even though Vatican II made no new doctrinal definitions, it spoke of many matters that were already part of the faith of the Church. The same is true of papal encyclicals. The fact that the popes have not used encyclical letters for promulgating solemn definitions does not mean that these letters contain no definitive teaching.

13. I have noted the complexity of this question in *The Reshaping of Catholicism* (San Francisco: Harper & Row, 1988), 102–3.

14. *L'Osservatore Romano* [English weekly edition], 2 July 1990, 5.

15. It is possible to read paragraph 24 of the instruction as dealing with two distinct categories of prudential intervention — the doctrinal and the disciplinary, but this distinction is not clearly expressed and may not, in fact, be intended. See Joseph Komonchak, "The Magisterium and Theologians," *Chicago Studies* 29 (1990): 307–29, at 322–23.

16. The term "irreformable," consecrated by the usage of Vatican I and Vatican II, means definitive, i.e., not subject to cancellation or reversal by any other body in the Church. As the reason for "irreformability," Vatican I assigned the charism of infallibility. The term "irreformable" was used previously in the Four Articles of the Gallican Clergy, condemned by Alexander VIII in 1690 (DS 2284).

17. I here use the term "reformable" simply as the opposite of "irreformable," and hence as equivalent to "nondefinitive." To prevent confusion, it should be clearly understood that a reformable statement may be certain and may contain abiding truth. The term "reformable" is not wholly felicitous. People spontaneously think that what *can* be reformed should be reformed, and that dissenters usually deserve to be praised as reformers. Thus some better term should probably be found, possibly "nondefinitive." I do not see that the double negative "nonirreformable" is any improvement.

18. The most exhaustive investigation of the so-called "reversals" of ordinary papal teaching by Vatican II is J. Robert Dionne, *The Papacy and the Church: A Study of Praxis and Reception in Ecumenical Perspective* (New York: Philosophical Library, 1987). Dionne maintains that reversals occurred in Catholic doctrine regarding non-Christian religions, religious freedom, the ideal of church-state relations, the identity (or nonidentity) between the Mystical Body of Christ and the Catholic Church, and the theology of church membership. On these and other issues, he contends, historical scholarship does not support the "maximalist" position that the ordinary magisterium of the pope is equipped with the charism of infallibility. To deny on principle that ordinary papal teaching can be corrected would be, in effect, to assert that all of it is definitive, and that none of it can pertain to the third and fourth categories in the CDF instruction.

19. *Human Life in Our Day* (Washington, D.C.: United States Catholic Conference, 1968), 18.

20. I am following the language of the normative Italian text which, as Father Komonchak points out, differs slightly at this point from the English version. See his "The Magisterium and Theologians," 313.

21. See Max Seckler, "Der Dialog zwischen dem Lehramt und den Theologen," *L'Osservatore Romano* [German-language edition], 19 October 1990), 6.

22. Using a slightly different concept of "dissent," the United States bishops, meeting on November 14, 1991, distinguished between the withholding of assent, private dissent, and public dissent. See "The Teaching Ministry of the Diocesan Bishop: A Pastoral Reflection," *Origins* 21 (January 2, 1992):

743–92. This statement was published too late for me to make use of it in this chapter.

23. One journalist-theologian complains that according to Cardinal Ratzinger "If we have any complaints with official doctrine, we are to communicate them to the proper authorities behind closed doors, in secret." So writes David S. Toolan in his report "A Disagreeable Bunch in the Bark of Peter," *America* 164 (February 2, 1991): 76–77, at 76. In a more serious vein, see Ladislas Orsy, "The Limits of Magisterium," *The Tablet* (London), 244 (August 25, 1990): 1066–69; see also his "Magisterium and Theologians — A Vatican Document," *America* 163 (July 21, 1990): 30–32.

24. "Observations on Doctrinal Congregation's Instruction," *Origins* 20 (September 6, 1990): 201–5, especially 204.

25. See Avery Dulles, "The Question of Dissent," *The Tablet* (London), 244 (August 18, 1990): 1033–34. Sullivan ("The Ecclesial Vocation," 65) agrees "in substance" with my position in that article.

26. See Komonchak, "The Magisterium and Theologians," 327–29.

27. "Doctrinal Responsibilities," II.B; *Origins* 19 (June 29, 1989): 104.

28. According to "Doctrinal Responsibilities" theological consultants "should be selected from as many segments as possible on the spectrum of acceptable theological opinion," ibid., 105.

29. The preparation of the Apostolic Constitution on Catholic Universities, *Ex Corde Ecclesiae* (*Origins* 20 [October 20, 1990]: 265–76), is an example of a successful procedure.

Chapter 8: Theology and Philosophy

1. This scholastic renaissance is well described in Gerald A. McCool, *Catholic Theology in the Nineteenth Century* (New York: Seabury/Crossroad, 1977).

2. English translation of 8th ed., *A Manual of Modern Scholastic Philosophy*, 2 vols. (London: Paul, Trench, Trubner & Co., 1916–17).

3. See John M. Oesterreicher, *Walls Are Crumbling: Seven Jewish Philosophers Discover Christ* (New York: Devin-Adair, 1952).

4. Herbert Spiegelberg, *The Phenomenological Movement: A Historical Introduction*, 3rd ed. (The Hague: Nijhoff, 1982), 433.

5. Accounts of Daniélou's positions and the ensuing debate may be found in Robert F. Harvanek, "Philosophical Pluralism and Catholic Orthodoxy," *Thought* 25 (1950): 21–52; also Gerald A. McCool, "The Explosion of Pluralism: The 'New Theology' Crisis," chapter 9 of his *From Unity to Pluralism: The Internal Evolution of Thomism* (New York: Fordham University Press, 1989).

6. Ralph M. Wiltgen, *The Rhine Flows into the Tiber: A History of Vatican II* (Devon: Augustine Publishing Co., 1978), 15–19 and passim. By the "European Alliance" he means a coalition of bishops of Germany, Austria, France, Holland, Belgium, and Switzerland, whom he considers responsible for the liberal majority of the commission elected on October 16, 1962.

7. *Acta synodalia* 1/4, p. 223.

8. John F. Kobler, *Vatican II and Phenomenology: Reflections on the Life-World of the Church* (Dordrecht: Nijhoff, 1985) 99, 135, 187–88. His remarks on Marcel are derived from Spiegelberg, *The Phenomenological Movement*, 452–53.

9. Mark G. McGrath, discussing the first part of the pastoral constitution *Gaudium et Spes* in *Vatican II: An Interfaith Appraisal*, ed. John H. Miller (Notre Dame, Ind.: University of Notre Dame Press, 1966), 429.

10. *Sources of Renewal: The Implementation of Vatican II* (San Francisco: Harper & Row, 1979), 35–41.

11. Text in Sacrosancti Oecumenici Concilii Vaticani II, *Constitutiones, Decreta, Declarationes* (Vatican City: Typis Polyglottis, 1966), 1065–66; cf. Kobler, *Vatican II and Phenomenology*, 142.

12. Text in Walter M. Abbott, ed., *The Documents of Vatican II* (New York: America Press, 1966), 716.

13. Kobler, *Vatican II and Phenomenology*, 100.

14. David Tracy, *Blessed Rage for Order* (New York: Crossroad, 1975), 47–48. Contrast idem, *Plurality and Ambiguity* (San Francisco: Harper & Row, 1987), 134, note 40.

15. In a 1972 statement on "Theological Pluralism" the International Theological Commission declared: "Dogmatic definitions ordinarily use a common language; while they may make use of apparently philosophical terminology, they do not thereby bind the Church to a particular philosophy." See International Theological Commission, *Texts and Documents 1969–85* (San Francisco: Ignatius, 1989), 89–92, at 91.

16. Congregation for the Doctrine of the Faith, declaration *Mysterium Ecclesiae*, AAS 65 (1973): 396–408, quotation from 403.

17. Abbott, *Documents*, 714.

18. Ibid., 717.

19. Ibid., 731.

20. These are two of the seven criteria for authentic doctrinal developments expounded by Newman in his *Essay on the Development of Christian Doctrine*. The International Theological Commission, in its recent statement "On the Interpretation of Dogmas," recalled all seven of Newman's principles; text in *Origins* 20 (May 17, 1990): 1–14, especially 13.

21. In the English translation the Italian *transfinalizzatione* is inaccurately rendered "transfiguration." See the pamphlet *Mysterium Fidei: On the Eucharistic Doctrine of Worship* (Glen Rock, N.J.: Paulist, 1966), no. 11, p. 30, and Gregory Baum's comment in the "Introduction," 10–11.

22. "Christ, the Trinity and Theology Today," *Origins* 1 (March 23, 1972): 665–68; also published as "Safeguarding Belief in the Incarnation and Trinity," *Catholic Mind* 70 (June 1972): 61–64.

23. Michael Polanyi, *Personal Knowledge: Towards a Post-Critical Philosophy* (New York: Harper Torchbooks, 1964), 115.

Chapter 9: Theology and the Physical Sciences

1. "Qu'est-ce que la foi?" *Revue du clergé français* 47 (1906): 449–73, 591–605.

2. "A Papal Address on the Church and Science," *Origins* 13 (June 2, 1983): 49–52, quotations from 51.

3. See Mario d'Addio, "Alcune fasi dell'istruttoria del processo a Galileo," *L'Osservatore Romano*, 2 March 1984, 3. Further materials may be found in *Galileo Galilei: Toward a Resolution of 350 Years of Debate, 1633–1983*, ed. Paul Poupard (Pittsburgh, Pa.: Duquesne University Press, 1987).

4. The message of John Paul II will be cited in this article from the text printed in *Physics, Philosophy and Theology: A Common Quest for Understanding*, ed. Robert John Russell, William R. Stoeger, and George V. Coyne (Vatican City: Vatican Observatory, 1988). Numerals in parentheses following the letter M refer to pages in that volume.

5. Ernan McMullin, "Religious Book Week: Critics' Choices," *Commonweal* 116 (March 10, 1989): 149.

6. Many such typologies have been proposed; for example, that by Arthur R. Peacocke in his introduction to *The Sciences and Theology in the Twentieth Century*, ed. A. R. Peacocke (Notre Dame, Ind.: University of Notre Dame Press, 1981), xiii–xv. See also Ian G. Barbour, "Ways of Relating Science and Theology," in *Physics, Philosophy and Theology*, 21–45. I am, in general, following Barbour's typology.

7. Quotation in Stanley L. Jaki, *The Relevance of Physics* (Chicago: University of Chicago Press, 1966), 499.

8. *Free Inquiry*, edited by Paul Kurtz, is published in Buffalo, New York, by the Council for Democratic and Secular Humanism.

9. Langdon Gilkey, *Creationism on Trial: Evolution and God at Little Rock* (San Francisco: Harper & Row, 1985).

10. Paul Tillich, *Systematic Theology* 1 (Chicago: University of Chicago Press, 1951), 130.

11. "A Common Quest for Understanding," in *John Paul II on Science and Religion: Reflections on the New View from Rome*, ed. Robert John Russell et al. (Notre Dame, Ind.: University of Notre Dame Press, 1990), 53–58, quotation from 54.

12. George A. Lindbeck, *The Nature of Doctrine* (Philadelphia: Westminster, 1984), 18.

13. C. P. Snow, *The Two Cultures and A Second Look* (Cambridge, England: Cambridge University Press, 1965).

14. Pius XII, encyclical, *Humani Generis* (*AAS* 42 [1950]: 571); ET (New York: Paulist, 1950), nos. 48–49, pp. 14–15. This passage has already been discussed in chapter 8 above, pp. 121, 128.

15. Pius XII is often quoted as having said in an address to the Pontifical Academy of Sciences in 1951 that modern science "has confirmed the contingency of the universe and also the well-founded deduction as to the epoch when the cosmos came forth from the hands of the Creator. Hence, creation took place in time" ("Modern Science and the Existence

of God," *Catholic Mind* 50 [1952]: 182–92, at 191). Yet in the same address the pope cautioned: "It is quite true that the facts established up to the present time are not an absolute proof of creation in time, as are the proofs drawn from metaphysics and Revelation in what concerns simple creation, or those founded on Revelation if there be question of creation in time. The pertinent facts of the natural sciences, to which We have referred, are awaiting still further research and confirmation, and the theories founded on them are in need of further development and proof, before they can provide a sure foundation for arguments which, of themselves, are outside the proper sphere of the natural sciences" (ibid., 190). John Paul II, in the statements I have seen, has likewise been reserved about the capacity of the physical sciences to establish or undermine the metaphysical and theological doctrine of creation. See John Paul II, "The Path of Scientific Discovery," *Origins* 11 (October 15, 1981): 277–80. Stephen W. Hawking, in his *A Brief History of Time* (New York: Bantam Books, 1988), 116 and 141, hypothetically proposes a scientific theory according to which creation would have no beginning and thus there would be no moment of creation. Pius XII, as quoted above, holds that neither metaphysics nor science, but only revelation, can establish the fact of creation in time.

16. Yves M.-J. Congar, *Diversity and Communion* (Mystic, Conn.: Twenty-Third Publications, 1985), 74–76. Robert J. Russell, in his "Quantum Physics in Philosophical and Theological Perspective," in *Physics, Philosophy and Theology*, 343–74, at 359–61, gives a number of other attempted applications of the principle of complementarity in the realm of theology. See my own observations above, p. 48.

17. Cf. Jacques Monod, *Chance and Necessity* (New York: Knopf, 1971); also Leo J. O'Donovan, "Science or Prophecy? A Discussion with Jacques Monod," *American Ecclesiastical Review* 167 (1973): 543–52.

18. Pius XII, *Humani Generis*, AAS 42 (1950): 575; ET, no. 65, p. 19. On the basis of the principles in the pope's message of 1987, Wolfhart Pannenberg suggests that the acceptance of an evolutionary perspective, as intimated in the new papal position, might lead to a revision of Pius XII's position on monogenism. See W. Pannenberg, "Theology and Philosophy in Interaction with Science: A Response to the Message of Pope John Paul II on the Occasion of the Newton Tricentennial in 1987," *John Paul II on Science and Religion*, 75–79, at 79.

19. Blaise Pascal, "Préface sur le traité du vide," in *Opuscules et lettres (choix)*, ed. L. Lafuma (Paris: Aubier, 1955), 50. My translation.

20. Max Planck, *Where Is Science Going?* (New York: W. W. Norton, 1932), 214.

21. For some testimonies see Stanley L. Jaki, "The Role of Faith in Physics," *Zygon* 2 (1967): 187–202.

22. Michael Polanyi, *The Tacit Dimension* (Garden City, N.Y.: Doubleday, 1967), 63.

23. Werner Heisenberg, *Tradition in Science* (New York: Seabury, 1983), chapter 1.

24. George A. Lindbeck, "Theological Revolutions and the Present Crisis," *Theology Digest* 23 (Winter 1975): 308–19.

25. Michael Polanyi, *Personal Knowledge: Towards a Post-Critical Philosophy* (New York: Harper Torchbooks, 1964), 207. For discussion, see Avery Dulles, "Faith, Church, and God: Insights from Michael Polanyi," *Theological Studies* 45 (1984): 537–50.

26. Michael Polanyi, *Science, Faith and Society* (Chicago: University of Chicago Press, 1946), quotation from 49.

27. The resemblances between theological doctrines and scientific theories are strongly emphasized (without their differences being ignored) by Nancey Murphy in her stimulating article "The Message of Pope John Paul II on Science and the Church: A Response," *John Paul II on Science and Religion*, 67–73.

28. Blaise Pascal, Pensées, no. 313, in *The Essential Pascal*, ed. Robert J. Gleason (New York: Mentor-Omega, 1966), 124. The reflections on the two infinites in no. 43 (pp. 33–40) likewise exhibit the reactions of this religious genius to the dawning scientific consciousness of the age.

29. Closing message "To Men of Thought and Science," in *The Documents of Vatican II*, ed. Walter M. Abbott (New York: America Press, 1966), 731.

Chapter 10: University Theology in Service to the Church

1. DS 1179.

2. John Paul II, *Ex Corde Ecclesiae*, par. 19; *Origins* 20 (October 4, 1990): 265–76, quotation from 269–70.

3. For an informative survey see Jacques Verger, *Les universités au Moyen Age* (Vendôme: Presses universitaires de France, 1973).

4. See Yves M.-J. Congar, *Vraie et fausse Réforme dans l'Eglise*, 2d ed. (Paris: Cerf, 1968), 461.

5. Robert N. Swanson, *Universities, Academics, and the Great Schism* (Cambridge, England: Cambridge University Press, 1979).

6. John Henry Newman, *The Idea of a University Defined and Illustrated* (Notre Dame, Ind.: University of Notre Dame Press, 1982), "Discourse 4," 74.

7. For data concerning the erection of such programs, see Claude Welch, *Graduate Education in Religion* (Missoula, Mont.: University of Montana Press, 1971), 230–31.

8. Vatican II, Declaration on Christian Education, *Gravissimum Educationis*, no. 10.

9. Quoted from Eberhard Bethge, "The Challenge of Dietrich Bonhoeffer's Life and Theology," *Chicago Theological Seminary Register* 51 (February 1961): 23.

10. Döllinger's address is reprinted in *Ignaz von Döllinger*, ed. Johann Finsterhölzl (Graz: Styria, 1969), 227–63. For an account in English see Wilfrid Ward, *The Life of John Henry Cardinal Newman*, 2 vols. (London: Longmans, Green, 1912), 1:562–67, 641–42.

11. Pius IX, letter, *Tuas Libenter*, December 21, 1863, ASS 8 (1874/75): 438ff.; excerpts in DS 2875–80.

12. Vatican II, *Gravissimum Educationis*, no. 10.

13. Vatican II, *Lumen Gentium*, no. 37; *Gaudium et Spes*, no. 62; Code of Canon Law (1983), can. 218.

14. *Ex Corde Ecclesiae*, par. 29; *Origins*, 271.

15. Sidney Hook defined academic freedom as "the freedom of professionally qualified persons to inquire, discover, publish and teach the truth as they see it in the field of their competence, without any control or authority except the control or authority of the rational methods by which truth is established. Insofar as it acknowledges intellectual discipline or restraint from a community, it is only from the community of qualified scholars which accepts the authority of rational inquiry" (*Heresy, Yes — Conspiracy, No* [New York: John Day, 1953], 154). Bishop Donald Wuerl in his "Academic Freedom and the University" (*Origins* 18 [September 8, 1988]: 208) regards this definition as typical of the current secular model. Richard P. McBrien in his "Academic Freedom and Catholic Universities" (*America* 159 [December 3, 1988]: 455), accuses Wuerl of giving a caricature. This difference of opinion indicates some lack of clarity in the current American concept of academic freedom.

16. Vatican II, *Dei Verbum*, no. 12.

17. John Paul II, "Catholic Higher Education," *Origins* 17 (October 1, 1987): 269. This statement in quoted in *Ex Corde Ecclesiae*, par. 28; *Origins*, 271.

18. Wuerl, "Academic Freedom," 210.

19. Newman, *The Idea of a University*, 345.

20. Ibid., 351.

21. Ibid., 360.

22. "A Dynamic Relationship of Theology and Science," *Origins* 18 (November 17, 1988): 375–78. On this letter see chapter 9 above.

23. *The Idea of a University*, 354–56.

24. John Paul II, "Catholic Higher Education," 269.

25. Christopher Driver paraphrases the British professor of comparative religion Ninian Smart as "arguing in effect that in today's pluralistic society, the comparative approach was the only possible one for a university" (*The Exploding University* [London: Hodder and Stoughton, 1971], 181). Driver explains how Smart's proposals and arguments, based on his conception of the secular university, were accepted by the University of Lancaster in 1970.

26. For a summary account of this development, see George M. Marsden, "The Soul of the American University," *First Things* 9 (January 1991): 34–47. See also James Tunstead Burtchaell, "The Decline and Fall of the Christian College," *First Things* 12 (April 1991): 16–29, and *First Things* 13 (May 1991): 30–38.

27. Text in Neil G. McCluskey, ed., *The Catholic University: A Modern Appraisal* (Notre Dame, Ind.: University of Notre Dame Press, 1970), 336.

28. These three categories are distinguished in Frank D. Schubert, *A Sociological Study of Secularization Trends in the American Catholic University: De-*

catholicizing the Catholic Religious Curriculum (Lewiston, N.Y.: Edwin Mellen, 1990); more briefly in Schubert's article "Theology without God: A New Study Documents the Secularization of the Catholic Curriculum," *Crisis* 7 (June 1989): 22–26.

29. See Ladislas Orsy, *The Church: Learning and Teaching* (Wilmington, Del.: Michael Glazier, 1987), chapter 4, "Teaching Authority, Catholic Universities, Academic Freedom," especially 113–21.

Chapter 11: The Teaching Mission of the Church and Academic Freedom

1. Vatican II, *Gravissimum Educationis*, no. 3.

2. United States Bishops, *Human Life in Our Day* (Washington, D.C: United States Catholic Conference, 1968), 18–19; quoted above p. 113.

3. See the discussion above, pp. 157–160 and the references given in note 15 to chapter 10.

4. James John Annarelli (*Academic Freedom and Catholic Higher Education* [Westport, Conn.: Greenwood Press, 1987], 99), quotes Walter P. Metzger: "The professional standing of a professor can only be established by experts, and these experts must be chosen from among his scholarly peers."

5. Annarelli (*Academic Freedom*, 102), quotes William J. Kilgore, chairman of a 1964 committee studying this question for the AAUP, as declaring that "each restriction [on academic freedom] might diminish the institution's academic effectiveness and standing." Kilgore adds that such restrictions may reach a point at which the institution will "cease to be an institution of higher education according to the prevailing conception."

6. See chapter 10 above.

7. John Henry Newman, *The Idea of a University* (Notre Dame, Ind.: University of Notre Dame Press, 1982), "Discourse 4," 53–74.

8. Annarelli asserts: "To establish limits that scholarly conclusions cannot transgress, or to impose an orthodoxy upon an entire university or particular department, is to contradict basic principles of academic freedom and to frustrate the exercise of the university's function" (*Academic Freedom*, 206).

9. Charles E. Curran, *Catholic Higher Education, Theology, and Academic Freedom* (Notre Dame, Ind.: University of Notre Dame Press, 1990). Curran quotes and responds to Kliever on p. 185.

10. Ibid., 182.

11. At this point I find myself in apparent disagreement with Curran, who maintains that academic peers would be the qualified judges, provided that they consulted widely and in depth with peers in the specific area of competence of the theologian being investigated (ibid., 185).

12. "Doctrinal Responsibilities: Approaches to Promoting Cooperation and Resolving Misunderstandings between Bishops and Theologians," *Origins* 19 (June 29, 1989): 97–110, quotation from 102.

13. As I have noted on p. 157 above, this right is recognized for theologians

in Catholic universities by John Paul II in the apostolic constitution *Ex Corde Ecclesiae.*

14. See *Ex Corde Ecclesiae*, par. 28; *Origins* 20 (October 4, 1990): 265–76, at 271.

Chapter 12: Method in Ecumenical Theology

1. *Unitatis Redintegratio*, no. 3.

2. *Ad Gentes*, no. 7. Compare *Dei Verbum*, no. 3, *Lumen Gentium*, no. 16, *Gaudium et Spes*, no. 22, and *Nostra Aetate*, no. 2.

3. Raimundo Panikkar, "Faith — a Constitutive Dimension of Man," *Journal of Ecumenical Studies* 8 (1971): 223–53.

4. Wilfred Cantwell Smith, *Faith and Belief* (Princeton, N.J.: Princeton University Press, 1979), 129.

5. Hans Küng et al., *Christianity and the World Religions: Paths of Dialogue with Islam, Hinduism, and Buddhism* (Garden City, N.Y.: Doubleday, 1986), xiv.

6. Wolfhart Pannenberg, *Theology and the Philosophy of Science* (Philadelphia: Westminster, 1976), 319, 365.

7. Wolfhart Pannenberg, "Toward a Theology of the History of Religions," *Basic Questions in Theology* 2 (Philadelphia: Fortress, 1971), 65–118, quotation from 115.

8. Wilfred Cantwell Smith, *Towards a World Theology: Faith and the Comparative History of Religion* (Philadelphia: Westminster, 1981), 130.

9. Ibid., 100.

10. Ibid. 118.

11. Ibid., 151.

12. See Frederick J. Crosson, "*Fides* and *Credere*. W. C. Smith on Aquinas," *Journal of Religion* 65 (1985): 399–412.

13. Cf. Thomas Aquinas, *Summa theologiae* 2–2.5.3c: "Formale autem objectum fidei est veritas prima secundum quod manifestatur in scripturis sacris et doctrina Ecclesiae quae procedit ex veritate prima."

14. Küng et al., *Christianity and the World Religions*, viii.

15. John Paul II, encyclical *Redemptoris Missio*, no. 56; quoted from *Origins* 20 (January 31, 1991): 541–68, at 557.

16. Hans Küng, *Theology for the Third Millennium: An Ecumenical View* (New York: Doubleday, 1988), 179. Küng's italics.

17. Ibid., 195.

18. Hans Küng, "Toward a New Consensus in Catholic (and Ecumenical) Theology," in *Consensus in Theology? A Dialogue with Hans Küng and Edward Schillebeeckx*, ed. Leonard Swidler (Philadelphia: Westminster, 1980), 1–17, quotation from 14.

19. See, for instance, Bernard Cooke, "The Experiential 'Word of God,'" *Consensus in Theology*, 69–74.

20. Peter Chirico, "Hans Küng's Christology: An Evaluation of Its Presuppositions," *Theological Studies* 40 (1979): 256–72, especially 266.

21. Raymond E. Brown, "The Contribution of Historical Biblical Criticism to Ecumenical Church Discussion," in *Biblical Interpretation in Crisis: The Ratzinger Conference on Bible and Church,* ed. Richard John Neuhaus (Grand Rapids, Mich.: Eerdmans, 1989), 24–49, quotation from 24. See chapter 5 above, pp. 78–80.

22. *Peter in the New Testament, Mary in the New Testament,* and *Righteousness in the New Testament.* For publication data, see above, chapter 5, note 29.

23. Vatican I in its constitution *Dei Filius,* chapter 3 (DS 3011), speaks of *verbum Dei scriptum.* Vatican II in *Dei Verbum,* nos. 9 and 24, uses similar language.

24. Karl Rahner, "Scripture and Tradition," *Theological Investigations* 6 (Baltimore: Helicon, 1969), 98–112. See also his article, "Scripture and Tradition," *Encyclopedia of Theology* (New York: Seabury/Crossroad, 1975), 1549–54. Walter Kasper in his *The Methods of Dogmatic Theology* (Glen Rock, N.J.: Paulist, 1969) holds that Scripture is "the *norma normans non normata*" (27).

25. Leo XIII, *Providentissimus Deus* (EB 114); Vatican II, *Dei Verbum,* no. 24; cf. *Optatam Totius,* no. 16.

26. "The Renewal of the Christian Tradition: The Report of the North American Section," in *Report of the Theological Commission on Tradition and Traditions,* Faith and Order papers 40, ed. Lukas Vischer (Geneva: World Council of Churches, 1963), 21.

27. *Dei Verbum,* no. 9.

28. Ibid., no. 10.

29. John Henry Newman, *Essay in Aid of a Grammar of Assent* (Garden City, N.Y.: Doubleday Image, 1955), chapter 10, section 2, no. 3, 330.

30. *Unitatis Redintegratio,* no. 4.

31. Reuel Howe, *The Miracle of Dialogue* (New York: Seabury, 1963), 49–50.

32. "Baptism, Eucharist and Ministry: An Appraisal," *Origins* 17 (November 19, 1987): 401.

33. On the unresolved differences between Anglicans and Catholics, see the Vatican response to the Final Report of ARCIC I (*Origins* 21 [December 19, 1991]: 441–47).

34. "The Importance of Being Catholic: A Protestant View," *First Things* 1 (1990): 25.

35. "Common Declaration," *Origins* 19 (October 12, 1989): 316–17, quotation from 317.

36. *Dialogue between Christians* (Westminster, Md.: Newman, 1966), 31.

Chapter 13: Theology and Worship

1. Translated from Denzinger-Schönmetzer, *Enchiridion symbolorum, definitionum et declarationum de rebus fidei et morum,* 36th ed. (Freiburg: Herder, 1976), no. 246.

2. *De vocatione omnium gentium,* I:12; PL 51:664–65; English translation, *The Call of All Nations,* Ancient Christian Writers, no. 14 (Westminster, Md.: Newman, 1952), 52.

3. See David M. Stanley, "Carmenque Christo quasi deo dicere," in his *The Apostolic Church in the New Testament* (Westminster, Md.: Newman, 1965), 95–118. In this chapter he analyzes the hymns in Phil. 2:5–11; Rev. 5:9–10, 12, 13; Eph. 5:12; 1 Tim. 3:16; Col. 1:13–20, 1 Pet. 1:3–5, and John 1:1–18.

4. David M. Stanley, "Liturgical Influences on the Formation of the Gospels," ibid., 119–39.

5. For the historical material in this and the following paragraphs see especially Geoffrey Wainwright, *Doxology* (New York: Oxford, 1980), here 228.

6. Tertullian, *De resurrectione carnis*, 8; PL 2:852.

7. "Nihil innovetur nisi quod traditum est" (DS 110).

8. Bernard of Clairvaux, Ep. 174:5; PL 182:334; Thomas Aquinas, *Summa theol.* 2:27:1.

9. *Comm. on 1 Cor.*, cap. 11, lectio 6.

10. Joseph A. Jungmann, *Die Stellung Christi im liturgischen Gebet*, 2d ed. (Münster: Aschendorff, 1962).

11. George Tyrrell, *Through Scylla and Charybdis* (London: Longmans, Green, 1907), 104–5.

12. *Collectio lacensis* (Freiburg: Herder, 1882), 6:837. I have modified the translation in *Papal Documents on Mary*, ed. William J. Doheny and Joseph P. Kelly (Boston: St. Paul Editions, 1981), 65.

13. Pius XII, "Munificentissimus Deus," quoted from *Papal Documents on Mary*, 308.

14. Edmund Schlink, *The Coming Christ and the Coming Church* (Philadelphia: Fortress, 1968), 16–95.

15. Yves Congar, *Diversity and Communion* (Mystic, Conn.: Twenty-Third Publications, 1985), 100.

16. Paul Knitter, *No Other Name* (Maryknoll, N.Y.: Orbis, 1985), 203.

17. Schlink, *The Coming Christ*, 143.

Chapter 14: Historical Method and the Reality of Christ

1. John P. Meier, *A Marginal Jew: Rethinking the Historical Jesus* (New York: Doubleday, 1991).

2. John Dominic Crossan, *The Historical Jesus: The Life of a Mediterranean Jewish Peasant* (San Francisco: HarperSanFrancisco, 1991).

3. Albert Schweitzer, *The Quest of the Historical Jesus* (New York: Macmillan, 1961), 3.

4. The criteria are discussed by Meier, *A Marginal* Jew, 168–84, and Crossan, *The Historical Jesus*, xxxi–xxxiv. In his footnotes Meier cites a large body of literature on the subject. The works of Norman Perrin and Harvey K. McArthur have been very influential.

5. Paul Hollenbach, "The Historical Jesus Question in North America Today," *Biblical Theology Bulletin* 19 (1989): 11–22, at 19 and 20.

6. John Dominic Crossan, *Jesus: A Revolutionary Biography* (San Francisco: HarperSanFrancisco, 1993).

7. Meier, *A Marginal Jew*, 237, n. 41; cf. 244–45, n. 76.

8. In my *Apologetics and the Biblical Christ* (Westminster, Md.: Newman, 1963), 6–10, I have given a fuller description of this "historicist" form of apologetics, with quotations from the works of Felder and Fillion.

9. See Joachim Jeremias, *New Testament Theology 1: The Proclamation of Jesus* (New York: Scribner's, 1971), 61–68.

10. The best single introduction to Pannenberg's thought on the historical Jesus is probably his *Jesus God and Man* (Philadelphia: Westminster, 1968). See also his discussion of the "methods of Christology" in volume 2 of his *Systematische Theologie* (Göttingen: Vandenhoeck & Ruprecht, 1991), 316–36.

11. Pontifical Biblical Commission, "Instruction on the Historical Truth of the Gospels," nos. 9–10; text in Joseph A. Fitzmyer, *A Christological Catechism: New Testament Answers* (New York: Paulist, 1982), 131–40, at 135–37.

12. John Henry Newman, *Essay in Aid of a Grammar of Assent*, chapter 10, sec. 2, §3 (Garden City, N.Y.: Doubleday Image, 1955), 329–30.

13. John Henry Newman, "Letter to the Duke of Norfolk" in *Newman and Gladstone: The Vatican Decrees*, ed. Alvan Ryan (Notre Dame: University of Notre Dame, 1962), 177.

14. See Ben F. Meyer, *The Aims of Jesus* (London: SCM, 1979), 110.

15. Unfortunately John P. Meier's article entitled "Jesus" in the *New Jerome Biblical Commentary* (Englewood Cliffs, N.J.: Prentice-Hall, 1990), 1316–28, is written from a perspective that prescinds from faith. The deficiency is partly offset by several later articles on "New Testament Thought" that take up New Testament Christology, miracles, and the resurrection of Jesus. But one misses in this commentary an article along the lines of Prosper Grech's "Jesus Christ in History and Kerygma" in *The New Catholic Commentary on Holy Scripture*, rev. ed. (London: Nelson, 1975), 822–37.

Sources

N.B. All the chapters of the present book are based on previously written articles, but they have been updated, modified, and in some cases notably expanded. The sources are as follows.

Chapter 1. Toward a Postcritical Theology
Prepared for conference on "Theology for the Third Millennium," Creighton University, Omaha, Nebraska, April 20–21, 1990. Published in *Theology for the Third Millennium,* ed. David G. Schultenover (Toronto Studies in Theology 56; Toronto: Edwin Mellen, 1991), 5–21.

Chapter 2. Theology and Symbolic Communication
Written in connection with an interdisciplinary seminar on Fundamental Theology and Communications under the auspices of the Gregorian University, Rome, and held at Villa Cavalletti, from September 28 to October 4, 1983. Previously unpublished.

Chapter 3. The Problem of Method: From Scholasticism to Models
Adapted, with omissions, from a paper, "Umrisse meiner theologischen Methode," in Johannes B. Bauer, ed., *Entwürfe der Theologie* (Graz, Austria: Styria, 1985), 51–70.

Chapter 4. Fundamental Theology and the Dynamics of Conversion
Reproduces with minor changes an article by the same title in *The Thomist* 45 (1981): 175–93.

Chapter 5. The Uses of Scripture in Theology
Laurence J. McGinley lecture, Fordham University, Bronx, New York, April 10, 1991. Previously unpublished.

Chapter 6. Tradition as a Theological Source
Delivered as a paper for United States Lutheran/Roman Catholic Dialogue, at Marydale Retreat Center, Covington, Kentucky, September 21, 1990. Previously unpublished.

Chapter 7. The Magisterium and Theological Dissent
Lecture at Franciscan University, Steubenville, Ohio, February 20, 1991. Published under the title "The Magisterium, Theology, and Dissent" in *Origins* 20 (March 28, 1991): 692–96.

Chapter 8. Theology and Philosophy
Based on an article "Vatican II and Scholasticism," *New Oxford Review* 57 (May 1990): 5–11.

Chapter 9. Theology and the Physical Sciences
Expanded version of article "Science and Theology," in *John Paul II on Science and Religion: Reflections on the New View from Rome,* ed. Robert J. Russell, William R. Stoeger, and George V. Coyne (Vatican City: Vatican Observatory, 1990), 9–18.

Chapter 10. University Theology in Service to the Church
Laurence J. McGinley inaugural lecture, Fordham University, Bronx, N.Y., December 6, 1988, and Lincoln Center, N.Y., December 7, 1988. Published as "University Theology as a Service to the Church" in *Thought* 64 (June 1989): 103–15.

Chapter 11. The Teaching Mission of the Church and Academic Freedom
From a lecture by the same title delivered at a symposium at Duquesne University, October 27, 1989, and published in the volume *Academic Freedom in a Pluralistic Society,* ed. Nicholas P. Cafardi (Pittsburgh, Pa.: Duquesne University Press, 1990), 10–19.

Chapter 12. Method in Ecumenical Theology
Based primarily on an article "Ecumenism without Illusions: A Catholic Perspective," *First Things* 4 (June–July 1990): 20–25. That article was based on a lecture, "Ecumenism since Vatican II: The Road Traveled and the Road Ahead," the annual Charles K. von Euw Lecture at St. John's Seminary, March 18, 1990.

Chapter 13. Theology and Worship
Written for a Symposium on the Theological Interpretation of Scripture held at North Park Theological Seminary, Chicago, October 9–11, 1992; published under the title "Theology and Worship: The Reciprocity of Prayer and Belief," in *Ex Auditu: An International Journal of Theological Interpretation of Scripture* 8 (1992): 85–94.

Chapter 14. Historical Method and the Reality of Christ
Delivered as Laurence J. McGinley Lecture, Fordham University, April 2, 1992, and published under the title "Historians and the Reality of Christ," *First Things* 28 (December 1992): 20–25.

Index